DANCES OF THE SELF IN HEINRICH VON KLEIST, E.T.A. HOFFMANN AND HEINRICH HEINE

To my parents

Dances of the Self in Heinrich von Kleist, E.T.A. Hoffmann and Heinrich Heine

LUCIA RUPRECHT
Emmanuel College, Cambridge University, UK

ASHGATE

Published by
Ashgate Publishing Limited
Gower House
Croft Road
Aldershot
Hampshire GU11 3HR
England

Ashgate Publishing Company
Suite 420
101 Cherry Street
Burlington, VT 05401-4405
USA

Ashgate website: http://www.ashgate.com

QM LIBRARY
(MILE END)

British Library Cataloguing in Publication Data
Ruprecht, Lucia, 1972–
    Dances of the Self in Heinrich von Kleist, E.T.A. Hoffman
    and Heinrich Heine
    1.Kleist, Heinrich von, 1777–1811 – Criticism and interpretation 2.Hoffmann, E. T. A.
    (Ernst Theodor Amadeus), 1776–1822 – Criticism and interpretation 3.Heine, Heinrich,
    1797–1856 – Criticism and interpretation 4.Dance criticism – Germany – History – 19th
    century 5.Modern dance – History – 19th century 6.Dance in literature 7.Aesthetics in
    literature
    I.Title
    830.9'3579'09034

Library of Congress Cataloging-in-Publication Data
Ruprecht, Lucia, 1972–
    Dances of the Self in Heinrich von Kleist, E. T. A. Hoffman and Heinrich Heine / Lucia
    Ruprecht.
        p. cm.
    Includes bibliographical references and index.
    ISBN 0–7546–5361–7 (alk. paper)
    1.   Kleist, Heinrich von, 1777-1811–Knowledge–Dance. 2.   Hoffmann, E. T. A. (Ernst
    Theodor Amadeus), 1776–1822–Knowledge–Dance. 3.   Heine, Heinrich, 1797–1856–
    Knowledge–Dance. 4. Dance–Germany–History–19th century. 5. Dance in literature. I. Title.
    PT2379.Z5R87 2006
    833'.6–dc22
                                                                                            2006003926

ISBN-13: 978-0-7546-5361-5
ISBN-10: 0-7546-5361-7

Printed and bound in Great Britain by Antony Rowe Ltd, Chippenham, Wiltshire.

Contents

List of Figures

Cover illustration: E.T.A. Hoffmann, pencil drawing of Kapellmeister Kreisler
in a fit of madness (1822) (by kind permission of the Staatsbibliothek Bamberg).

Acknowledgements

My deepest thanks and greatest debt go to Andrew Webber, who supervised the dissertation on which this book is based. Without our dialogues my work would not have taken on its present shape. In addition, various colleagues and friends accompanied its development over the last years. While I have been able to incorporate many of their insights, for the remaining blindnesses I alone am responsible. I have received expert advice from Hans-Jochen Marquardt, Ben Morgan, Roger Parker, Roger Paulin, Nicholas Saul, Ricarda Schmidt and Mary Ann Smart. Marion Kant, Joellen Meglin and Giannandrea Poesio gave me valuable feedback on dance-related questions. Cornelia Blasberg encouraged me to pursue this project in the first place; Gabriele Brandstetter and Gerhard Neumann offered their interest and support at its late stages. I wish to thank Hilary Brown, Jonathan Conlin, Stefan Ecks, Anke Kramer, José de Paiva and Jan Söhlke for reading and discussing parts of this book with me. The team at Ashgate has been efficient and helpful throughout the production process. I am especially grateful to my editor, Ann Donahue, who believed in the potential of my work from our first email exchange, and for the constructive criticism I received through reader reports. Chantal Wright kindly translated the more obscure German sources. Helena Sedgwick's competence saved me many hours of copy-editing. Finally, I should like to thank my parents, for all their encouragement; and Jens Schindler, whose outspoken and unspoken companionship remains a constant inspiration.

I have received generous financial support from the Studienstiftung des deutschen Volkes, the Arts and Humanities Research Board, the Tiarks Fund of the Department of German at the University of Cambridge, and Gonville and Caius College. Some of the work was undertaken during a Research Fellowship at Churchill College, Cambridge. I am grateful to the following libraries and research institutions for the use of their resources: the Berlin Staatsbibliothek, the Dance Archives Cologne, the British Library in London, the New York Public Library, the Derra de Moroda Dance Archives in Salzburg, and the University Library at Cambridge. Extracts of earlier versions of the chapters have already appeared under the following titles elsewhere: 'Tanz-Fiktionen gegen den Strich: Heinrich von Kleist, E.T.A. Hoffmann, Heinrich Heine', *Jahrbuch Tanzforschung*, 12 (Hamburg: Lit, 2002), 553–68; 'Körperbewegung – Sprachbewegung: Kleists *Über das Marionettentheater* aus tanzästhetischer Perspektive', in *Internationale Konferenz 'Heinrich von Kleist'*, ed. by Hans-Jochen Marquardt and Peter Ensberg (Stuttgart: Heinz, 2003), 143–58; 'Heinrich Heine's *Florentinische Nächte*: A Tale of Transgression', in *Field Studies:*

German Language, Media and Culture (CUTG Proceedings 5), ed. by Holger Briel and Carol Fehringer (Oxford: Peter Lang, 2005), 139–55.

List of Abbreviations

The following abbreviations have been used for key texts:

BL Heinrich Heine, *The Baths of Lucca*, in *The Sword and the Flame: Selections from Heinrich Heine's Prose*, ed. by Alfred Werner (New York: Thomas Yoseloff, 1960), pp. 356–424, by page number.

DHA Heinrich Heine, *Historisch-Kritische Gesamtausgabe der Werke*, ed. by Manfred Windfuhr et al., 16 vols (Hamburg: Hoffmann und Campe, 1973–97), by volume and page number.

DKV Heinrich von Kleist, *Sämtliche Werke und Briefe*, ed. by Ilse-Marie Barth, Klaus Müller-Salget, Stefan Ormanns and Hinrich C. Seeba, 4 vols (Frankfurt am Main: Deutscher Klassiker Verlag, 1987–97), by volume and page number.

FN Heinrich Heine, *Florentine Nights*, in *The Sword and the Flame*, pp. 101–51, by page number.

HB E.T.A. Hoffmann, *Princess Brambilla*, in *The Golden Pot and Other Tales*, transl. by Ritchie Robertson (Oxford: Oxford University Press, 1992), pp. 119–238, by page number.

HS E.T.A. Hoffmann, *The Sandman*, in *The Golden Pot and Other Tales*, pp. 85–118, by page number.

MT Heinrich von Kleist, *On the Marionette Theater*, transl. by Roman Paska, in *Fragments for a History of the Human Body Part I*, ed. by Michel Feher (New York: Zone, 1990), pp. 415–21, by page number.

S Friedrich Schiller, *Gracefulness and Dignity*, transl. by Leon Richard Liebner (University Microfilms International, 1979), by page number.

SE *Standard Edition of the Complete Psychological Works of Sigmund Freud*, ed. by James Strachey in collaboration with Anna Freud, 24 vols (London: Hogarth Press, 1953–74), by volume and page number.

SW E.T.A. Hoffmann, *Sämtliche Werke*, ed. by Wulf Segebrecht et al., 6 vols (Frankfurt am Main: Deutscher Klassiker Verlag, 1985–), by volume and page number.

All translations of texts which are not available in English are Chantal Wright's (*CW*) or my own.

Introduction

When he wanted to dazzle his audience completely he would suddenly and unexpectedly spring from the ground, whirling his two legs about each other with bewildering swiftness in the air, as it were trilling with them, and then, with a subdued bump, which nevertheless shook everything within him to its depths, return to earth. (Thomas Mann, *Tonio Kröger*)

There is a fundamental remoteness between dance as one of the most physical and literature as one of the most abstracted of arts. Yet writers and theorists have time and again tried to bridge the gap with metaphorical connections, swaying in the sounds and rhythms of the 'verbal dance' of a poetry recital,[1] or admiring the *écriture corporelle* of the ballerina.[2] Figures like Thomas Mann's dance-master François Knaak of the novella *Tonio Kröger* (1903) reflect the increasing attention of German writers to corporeal expression at the beginning of the twentieth century, which in turn has been acknowledged in the academic literature. This focus on the age of modernism, however, possesses a prehistory, which has received little systematic consideration.[3] It is the motivation of this book to analyse that which went before, when dance was less popular with the intellectual public. At its centre are three authors – Heinrich von Kleist, E.T.A. Hoffmann and Heinrich Heine – who offer fascinating insights in the interface between German literature and the aesthetic and practice of dance theatre. The exploration and theoretical evaluation of their works within an interdiscursive and intermedial context not only sheds new light on a number of their writings, it also opens up new pathways for understanding Western theatrical dance's theoretical and historical continuum.[4]

---

1   Paul Valéry, 'Philosophy of the Dance', in *The Collected Works of Paul Valéry*, ed. by Jackson Mathews, 15 vols (London: Routledge and Kegan Paul, 1958–75), XIII (1964), 197–211 (p. 208).

2   Stéphane Mallarmé, 'Ballets', in *Igitur, Divagations, Un coup de dés* (Paris: Gallimard, 1976), pp. 191–7 (p. 192).

3   There is a strong focus on the turn of the century in research on German literature and dance; pathbreaking here is Gabriele Brandstetter, *Tanz-Lektüren: Körperbilder und Raumfiguren der Avantgarde* (Frankfurt am Main: Fischer, 1995). See also Gregor Gumpert, *Die Rede vom Tanz* (Munich: Fink, 1994).

4   Two major recent monographs in French studies carve out the potential of juxtaposing dance as historical cultural practice with its literary representation: Sarah Davies Cordova's *Paris Dances: Textual Choreographies in the Nineteenth-Century French Novel* (San Francisco: International Scholars Publications, 1999); and Felicia McCarren's *Dance Pathologies: Performance, Poetics, Medicine* (Stanford: Stanford University Press, 1998).

Modernist authors often received direct impulses from their experience of dancers. The rise of modern dance provided writers with fresh impulses in a period of unsettlement where traditional modes of perception, representation and communication were no longer satisfactory. Not least because the capacities of their own medium were challenged, authors turned to other modes of expression for inspiration. Dance was idealised in ways that frequently told more about the literary agenda than about the bodily event in its performance context. However, the situation in the first decades of the nineteenth century presents us with a different picture. Rather than delight, the pre-Romantic ballets that were performed on Germany's stages caused boredom, if not aversion, as bluntly articulated by Kleist and Hoffmann. Even the Romantic ballet in Paris, one of the zeniths in the history of Western theatrical dance, failed to enchant the sceptical beholder. The art of the ballerinas performing *La Sylphide* or *Giselle*, immortalised by the praise of the French writer and balletomane Théophile Gautier, yielded to Heine's critical eye. Moreover, although French dance criticism celebrated ballet as the one universal language superior to any other form of expression, the art of writing was never seen to be at stake. The first half of the nineteenth century hardly produced documents of a crisis of representation formulated as sharply as Hugo von Hofmannsthal's famous *Letter to Lord Chandos* of 1902 that is representative of the turn of the century's enthusiastic reception of the 'silent' arts. The literary texts chosen here, albeit no less self-reflexive than those written around 1900, are subtler in their criticism of verbal expression. They strike a fragile balance between the immediacy of embodiment, and the representational modes of language. Without having much enthusiasm for what was concretely practised in the theatres, the writers nevertheless responded in highly original and complex ways to the dance pieces they saw.

Kleist, Hoffmann and Heine engage in modes of understanding physical movement that are neglected under the regime of eighteenth-century aesthetic theory, and of classical ballet, setting the human, frail and expressive body against the smoothly idealised neoclassicist ideal. Despite being aware of the paradox of approaching a form of expression that has been described as lying beyond or before language, they create written dances that unfold their power precisely because they surpass actual bodies and actual theatres. The visions of the writers go counter to the official aesthetic of ballet as it could be witnessed on stage, in theoretical or critical writings and dance technique manuals. The contextualisation of the literary texts aims to show how these other discourses are not merely represented or reflected, but rethought, worked over and radically reassessed in the writings of the three authors. Their literary counter-vision to ballet is twofold. Firstly, the writers turn to various types of alternative aesthetics of movement that draw little on the classical school, but feed upon popular traditions such as the puppet theatre, the *commedia dell'arte*, and the cancan. These other modes of movement, taking their peculiar shapes in the texts, testify to striking insights into both the expressive and the formalist potential of dance beyond the ways it was actually practised at the time.[5] Unfolding its epistemological power under the guise of literary imagination, literature becomes an archive of knowledge about the moving body. Deconstructing myths of beauty and perfection, it recreates physical performances in ways that were not intended by the politics of the dominant aesthetic canon.[6] Secondly, the literary texts distinguish themselves from the discourse of aesthetic theory and dance manuals through their narrative approach to bodily movement. By using literary devices like self-reflexivity and rhetorical playfulness to great effect, they do not impoverish, but enhance the artistic experience for the reader of the imaginary dance. Writing dancing, the authors formulate an alternative, literary and psychologically charged aesthetic of dance that is nothing less than a set of performative exercises for the articulation of cultural and personal narratives embodied in dances of the self.[7]

Let us go back to Mann's paradigmatic literary dance-master François Knaak for a moment in order to introduce this act of dancing the self. A descendant of those dance-masters whose manuals will be consulted shortly, François Knaak enters the literary stage almost one century after Kleist's exemplary dancer Herr C. His performance, however, illustrates those aspects of physical conduct which will be at the centre of this study. Although not exactly a classical dancer, Knaak possesses the aplomb of stunningly graceful demeanour, his steps sparkling with sheer bodily perfection. His name, his looks and his technique astound and bemuse. They master the art of illusion to greatest effect. While his first name in sound and content indicates his alliance with the nation of ballet – France – the German 'Knaak' may have been taken on to add some bourgeois respectability to a potentially flimsy profession. However, perhaps the 'François' is fake instead, meant to give credibility to a dancer called Knaak, a name evocative of the sounds generated by creaky, jerky movement? The forename is also only an 'e' away from its female version, and Knaak's gender poses a riddle indeed: 'How marvelously the silky black frock-coat fitted his chubby hips! His trouser-legs fell down in soft folds upon his patent-leather pumps with their wide satin bows, and his brown eyes glanced about him with languid pleasure

---

5   While I accentuate literature's capacity to function as a cross-current to actual aesthetic practices, and so to formulate untimely insights, Viktor Junk points out the importance of literature as a historical source for the investigation of dance, in *Grundlegung der Tanzwissenschaft* (Hildesheim: Olms, 1990), p. 61.

6   See Marianne Henn and Holger A. Pausch, 'Introduction: Genealogy and Construction of Body Identity in the Age of Goethe', in *Body Dialectics in the Age of Goethe*, ed. by Marianne Henn and Holger A. Pausch (Amsterdam: Rodopi, 2003), pp. 9–21 (p. 18).

7   My literal use of 'writing' differs from the one Susan Leigh Foster develops in *Reading Dancing: Bodies and Subjects in Contemporary American Dance* (Berkeley: University of California Press, 1986). Inspired by Barthes's notion of the 'writerly' text, Foster considers the body's movements as a text co-written by the performer and the interpreter. When she talks of 'writing dancing', she thus refers to the reading of dance as an active process where the viewer interacts with the choreographer and the dancer in the interpretative practice.

in their own beauty.'[8] Knaak's eyes, declares the narrator in another passage, were no instruments of penetrating perception, but attributes entirely of his body – they know nothing apart from the fact that they are brown and beautiful – and yet their possessor, this monster of self-forgetful embodiment, is extraordinarily literate in his ways: '*J'ai l'honneur de me vous représenter*', he starts, not just presenting, but re-presenting himself in an admirable posture.[9] This makes clear that the ensuing lesson will not be about the correct use of French, but about bodily representation, not only scrutinising the comportment of the pupils, but also displaying the skills of their master. He physically performs his selfhood, and therefore cultivates and disciplines his body with great care, before setting out to discipline others. Knaak's dance performance is brilliant; yet it entails unsettling effects, not least because of its inherent ambiguity. His regime lacks success: the less adept bodies of his pupils stumble and fall on the dance floor, or, in the case of Tonio himself, mix up male and female parts. The master's mission to install a clear psycho-cultural symbolic order of ideal moves and gender roles through his dancing lessons leaves something to be desired.[10]

Dances of the self involve the body in a signifying activity where physicality, even if constantly implied, does not only speak of itself, but of processes of cultural discipline and codification, their success or their failure, and of complex psycho-physical links. Through a style of movement, the body tells of the subjection to cultural and historical norms and ideals, how they shape the individual performance, or how this performance resists given codes. Dance, especially as recreated in the literary text, becomes a performed narrative of the subject; or in other words, a specific apparatus within the cultural processes that form subjectivity. At the same time, it functions as a metaphor for the fact that this subjectivity is an inherently repetitive, dynamic activity rather than a given state. While sometimes embedded in scenes of group dancing, dance as theatrical solo performance, or as dialogic encounter of the *pas de deux*, will therefore be the focus of my investigations. Set between 'trill' and 'bump', between the airy space of idealised representation and the referential ground of the fallible body, the written dances which will be considered in this book bear testimony to the fact that the nimbly leaping body is always also the falling body, the body which is shaken, shocked, distressed by traumatic wounds.

---

8   Thomas Mann, Tonio Kröger, in *Death in Venice and Other Stories*, transl. by H.T. Lowe-Porter (London: Secker and Warburg, 1979), pp. 85–120 (93).

9   Ibid.

10 Compare Andrew Webber's observations on François Knaak in 'Mann's Man's World: Gender and Sexuality', in *The Cambridge Companion to Thomas Mann*, ed. by Ritchie Robertson (Cambridge: Cambridge University Press, 2002), pp. 64–83 (pp. 71–2).

Chapter 1

Dance, Writing and Trauma

You're walking. And you don't always realize it, but you're always falling. With each step, you fall forward slightly. And then catch yourself from falling. Over and over, you're falling. And then catching yourself from falling. And this is how you can be walking and falling at the same time. (Laurie Anderson, *Big Science*)

Ballet and the Neoclassicist Tradition

Classical ballet is a virtuoso form of highly cultivated physical expression that rests on the control and stylisation of the natural body.[1] Surpassing physical limits in stunningly beautiful movements, it represents human dreams of freedom and transcendence, achieved through a relentless regime of bodily knowledge and discipline. In this book, it serves as a backdrop to the dance performances which are created in the literary texts, and shows how some of the literary topics have been transposed to the stage. It offers a matrix of formalisations of the body and its comportment, producing physical images of the ideal subject that casts its shadow on the less ideal protagonists of the writings. It is a form of dance that hardly enters the literary texts at all. However, ballet is part of an aesthetic tradition against which the literary authors form their own narratives. As a cultural practice that became a profession at the end of the seventeenth century, was refined over the course of the eighteenth century and codified at the beginning of the nineteenth century, it is deeply embedded in the neoclassicist discourse on the body.

One of the main representatives of this discourse is the scholar and dedicated amateur of the arts Johann Joachim Winckelmann. His *Gedanken über die Nachahmung der griechischen Werke in der Malerei und Bildhauerkunst* (Reflections on the Painting and Sculpture of the Greeks, 1755) established a prescriptive aesthetic of the beautiful body modelled after classical Greek sculpture. Winckelmann's ideal of beauty is defined by the smooth, harmonious shapes of the marble statues of antiquity. More than the sensual, it is the gymnastic-ascetic aspect of the body that is of interest. Modest curves, avoidance of any irregularities or protuberances, and the non-existence of orifices achieve the unity of the body image, the acclaimed

---

1   When ballet is mentioned in what follows, it will be with reference to the technique known as classical school, or *danse d'école*, of Western theatrical dance, which developed primarily in France, and goes back to the sixteenth-century tradition of court ballet. While it also denotes forms of non-Western theatrical dance, 'classical dance' will be used here with reference to the 'French school'.

uninterrupted lines, epitomised in the Greek profile. The whiteness of the stone, mistaken as an original feature of the Greek models, added to the aspect of purity created by the omission of anything that could indicate the organic. Apart from the hair on their heads, the sculptures are obviously hairless; subtle allusions to the genitals reduce the link to the physiological and procreative functions of the body. In Winckelmann, the gaze that traces the outline of sculptures leads to a sense of distance even in the most erotic descriptions: the eye discovers a beautiful body that transcends nature and elevates the onlooker to the realm of the spiritual. Physical features become transparent and allow for allegorical interpretation. Gautier's dance criticism, which will be discussed in detail in Chapter 4 on Heine, resounds heavily with Winckelmann's thought. The comparison of the dancers with Greek statuary enabled the critic to use sensual vocabulary which at once articulated the erotic potential of the public display of bodies and introduced a dandyesque distancing gesture from the vulgar aspects of physical love.[2] However, building a striking contrast to the corseted and tightly covered silhouettes of eighteenth-century bodies, the statue paradoxically enabled the modern gaze, distorted by civilization, to rediscover the 'natural' body in art. The allegedly unspoiled, yet extremely formalised Greek shape of course testified to a notion of nature that was itself extraordinarily civilised. The inherent contradiction of the claim for the natural that by definition had to be beautiful runs through eighteenth-century aesthetics. We will encounter it in Friedrich von Schiller's definition of grace, and find its influence on choreographers like Jean-Georges Noverre, who saw the 'natural' side of dancing in its gestural potential of evoking sentiments and passions in a sincere, yet always elegant manner.

It is significant that the idealisation of the body was not restricted to its visual aspect, which is predominant in Winckelmann's writings. Johann Gottfried Herder shifts the attention from the sense of sight to the sense of touch. This change of emphasis is intended to do justice to the three-dimensional object, to the corporeality of the sculpture, yet it results in equally stylised depictions of the body. Herder writes in his 1778 essay *Plastik* (Sculpture):

> The living, embodied truth of the three-dimensional space of angles, of forms and volume, is not something we can learn through *sight*. This is all the more true of the essence of sculpture, *beautiful* form and *beautiful* shape, for this is not a matter of color, or of the play of proportion and symmetry, or of light and shadow, but of *physically present, tangible truth*.[3]

Herder's descriptions of sculpted bodies do not exclude their sensual aspects; however, sensuality is only legitimised through beauty. Even more than for the visual

---

2   See Maribeth Clark, 'Bodies at the Opéra', in *Reading Critics Reading: Opera and Ballet Criticism in France from the Revolution to 1848*, ed. by Roger Parker and Mary Ann Smart (Oxford: Oxford University Press, 2001), pp. 237–51.

3   Johann Gottfried Herder, *Sculpture: Some Observations on Shape and Form from Pygmalion's Creative Dream*, ed. and transl. by Jason Gaiger (Chicago: University of Chicago Press, 2002), p. 40.

experience, roundness and smoothness are prerequisites for the aesthetic experience of touching.[4]

The celebration of idealised nudity, whether as visual or haptic delight, makes the naked body disappear. The stylisation of the marble statue stands for a process that creates the aesthetic body as an object for aesthetic pleasure by decidedly excluding the too-close, the too-real, the potentially abject.[5] The sculpture becomes the incorporation of a body that has nothing to hide beneath its skin, and nothing that could alter its smooth outline from underneath. Even the smallest uneven patches caused by veins and cartilage have to be avoided as they recall the fact that all matter is prone to death. To quote again from Herder's *Sculpture*:

> The veins in the hands, the cartilage in the fingers, the knee-pan must be softened and veiled in the fullness of the whole. If not, the silent sense of touch that feels things in the dark will register the veins as wriggling worms and the cartilage as protruding growths. Rather than being experienced as belonging to the fullness of a *single* body, they will be perceived as independent, separate entities that prefigure the ultimate demise of the body, from which they should therefore be removed.[6]

The aesthetic ideal of an invulnerable surface seems to constitute a counter-image to the intrusion into the body by its anatomical dissection which was another paradigmatic discourse of the eighteenth century. While the scientific fragmentation reduces the body to dead matter, the unity of the outline preserves the integrity of the person who *is* her or his body. Yet although invoking entirely different sights of the body, both phenomena pertain to a process of objectification that aestheticises the organic. Whether for reasons of beauty, knowledge or control, the body is charted, measured and shaped: in art, in aesthetic theory, in medicine and not least in the technique of classical dance.

The safely sealed body rules out that which would hint at forms of pleasure beyond the aesthetic, namely the bodily acts of eating and non-idealised sexual activity, both recalling the biblical Fall where they are employed as emblems of human disobedience and shame. Like those a little too realistically depicted details of the human skin, they are representative of the body's mortality; moreover, they point to the crude facts that it has to be fed and is dependent on reproduction. The neoclassicist ideal of beauty is thus characterised by the utmost distance to the two moments of human life that most relentlessly represent the transient quality of the body, birth, and even more so, death. Beauty is typified in the eternal spring of the youthful figure, equally far away from its beginning and its end. It is an androgynous ideal, moulded after slender young men, or pubescent women, displaying contours

---

4 See Helmut Pfotenhauer, 'Gemeißelte Sinnlichkeit: Herders Anthropologie des Plastischen und die Spannungen darin', in Pfotenhauer, *Um 1800: Konfigurationen der Literatur, Kunstliteratur und Ästhetik* (Tübingen: Niemeyer, 1991), pp. 79–102.

5 See Winfried Menninghaus, *Ekel: Theorie und Geschichte einer starken Empfindung* (Frankfurt am Main: Suhrkamp, 2002), especially pp. 76–159.

6 Herder, 54.

that hint the least at the visible changes taking place in bodies due to age or procreation. In Gautier's dance writings, it is thus the hermaphroditic type that best fits his expectations of the perfect dancer's body.[7]

While perpetuating the neoclassicist ideal in the moulding of a dancer's anatomy, classical ballet adds an important aspect to the tradition: the harmonious lines and proportions of Greek statuary had to be transposed into movement. It was the dancer, choreographer and dance scholar Carlo Blasis who developed the systematic transposition of neoclassicist aesthetic to the art of dance, tacking stock of poses and steps in his 1830 'grammar' of ballet, *The Code of Terpsichore*.[8] In doing so he followed rules which not only draw on a unique knowledge of the anatomical and physical laws of movement, but also represent those values which have been summarised above as the attempt to transcend the organic, sexualised body. The code of ballet values the vertical over the horizontal, lightness over weight and balance over fall, producing geometric poses and body lines through the interplay of a motionless centre and mobile extremities. The technique is thus based on the vertical alignment of the body in space, and on wide-ranging yet clear-cut movements and poses of the legs and arms. The torso is largely stable, functioning as connection between the limbs and the head with the movement-generating centre approximately at the height of the sternum.[9] The forces of gravity seem to be mastered in the *équilibre*, the balancing of apparently unstable poses that works through a clear centring, and the harmonious interaction of all parts of the body. The dancer is symmetrically orientated along the vertical axis, and placed on stage according to the rules of the central perspective, incorporating a controlled and upright subject whose mind artfully governs the body. The maximal frontal legibility of the body is established through legs that are permanently turned out in the hip joints; the organic body disappears behind the geometric grid which determines its every aspect.[10] The classical dancer's hips, a mere hinge to facilitate the movement of the legs, are certainly no source of motion, and practically rendered non-existent by the modalities of the technique.

---

7   See p. 113 f.

8   Carlo Blasis, *The Code of Terpsichore: The Art of Dancing*, trans. by R. Barton (London: Bull, 1830).

9   Compare, in contrast, Foster's description of the use of pelvic sexual energy by the modern choreographer Martha Graham, in *Reading Dancing*, p. 81; for the changing use of the torso throughout dance history, see Kattrin Deufert and Kerstin Evert, 'Der Torso im Tanz: Von der Destabilisierung des Körpers zur Autonomie der Körperteile', in *Körperteile: Eine kulturelle Anatomie*, ed. by Claudia Benthien and Christoph Wulf (Hamburg: Rowohlt, 2001), pp. 423–38.

10   For the visibility of the dancer that is achieved by the 'turn out', see Adrian Stokes, 'Tonight the Ballet', in *What is Dance? Readings in Theory and Criticism*, ed. by Roger Copeland and Marshall Cohen (New York: Oxford University Press, 1983), pp. 244–54; for the disappearance of the body in the pattern of the classical technique, see Francis Sparshott, *Off the Ground: First Steps to a Philosophical Consideration of the Dance* (Princeton: Princeton University Press, 1988), p. 355.

In eighteenth-century thought on statuary, however, aesthetic minds were preoccupied with the question that addressed the play between motion and stillness from the opposite end: how could movement be recreated in stone? The insistence on motion captured by the sculptor, and on the specific beauty of this endeavour, found its most characteristic expression in the discussion of the Laocoon statue, most prominently led by Winckelmann, Herder, Lessing and Goethe. Widely regarded as the perfect work of art, Laocoon nevertheless questions the common neoclassicist idealisations. Indeed, the tenuousness of these idealisations seems to be at its acutest in the texts on this sculpture.[11] It centres on a middle-aged body, depicting a moment of utmost danger that links the powerful physical appearance to pain and imminent death. In a careful analysis of eighteenth-century writings, Simon Richter has shown that the relation of pain and beauty is crucial to the neoclassicist aesthetic, claiming that this aesthetic 'simultaneously conceals *and is dependent on* some form of the dynamics of the infliction of bodily pain'.[12] The tension between neoclassicism's concealment of, and dependency on, bodily pain, is perhaps best illustrated in Goethe's 'On the Laocoon Group'. Here, Goethe explains in detail why the harmonious counterpoints and proportions within the sculpture, and therefore its beauty, result from the snake's lethal bite. At the same time he denies that the artist may have tried to represent a state of agony, but insists on witnessing the last moments of physical health and splendour.[13]

The extensive debate on Laocoon is characterised by a succession of idealisations that determined its tone from the first authoritative reference onwards. Not only is the allegedly agonising human body idealised in its sculpted copy; the historical discourse and the aesthetic response also idealise the sculpture. Even before it was rediscovered, its canonical value was established by Pliny's praise in his *Natural History*, which also gave rise to the myth that the Laocoon group was made out of one block of stone, encouraging the aesthetic insistence on the sensual and spiritual 'whole', the 'unity' of the work of art.[14] Sensual and spiritual unity is seen as both precondition and expression of beauty, and beauty is imperative because it is summoned to prove or evoke certain effects: the great and stalwart soul in Winckelmann, the right reactions, namely pity, in Lessing, and the evidence of aesthetic mastery in Goethe. Beauty makes the work of art instructive and enjoyable, while ugliness only leads to disgust or avoidance, which jeopardise both education and aesthetic pleasure. As Lessing has it:

---

11 For a detailed discussion of the double-sidedness of eighteenth-century aesthetic theory, as exemplified in the complementarity of beauty and the sublime, see Carsten Zelle, *Die doppelte Ästhetik der Moderne: Revisionen des Schönen von Boileau bis Nietzsche* (Stuttgart: Metzler, 1995).

12 Simon Richter, *Laocoon's Body and the Aesthetics of Pain: Winckelmann, Herder, Lessing, Moritz, Goethe* (Detroit: Wayne State University Press, 1992), p. 11.

13 See Johann Wolfgang Goethe, 'On the Laocoon Group', in Goethe, *Essays on Art and Literature*, ed. by John Gearey, transl. by Ellen von Nardroff and Ernest H. von Nardroff (New York: Suhrkamp, 1986), pp. 15–23.

14 See Richter, p. 13.

[Laocoon's] scream had to be softened to a sigh, not because screaming betrays an ignoble soul, but because it distorts the features in a disgusting manner. [...] Imagine him screaming, and then look! From a form which inspired pity because it possessed beauty and pain at the same time, it has now become an ugly, repulsive figure from which we gladly turn away.[15]

In the still-seminal analysis of *Discipline and Punish*, Michel Foucault investigated the link between education, observation, and a core of pain from a socio-historical perspective. He explored the various techniques that have been used to subject, train, observe and classify the human body so that it takes on its proper functions within society.[16] Extending Foucault's analysis to the realm of aesthetics, one feels inclined to argue that the neoclassicist tradition tried to ensure the body took on its proper aesthetic functions, that is educate and please through beauty; a form of beauty, however, that first of all had to be produced by dint of artful skills. Here, the technique of classical ballet can be considered the result of a particularly effective disciplinary regime applied to the living body that sought to match the sculpted models.[17] This meant entering a fight against nature which demanded not only refined insights into the potential of bodily movement, but also drastic practices to implement this knowledge. Indeed, the training of the classical dancer strongly recalls the production of the docile body in military training as Foucault has investigated it for the seventeenth and eighteenth centuries. Exercises that are devised in order to turn dancers' bodies into efficient instruments, and a system which ranks them hierarchically on a scale from *élève* to *étoile*, facilitating their observation, recognition and evaluation, make the *corps de ballet* comparable to the military corps.[18] The practices of military drill that are echoed in ballet exercise, characterise methods of training for a technique that asked from its disciples to perform steps and poses with the highest degree of precision and synchronicity.[19] While there are a number of correspondences between the training of the armed

15 Gotthold Ephraim Lessing, *Laocoon: An Essay on the Limits of Painting and Poetry*, transl. by Edward Allen McCormick (Baltimore: Johns Hopkins University Press, 1984), p. 17.

16 Michel Foucault, *Discipline and Punish: The Birth of the Prison* (London: Penguin, 1977).

17 'The Subjection of the Body as Subjection of Nature' (*Naturbeherrschung am Menschen*) is the telling title of Rudolf zur Lippe's materialist history of dance, written under the premises of the Frankfurt school's critical theory; I: *Körpererfahrung als Entfaltung von Sinnen und Beziehungen in der Ära des italienischen Kaufmannskapitals*; II: *Geometrisierung des Menschen und Repräsentation des Privaten im französischen Absolutismus* (Frankfurt am Main: Suhrkamp, 1974).

18 Michel Foucault, *Discipline*, especially Chapter III: 'Discipline'. For the relation between ballet and Foucault's notions of discipline and observation, see also Gerald Siegmund, 'Gedächtnisraum: Die Ballette William Forsythes', *Jahrbuch Tanzforschung*, 12 (2002), 397–411 (pp. 398–9).

19 See Dorion Weickmann, *Der dressierte Leib: Kulturgeschichte des Balletts 1580–1870* (Frankfurt: Campus, 2002), pp. 29, 37, 146, 155.

forces and ballet exercise, the following description may serve as an example. The system of military command is interchangeable with the customs in ballet class; both forms of education aim at producing automatised physical reactions:

> From the master of discipline to him who is subjected to it the relation is one of signalization: it is a question not of understanding the injunction but of perceiving the signal and reacting to it immediately, according to a more or less artificial, prearranged code. Place the bodies in a little world of signals to each of which is attached a single, obligatory response: it is a technique of training, of *dressage* [...].[20]

The association with the *res militaria* is embedded in the history of classical dance. For the Renaissance courtier, dancing skills were not only necessary to acquire graceful comportment, they also prepared the body for military service, which was a compelling reason for taking dancing lessons; a reason that was still stated in the founding decree of the Académie Royale de la Danse in 1671. Of particular interest here is the role of aesthetics in the symbolisation of power, which persisted in the military even when its association with dance had become obsolete. Indeed, by 1800 it was within the institution of the armed forces that men's display of their drilled, classical bodies indicated superiority, while it became increasingly problematic on the dance stages.[21] Theatre turned to favouring the female body, and with it an economy of vision that objectified the performer.

Dances of the Self

Eighteenth-century aesthetic writers focus on the embodiment of an ideal. The aesthetic style gains its full meaning only by being understood as the representation of rational humanity in its most ideal state, embodied in the conscious and thinking subject as central force of agency. The uninterrupted, closed outline celebrates those physical and psychic boundaries that, after Mary Douglas and Julia Kristeva, keep this subject intact by installing order, system and identity.[22] Pain and its associated ugliness in the eighteenth-century discourse are as threatening because they are not only a disruption of unity, but also a disruption of the self as inherently rational and in control. If Laocoon's scream had been depicted, it would have distorted his face in an unbearable manner, and disadvantageously altered the material surface of the work of art; but it also would have opened up the organic depths of the throat – organic depths that stood for the other of reason:[23] 'The wide-open mouth, aside

---

20 Foucault, *Discipline*, p. 166.

21 See Daniel Purdy 'Sculptured Soldiers and the Beauty of Discipline: Herder, Foucault and Masculinity', in Henn and Pausch, *Body Dialectics*, pp. 23–45.

22 Mary Douglas, *Purity and Danger: An Analysis of the Concepts of Pollution and Taboo* (London: Routledge, 1966); Julia Kristeva, *Powers of Horror: An Essay on Abjection* (New York: Columbia University Press, 1982).

23 For a general account of the repression of the body in eighteenth-century rationalist thought, see the seminal study by Hartmut and Gernot Böhme, *Das Andere der Vernunft: Zur*

from the fact that the rest of the face is thereby twisted and distorted in an unnatural and loathsome manner, becomes in painting a mere spot and in sculpture a cavity, with most repulsive effect'.[24] In neoclassicism, the perfect body is valued because it is the image of the perfect self. Pain, the unacknowledged core of the ideology of the beautiful, unsettles the self while unsettling beauty, and thus has to be suppressed in discourse.

Psychoanalytic criticism draws attention to this function of images in the construction of a bodily identity. Sigmund Freud's thesis of the self being, in the first instance, a bodily self, led to the notions of the 'body-ego', and the body image,[25] whose coherent moulding, allowing the individual to (mis)recognise her- or himself in its outlines, has been emphasised by Jacques Lacan as a crucial step in the formation of the subject.[26] The psychoanalytic concept of the body image refers in general to the unconscious aspects of bodily experience, and to imaginary representations of one's own body. Taking up these threads, Didier Anzieu has developed the notion of the *Moi-peau*, explaining the skin as an organ where psychic and bodily functions of exclusion and inclusion, unity and fragmentation are woven into each other.[27] Given that the instalment of boundaries through body images is not a choice, but a necessity that secures psychic stability, we can think of these images as symbolical constructions representing, and effectuating, the constitution of subjectivity. Iconographical models of the body such as the neoclassicist one are read here as cultural reflections of the constitution of subjectivity through body images. Representations of corporeal completeness and efficiency, then, may organise a 'culture's establishment of an ideal identity', as Susan Gustafson puts it in her Lacanian analysis of neoclassicism.[28]

Although propagating a notion of autonomy that is diametrically opposite to the reformulations of subjectivity which have focused on the subject's conditionality and heteronomy, the neoclassicist body image can of course be read against its own grain. It powerfully talks of those regimes, whether psycho-social, sexual, linguistic,

---

Entwicklung von Rationalitätsstrukturen am Beispiel Kants (Frankfurt am Main: Suhrkamp, 1985).

24 Lessing, p. 17.

25 Compare Freud's footnote in 'The Ego and the Id': 'the ego is ultimately derived from bodily sensations, chiefly from those springing from the surface of the body', in Sigmund Freud, 'the Ego and the Id', in *Standard Edition of the Complete Psychological Works of Sigmund Freud*, ed. by James Strachey in collaboration with Anna Freud, 24 vols (London: Hogarth Press, 1953–1974), IXX (19), pp. 3–66 (p. 26, footnote 1); for a general account of the psychoanalytic notion of the body image, see Claudia Benthien, *Im Leibe wohnen: Literarische Imagologie und historische Anthropologie der Haut* (Berlin: Spitz, 1998), pp. 59–67.

26 Jacques Lacan, 'Le stade du miroir comme formateur de la function du Je', in *Écrits* (Paris: Seuil, 1966), pp. 93–100.

27 Didier Anzieu, *The Skin Ego* (New Haven: Yale University Press, 1989).

28 Susan E. Gustafson, 'Beautiful Statues, Beautiful Men: the Abjection of Feminine Imagination in Lessing's Laokoon', *PMLA*, 108.5 (1993), 1083–97 (p. 1087).

aesthetic or disciplinary, that are at work in the shaping of subjectivity, and leave their traces on the body. Foucault understands the formation of subjectivity as a process that attaches attributes to the body, equips it with experience, brands it with distinguishing marks and fills it with meaning. While Foucault establishes the conditions of possibility for the body as an object of domination through a network of practices, Judith Butler further elaborates on the performativity of these practices. Her approach to the body will lead us from monuments to movement, from images to dances of the self.

Movement means, in the first instance, no more than itself. It is a concrete physical effort articulating a specific kinetic energy, which brings about a figuration of the body, or of several bodies, in space. Rather than to a written document, a dance piece could be compared to the act of reciting. This activity gains its unique artistic potential from the complex interlacing of the somatic and the semiotic dimensions of the moving body, of the sheer materiality and kinetic energy, and the power of signification, whose predominance over each other shifts according to different historical and cultural styles of movement. As Susan Leigh Foster summarises, the dancing body 'can be a voice through which the interior feelings and desires of the subject are made manifest, or it can simply enunciate itself. It can house a lexicon of abstract forms, or it can serve as the site at which images of the world come into being. Or it can comment on its own capacity to signify any of these things.'[29]

More than anything else, all forms of dance are performances. At a time when no one would label it performance theory, Paul Valéry thought about art as performed action. Dance becomes the model through which the philosopher approaches the other arts. In his 1936 essay *Philosophy of the Dance*, Valéry writes:

> All action which does not tend toward utility and which on the other hand can be trained, perfected, developed, may be subsumed under this simplified notion of the dance, and consequently, *all the arts can be considered as particular examples of this general idea*, since by definition all the arts imply an element of action, the *action which produces*, or else manifests, the *work*.[30]

He goes on to identify the body in dance as 'charged with motor energy', 'both mover and moved', entering into 'a kind of life that is at once strangely unstable and strangely regulated, strangely spontaneous, but at the same time strangely contrived and, assuredly, planned'.[31] Valéry's thinking of dance becomes the thinking of the body-as-movement both free and determined by rules, and as such prefigures aspects of Butler's approach to performativity and performance.[32] The performative

---

29 Foster, *Reading Dancing*, p. 227.

30 Valéry, pp. 207–8.

31 Ibid., pp. 203–4.

32 See Judith Butler, *Gender Trouble: Feminism and the Subversion of Identity* (London: Routledge, 1990); *Bodies that Matter: On the Discursive Limits of 'Sex'* (London: Routledge, 1993). For a discussion of the theoretical calibration of the terms 'performance' and

dimension – the embodied, event-like, yet rule-bound character – is at the heart of the art of movement.

Reformulating J.L. Austin's concept of the performative utterance that does not, in the first instance, refer to an established extra-linguistic reality but produces or enacts that which it names, Butler shows the body and its gender attributes as practices which 'effectively constitute the identity they are said to express or reveal'.[33] In order to transpose her theory onto dance, I will heighten its implicit theatrical aspects, focusing on Butler's early accent on performance as 'embodiment' or 'corporeal style'.[34] Gender, then, is one corporeal style along with, and generated by, the gesture, movement, dress or body shape that also characterise dance theatre.[35] Butler's notion of performativity is indebted to Foucault's work on the practices of subjection; yet it challenges the misconception of the 'mute' body as a pre-symbolic site awaiting disciplinary inscription that was fostered in the reception of his writings.[36] We never face the dancing body as 'mute' material, for it is always already involved in a signifying activity.[37] Comparable to the enactment of choreography, performativity exposes the formation of subjectivity as dynamic yet regulated process of repetition of norms and codes in a reiterative and citational practice. In our context, these given norms are those body images and conventions of movement which are prescribed by neoclassicist aesthetics and the classical code of dance; they are perpetuated by practices of imitation and copying in dance exercise and performance.

Partaking in the formation of subjectivity, the body is both a vulnerably organic entity and productively involved in the economy of cultural signification, its dance is both material activity and conceptual object. Performativity therefore allows the

---

'performativity', see Mieke Bal, 'Performance and Performativity', in *Travelling Concepts in the Humanities: A Rough Guide* (Toronto: University of Toronto Press, 2002), pp. 174–212.

33 Butler, *Gender Trouble*, p. 141.

34 See Judith Butler, 'Performative Acts and Gender Constitution: An Essay in Phenomenology and Feminist Theory', in *Performing Feminisms: Feminist Critical Theory and Theatre*, ed. by Sue-Ellen Case (Baltimore: Johns Hopkins University Press, 1990) pp. 270–82 (p. 273).

35 Although Judith Butler distanced herself from readings of her work that associate her view with theatre, and reinforced increasingly the performative dimension of mere speech, the theatrical aspect of her argument seemed to some critics of her work among the most plausible ones, and has developed a certain dynamic of its own in the reception; see Martha C. Nussbaum, 'The Professor of Parody', *The New Republic*, 22 October 1999, <http://www. tnr.com/archive/0299/022299/nussbaum022299.html> (accessed December 2002); see also Sybille Krämer and Marco Stahlhut, 'Das "Performative" als Thema der Sprach- und Kulturphilosophie', *Paragrana*, 10/1 (2001), 35–64 (p. 50).

36 'The body is not passively scripted with cultural codes, as if it were a lifeless recipient of wholly pre-given cultural relations. But neither do embodied selves pre-exist the cultural conventions, which essentially signify bodies. Actors are always already on the stage, within the terms of the performance'; Butler, *Performative Acts*, p. 277.

37 See Marcel Mauss's study 'Les techniques du corps', which is among the first attempts to analyse modes of movement as culturally codified; in *Journal de Psychologie*, 3–4 (1935), pp. 271–93.

dancing body to be placed beyond the dichotomy between symbolic inscription and corporeal emancipation as a practice on a continuum between matter and metaphor. While the discursive network within which the self is trapped in the Butlerian model questions any traditional understanding of agency as a core quality of the self-actuating subject, it does leave open some loopholes for transformation. Here, Jacques Derrida's concept of reiteration or iterability comes into play: Derrida defines agency in terms of an unstable interaction between the recurrence of the conventional and the appearance of the new through variation and difference.[38] In terms of the dancing body, this means that its creative and possibly subversive potential does not stem from the escape into the alleged authenticity and presence of matter, but from the variation of the repetitive signifying practice in the performance, more succinctly from the modalities through which it invokes, re-enacts, parodies or expands given conventions. The following chapters propose to engage with these performances as dances of the self, incorporating choreographies which point up the writers' visions of what dance movement can achieve. The notion of choreography, encompassing both a regulatory system and the possibilities of personal interpretation, conveys the dual value of performance, affirmation and resistance.[39]

Performance theory challenges a notion of subjectivity that differentiates between being, and appearing or acting. For the dancing body in particular, the negotiation between essentialist and constructionist positions inherent in this theory proves helpful. Performatively realising itself, the body is, on the one hand, no pre-given entity beyond codification, while one equally cannot deny, on the other hand, its materiality and presence:

> But the dancer's body is not merely a written-upon page; it is more accurately described as an artifact, of blood, flesh, organs, bone and skin, arduously and meticulously constructed. Social and political values are not simply placed or grafted onto a neutral body-object like so many old or new clothes. On the contrary, ideologies are systematically deposited and constructed on an anatomical plane, that is, in the neuromusculature of the dancer's body.[40]

---

38 See Jacques Derrida, 'Signature, Event, Context', in *Limited Inc.*, transl. Samuel Weber, (Evanston: Northwestern University Press, 1988), pp. 1–23.

39 I am indebted to Susan Leigh Foster and Janet Wolff here, who also argue that the metaphor of choreography works generally better than performance to indicate the traditions and codes people reproduce or upset, as well as the performative enactment of gender, class, or ethnic identities; see Susan Leigh Foster, 'Choreographies of Gender', *Signs: Journal of Women in Culture and Society*, 24 (1998), 1–33; Janet Wolff, 'Dance Criticism: Feminism, Theory and Choreography', in *Resident Alien: Feminist Cultural Criticism*, ed. by Janet Wolff (Cambridge: Polity Press, 1995), pp. 68–87.

40 Elizabeth Dempster, 'Women Writing the Body: Let's Watch a Little How She Dances', in *Bodies of the Text: Dance as Theory, Literature as Dance*, ed. by Ellen W. Goellner and Jaqueline Shea Murphy (New Brunswick: Rutgers University Press, 1995), pp. 21–38 (p. 23).

In dance, materiality and presence manifest themselves in weight, sweat, breath, blood; and also in the failure to comply with the prescribed ideal of the classical code which is so crucial to the literary authors considered here. The child's identification with the body image as delineated by Lacan, the Butlerian subject's repetitive enactment of gender norms or the body's attempt to match the classical code are from the outset both stabilising and inadequate. The framework within which the subject can position itself leads at the same time to the assimilation of norms that are based on rational stylizations which force the subject into alienating practices. The art of ballet testifies to this dialectic between control and alienation that characterises understandings of culture as formulated by Max Horkheimer and Theodor W. Adorno, further developed in Norbert Elias's work on strategies of social discipline, and reassessed by Foucault in his concentration on the pervasive networks of concrete practices of subjection. A cultural history of nineteenth-century ballet should undoubtedly be informed by these theories.[41] Yet it would also need to include dance as an elaborate system of applied knowledge, as aesthetic, performative practice with a distinct critical potential, and as form of physical expenditure that counteracts the economical logic of the capitalist state. Here, the focus on subjection in the presentation of classical dance has been chosen as it echoes the stance of the three authors whose work is at the centre of this study. In their eyes, dance does not fulfil its subversive potential on the ballet stages. To do so, it needs the literary stage.

Kleist shows the classical technique as a force of normalization and *dressage*, as a law, however, which produces failure. This view of ballet as a crippling discipline might not least be rooted in the author's own experiences in the Prussian military. Yet Heine's cultural theory of ballet, too, draws on the repressive mechanisms of culture; both he and Hoffmann will turn to genuinely different modes of dance, highlighting potentials of movement that are excluded, or civilised, by the classical tradition. Without getting carried away by anarchic outbreaks of kinetic energy, the authors formulate unorthodox dances as modes of performance that reintroduce a certain form – however contested – of agency, and shape the subjectivity of their characters. They turn their attention away from the idealisation and its exclusions to the pathological implications of the psycho-somatic unity in showing how pain is written on, and expressed in, the body. In their texts, psychic suffering is reflected in physical appearance and movement: Hoffmann's driven dances, and his fragmented, grotesque bodies full of bulbous protuberances and gaping orifices are among the most striking examples of the Romantic response to the beautiful shapes of neoclassicism. In the novella *Der Sandmann* (The Sandman), the writer's combination of the tradition of Graecophilia with that of the automaton, epitomised in his doll Olimpia, draws the connection between the perfection of the classical body, and the perfection of the machine, and thus pushes the inherent artificiality of the neoclassicist ideal to the edge. Olimpia is as faultless as she is mindless. By pulling apart the doll, and confronting flawless functionality with his protagonist's repetition

---

41 As Dorion Weickmann's *Der dressierte Leib*, albeit too exclusively, proves.

compulsion, Hoffmann brings the repressed underside of those idealisations – the fragmentary, the abject, the irrational, the pathological – to the surface.[42]

Hoffmann's conflation of the ideal shape of Greek sculpture with the perfection of the automaton is complemented by Kleist's choice of the marionette for demonstrating accomplished grace; both literary acts are highly subversive. Contrary to its positive connotation in Julien Offray de la Mettrie's *L'Homme machine* (Machine Man), which is representative of the materialist strand of eighteenth-century philosophy, the automaton strikes a decidedly negative note in aesthetic thought. Here, the organic unity of the beautiful work of art that represents the autonomous subject is seen as standing against the heteronomous power structures of the machinery of late absolutism.[43] Moreover, the aesthetic ideology of the natural has to exclude artificiality from its discourse. Kleist's and Hoffmann's union of the beautiful and the mechanical does not only point towards this paradoxical tension between nature and art, it also teases out myths of omnipotence and invincibility that underlie the neoclassicist imagination. Classical ballet, then, also represents a form of self-empowerment entailed by the deliberate production of the superior 'natural' body through technique.[44] This process actually resounds with the eighteenth-century dream of the automaton that elevates man to the position of divine creator, reinstalls redemption by the transcending of the flesh, and seeks to secure a form of artificially created immortality.[45] It betrays a desire for mythically refashioning the human body, outside and beyond its biological limits. In this sense, the idealisation of the *homme machine* and the perfect proportions of the sculpted body image are but two sides of the same coin.

In the authors considered here, however, the super-human or non-human perfection of statuary and automata is also uncannily close to the 'perfect' regime of a haunted psyche that is pathologically obsessed with compulsive re-enactments of a traumatic scene. Or to use Freud's terms: rather than enhancing narcissistic desires for omnipotence and immortality, man turned into automaton falls prey to the destructive forces of the death drive. The literary texts show the practice of

---

42 See Nicholas Saul, 'From "Ideendichtung" to the *Commercium Mentis et Corporis*: The Body in German Literature around 1800', *German Life and Letters*, 52/2 (1999), 116–22.

43 See Carsten Zelle, 'Maschinen-Metaphern in der Ästhetik des 18. Jahrhunderts (Lessing, Lenz, Schiller)', *Zeitschrift für Germanistik*, 3 (1997), 510–20 (p. 515).

44 See Martina Leeker, 'Maschinen – Gnosis – Tanz', *Jahrbuch Tanzforschung*, 10 (2000), 33–66 (p. 37), and also Jean-Claude Beaune, 'The Classical Age of Automata: An Impressionistic Survey from the Sixteenth to the Nineteenth Century', in *Fragments of a History of the Human Body*, Part I, ed. by Michel Feher (New York: Zone, 1990), pp. 431–80 (p. 475).

45 On the metaphysical promise that is attached to the automaton, see Bernhard Dotzler, 'Die Wiederkehr der Puppe: Szenenwechsel im Fin de Siècle', in *Puppen, Körper, Automaten: Phantasmen der Moderne*, ed. by Pia Müller-Tamm and Katharina Sykora (Cologne: Oktagon, 1999), pp. 234–47 (p. 234).

dance oscillating between serene control of, and obsessive surrender to the body, incorporating both the dream and the curse of the machine.[46]

Not least by letting the neoclassicist ideal turn against itself, responding to repeatability with repetition compulsion, Kleist, Hoffmann and Heine draw attention to the psychic vulnerability of human beings. This is reflected in bodies which are characterised by their mutability and mortality, and by their resistance against norms. They are susceptible to gender trouble, trauma, abuse and infection, and they also fail to dance to perfection, in short, bodies which represent the variety and fallibility that the vision of the beautiful machine tries to overcome. Hayden White has illustrated the psycho-somatism at work in such vulnerability. He elaborates on the assumption that drives are psychic representatives of organic forces.[47] Without going into the details of Freud's definition of drive, here, the psycho-physical line of thought in White's argument is of interest. Departing from Freud's supposition that the articulation of drives such as love, hate, mastery, self-preservation and the like may display the effects of a number of different 'emplotments', he speculates that each of these fates produces a different kind of body – 'it being understood that by "body" we will mean the totality of somatic effects produced by the psychical representation of an organic force'.[48] Freud's examples of 'emplotments' are thus being linked to different somatic repercussions:

> repression to the 'mechanical body', recognizable by its tics and obsessional behaviour, sublimation to the well-organized 'serene body', the turning back onto the subject to the 'masochistic body' that inflicts pain upon itself, and the transformation of affects into their opposite to the 'divided body' of the 'Jekyll and Hyde syndrome'.[49]

The dance narratives of Kleist, Hoffmann, and Heine tell the body's plots. They incorporate the pathological implications that grow out of a vulnerable or wounded psyche, thus being part of what Elisabeth Bronfen has termed 'the persistent production of narratives commemorating the impact of traumatic vulnerability at the core of our psychic and aesthetic representations'.[50] In the context of this book, the notion of 'trauma' is used in some instances to get a grasp on specific afflictions that haunt the literary protagonists. More generally, however, it provides a conceptual framework for dealing with the constitutive experience of loss and separation that informs psychoanalytical approaches to the formation of subjectivity. Peggy Phelan

---

46 Felicia McCarren follows the nexus between movement and technology from the turn of the century through the 1930s in her *Dancing Machines: Choreographies of the Age of Mechanical Reproduction* (Stanford: Stanford University Press, 2003).

47 Hayden White, 'Bodies and Their Plots', in *Choreographing History*, ed. by Susan Leigh Foster (Bloomington: Indiana University Press, 1995), pp. 229–34.

48 Ibid., p. 230.

49 Ibid.

50 Elisabeth Bronfen, *The Knotted Subject: Hysteria and its Discontents* (Princeton: Princeton University Press, 1998), p. 12.

transposes this onto physical terms; she speaks of an 'amputated body', cast from the womb, 'whose [...] very mortality' determines the being of every person.[51]

The technique of classical ballet as a system that is defined by closure and order rests on the concealment of the cultural trauma of the fallible organic body and its illicit desires. The fact that ballet's story-lines, in turn, often stage topics such as death and desire, would be a fascinating field for enquiry in itself; here, however, the focus is on how writers' dances revisit the site of the trauma. Along the lines of what may be called a hysterical conversion, the bodily performances in the literary texts bear testimony to, and articulate, an unspeakable, whether ineffable or censored, wound. As Bronfen has it, the 'conversion of psychic anguish into a somatic symptom can be interpreted as the enactment of a message in code', a message about the vulnerability of representation, of identity, and of the body.[52] By turning dance into a form of symptomatic expression, the writers reclaim the embodied meaning that they find lacking in what was actually practised on early nineteenth-century stages. While Felicia McCarren's stimulating study *Dance Pathologies* presents the alliance of dance and illness in the second half of the nineteenth century as a cultural stigma, it casts a somewhat different light in this book. In the texts explored here, the capacity to embody the full range of human experience in modes that transgressed the aesthetic canon expands the creative potential of dance instead of ostracising it.[53]

However, being to varying degrees the enactment of suffering, physical movement also becomes a technique which, by installing some forms of agency and control, stabilises the subject in a way that goes beyond the mere reiteration of norms dictated by a cultural or psychic matrix. In addition to its symptomatic role, dance acquires a curative function. Movement as a technique that potentially heals can be thought, then, as an expressive act that overcomes the painful repetitions of traumatic suffering. As the psychoanalyst Daniel Sibony writes:

> The body is the site that remembers trauma, physical shock that has been experienced and discarded for being impossible to integrate; here, speech and phantasmas are negotiated in *physical* terms. But the body is even more than that: it is the source of phenomena that refuse to repeat, that speak differently, through gesture and movement.[54]

These acts of movement thus represent possibilities of resistance and displacement due to the individual creative performance: it is ironically precisely movement 'that does not repeat', that fails to match the classicist ideal, which becomes an empowering force. As practices that take care of their performers, the written dances evoke Foucault's concept of the technologies of the self. This strand of his late writings complements his earlier work on subjection: the idea of the body's malleability remains, yet while he concentrated on how power moulds the subject

---

51 Peggy Phelan, *Mourning Sex: Performing Public Memories* (London: Routledge, 1997), p. 5.

52 Ibid., p. xii.

53 See McCarren, *Dance Pathologies*, especially pp. 42–7.

54 Daniel Sibony, *Le corps et sa danse* (Paris: Seuil, 1995), p. 61.

in works like *Discipline and Punish*, he then turned to the ways in which the subject moulds itself. Detached from Foucault's contested gendering of the practices of self-care, and from his understanding of their function in antiquity, they shall serve here to build up a systematic approach to the dancing subject in literature. The technologies constitute an 'art of existence', allowing the individuals:

> to effect by their own means or with the help of others a certain number of operations on their own bodies and souls, thoughts, conduct and way of being, so as to transform themselves in order to attain a certain state of happiness, purity, wisdom, perfection, or immortality.[55]

Rather than the messianic tone in which the programme of the *souci de soi* is uttered, the fact that Foucault maintains the idea of controlling the body, and the self, while formulating his idea of an autonomous subject, is important when transposing his model to the practice of dance. Literary criticism often contents itself by pointing out the Dionysian, rule-breaking aspect of bodily movement, as if its performativity by definition enabled it to escape power. Against this background, the concept of technology is particularly helpful to achieve a more balanced view. The subjects of the narratives enact what they are, and sometimes come to understand themselves, in rule-bound creative action. As with an improvisation that unfolds new possibilities of movement precisely through a prescribed set of limits – whether these are certain mental images, some sort of plot, points in space, qualities of movement, or the interaction with another person – dance becomes a way to develop agency within cultural and psychic power structures. Thus, the writers' answer to the artful classical tradition of ballet is artful in itself. This is perhaps one of the reasons why versions of the dance-master play a rather prominent role in some of the texts. They come to indicate both a tyrannical psychic regime, and an enabling force that teaches the individual how and where to move.

Figures of the Text

How, then, are the dances of the self written? When aligning the textual and the corporeal, what is ultimately at stake are the specific representational modes of different media, and, by extension, the issue of representation itself. Without the assumption that there is a textual aspect in the bodily performance, and a performative aspect in the text, the following explorations would not be possible. Yet without the respective specificities of the textual and the performative, of text and dance, they would not be challenging.[56] The effort to describe dance leads language to its limits.

---

55 Michel Foucault, *Technologies of the Self: A Seminar with Michel Foucault*, ed. by Luther H. Martin and others (London: Tavistock, 1988), p. 18.

56 Compare Gabriele Klein's and Christa Zipprich's introduction 'Tanz Theorie Text: Zur Einführung', *Jahrbuch Tanzforschung*, 12 (2002), 1–14, and Gabriele Wittmann, 'Dancing is not Writing: Ein poetisches Projekt über die Schnittstelle von Sprache und Tanz', *Jahrbuch Tanzforschung*, 12 (2002), 585–96.

In one of the climactic moments of Hoffmann's *Prinzessin Brambilla*, for instance, what is narrated, a breathless *pas de deux*, asphyxiates the narration that peters out in a sequence of dashes. In speaking about dance, literature rethinks itself: the dance motif becomes a metaphor for literary writing, its conditions, possibilities and limits. In this self-reflection, literature gains a performative quality; it refers to its own capacity for creating meaning, to the 'how' of its rhetorical procedures, and not only to the 'what' of its content. Texts are performative in as far as they 'enact' what they describe. The close readings proposed here attempt to tease out the dynamic of literary staging where figurative language and narrative structure interact to heighten the processual character of a text instead of its definitive shape, where, for instance, the recurrent use of words or figures counteracts, rather than enhances, narrative closure.

My readings set out from this productive interface between two media.[57] They identify three different literary visions of bodily motion that distinguish themselves not only through their general opposition to the official discourse, ballet, but also through their particular understandings of dance. The different aesthetics of movement enter into a productive interaction with equally distinctive poetics. This relation will be carved out by highlighting three rhetorical paradigms – paradox, irony and allegory. While they are at work across the texts of the three writers, they have been singled out for each of them respectively in order to further describe the specificities of their approaches.

The difficulty of representing something that goes, at least partly, beyond representation is doubly given in the texts considered here. Both embodiment and the impact of trauma resist exhaustive narration. The traumatic is traumatic precisely because it defies consistent representation and cognition, as Cathy Caruth has shown.[58] The wound of the fallible body and its unspoken desires as a cultural trauma underlying myths and practices of perfectibility haunts the literary texts; it also materialises in the more concrete afflictions and compulsive lives of the protagonists. Their specific traumatic experiences are indeed defined by an initial unknowability: an overwhelming event happened too early in the life to be remembered, or it is met with the refusal to acknowledge its occurrence, leading to fits of fainting, attacks of sleep, or states of half-consciousness. And yet – or indeed, therefore – this event persistently recurs to unsettle the ones who experienced, or rather refused to experience it initially. The persistence of trauma articulates itself in

---

57 Their scope varies therefore considerably from Roger Müller-Farguell's *Tanz-Figuren: Zur metaphorischen Konstitution von Bewegung in Texten – Schiller, Kleist, Heine, Nietzsche* (Munich: Fink, 1995). While my approach is shaped by the exploration of dance as a historical physical practice in its own right, in order then to trace the reassessment of this practice in literature, Müller-Farguell exclusively enquires into dance-like processes in poetic language. His analysis embarks on a general investigation of a fairly disembodied notion of movement. However, his attempt to single out typical figurative strategies that mediate between the figures of dance and the rhetorical figurations of the text proves helpful.

58 Cathy Caruth, *Unclaimed Experience: Trauma, Narrative, and History* (Baltimore: Johns Hopkins University Press, 1996).

a narrative memory as it is displayed, it will be argued, in Kleist's, Hoffmann's and Heine's texts. By their specific depictions of dance, and by the modes in which they depict it, the narratives bear testimony to this repetition compulsion, or else present the narration as a potentially curative tool that rhythmically works through, rather than repeats, the painful wounding.[59]

The alignment of language and dance leaves a residue of unrepresentability, of recalcitrant tensions that may be tracked in the individual case, but never resolved entirely. Language shows dance as much as hiding it; this is not because dance is beyond the symbolic, but rather because it constitutes an alternative symbolic order which is not congruent with the symbolic order of language. Dance 'speaks', yet it speaks otherwise. The rhetorical figures which are at stake in my close readings all have in common that they, too, 'speak otherwise'; as rhetoric categories of an intermedial character, they echo the dances which are described by the writers. Moreover, both the processes of verbalisation and of choreography are at once forces that alienate and techniques that heal. Writing recalls the dances it displays by becoming itself the medium of imitation, or compulsive repetition, by enacting a subversive performance, or by being the voice that works through a traumatic experience, bearing testimony to the vulnerable body. As talking and movement cure, language and dance are potentially recuperative arts and skills.

The following analyses of literature, dance and aesthetics thus unfold a multi-layered argument which draws on Foucault's investigation of practices of subjection and self-care, on Butler's theory of performance, and on theoretical explorations of the association between trauma and narrative. While the theories necessarily shaped my view of the material, the material in turn started to mould the theories, and made them interact in unforeseen ways. The notions of discipline, trauma and performance help to approach the dancing body in literature: bound to the imitative performance of cultural patterns, and idealised by aesthetic norms, ruled by the discipline of psychic automatisms, and empowered by creative choreographies.

---

59 See Shoshana Felman and Dori Laub, *Testimony: Crises of Witnessing in Literature, Psychoanalysis, and History* (London: Routledge, 1992).

Chapter 2

Heinrich von Kleist and the Mechanics of Grace

For equanimity is the virtue
But of the athletes. We human beings are not paid
for demonstrating our falls. – Yet we are meant
to show that we can rise in dignity.
(Heinrich von Kleist, *Die Familie Schroffenstein*)

Heinrich von Kleist's credibility as a dance writer stems from an undoubtedly singular text: *Über das Marionettentheater* (On the Marionette Theatre), published in the writer's journal *Berliner Abendblätter* (Berlin Evening Gazette) in 1810. The short dialogue is as alluring as it is perplexing. A dancer, Herr C., persuades an acquaintance of the superior grace of a marionette. This grace is explained by simple physical principles: 'Each movement, he said, had its center of gravity; it sufficed to control this point within the interior of the figures; the limbs, which were nothing but pendula, followed by themselves in a mechanical way without further assistance.'[1] An elaborate mathematical analysis of the puppet's movement follows. At the centre of the scientific discussion is the fact that the marionette is not human, that its body is weightless and lacks a person's consciousness and affects. Both stand in the way of perfectly calibrated dance, as evidenced in the clumsy performance of real ballet dancers. In Kleist's text, these dancers do not meet the aesthetic target. The balletic embodiment of neoclassicist beauty is thwarted by incompetence; yet the ideal itself, here the marionette, is haunted by its uncanny, dysfunctional double, dancing with prosthetic limbs: 'have you heard of those mechanical legs that English artists fabricate for unfortunates who have lost their limbs?' (*MT*, 417). The neoclassicist core of pain, so evident in the Laocoon group, is equally present in the text's second example of grace. Yet again we are confronted with the idealisation of injury, now in the sculpture of the youth drawing a splinter from his foot. And the allusion to wounding returns in the third anecdote that praises the sovereign grace of the bear who defends himself in a potentially lethal fencing match. Kleist thus names the consequences of the neoclassicist era: flawless beauty of movement or body is not only a mortifying ideal, it is also deeply compromised. The latter, however, brings the ideal closer to a more human range of comportment in the shape of the text's

---

1   English translation of *Über das Marionettentheater* by Roman Paska, in *Fragments for a History of the Human Body Part I*, ed. by Michel Feher (New York: Zone, 1990), pp. 415–21 (p. 415).

counterexamples to perfection: jerky performers, a young man who compulsively fails to imitate the desired sculptural pose, and a fencer who is helplessly over-challenged by his task.

Yet *Über das Marionettentheater* has even more on offer. Wrapping up the eighteenth-century discussions of beauty by uncovering their paradoxical quality, it presents us with an intricate paradoxical argument itself. As will be discussed later in this chapter, the narrative discourse follows, more precisely performs, the dialectic of idealizations and their traumatic underside. It does so by unfolding the polarised yet constantly intertwined metaphorical fields of mastery and failure, epitomised in the interaction of weightlessness and weight in the marionette's dance. Along the way, Kleist develops a formalist aesthetic of successful movement which stands in stark contrast to what audiences were used to seeing on stage at the time. The formalist vision recurs, metaphorically charged, in choreographies of 'standing upright' and 'falling' which are significant throughout Kleist's *œuvre*.[2] Before taking a closer look at these dances of the self, two important contexts deserve our attention: Friedrich Schiller's account of eighteenth-century discourses on grace,[3] and actual theories and practices of ballet around 1800, which Kleist may have experienced as a spectator.[4]

Aesthetics and Dance *c.* 1800

The following excursus on Schiller's ideas on grace complements the discourse on sculptural beauty in neoclassicism as outlined in the previous chapter. Grace is defined, after Schiller's well-known statement, as beauty of movement. Like the idealised Greek body shape, it is endowed with a moral mission; and it gives evidence of the same conflation of nature and discipline which is at the heart of the sculptural aesthetic. Schiller's main treatise on the problem, *Über Anmut und Würde* (Gracefulness and Dignity) appeared in 1793. It is thus highly probable that Kleist was familiar with this text when he wrote *Über das Marionettentheater*.

---

2   My approach is indebted to Helmut J. Schneider, 'Standing and Falling in Heinrich von Kleist', *MLN*, 115 (2000), 502–18, which stimulated me to look more closely at Kleistian choreographies.

3   See Gail K. Hart, 'Anmut's Gender: The *Marionettentheater* and Kleist's Revision of *Anmut und Würde*', *Women in German Yearbook*, 10 (1994), 83–95; see also Helmut J. Schneider, 'Deconstruction of the Hermeneutical Body: Kleist and the Discourse of Classical Aesthetics', in *Body & Text in the Eighteenth Century*, ed. by Veronica Kelly and Dorothea von Mücke (Stanford: Stanford University Press, 1994), pp. 209–26.

4   An article by Bettina Clausen and Harro Segeberg seems to be the only study on *Über das Marionettentheater* which mentions dance in concrete terms; they investigate early nineteenth-century ballet as a profession from a sociological point of view, in 'Technik und Naturbeherrschung im Konflikt: Zur Entzerrung einiger Bilder auch über Kleist und Goethe', in *Technik in der Literatur*, ed. by Harro Segeberg (Frankfurt am Main: Suhrkamp, 1987), pp. 33–50.

Arguing against the subjectivist turn in Kant's *Critique of Judgement, Gracefulness and Dignity* tries to regain an objective notion of the beautiful. The essay thus invokes the goddess Venus as absolute benchmark of feminine beauty; in order to fulfil this ideal, her build has to be matched by her bodily conduct, symbolised by the three graces that keep her company. Grace is that special something which makes the goddess truly charming: it is 'beauty of movement'.[5] What makes a movement beautiful, then? In earlier thoughts on the topic in his *Kallias* letters, Schiller had illustrated beautiful movement with the iconographical figure of an undulated line, probably with reference to Hogarth's line of beauty.[6] In Hogarth's as well as in Schiller's eyes, this line is beautiful because it incorporates freedom, since one could not say at which point precisely it changes direction. Thus 'gracefulness is the beauty of the entire form under the influence of Freedom' (*S*, 19). This freedom, however, can only be gained by a person who is at one with herself, who is able to reunite duty and inclination so that everything she wants is by definition morally flawless; in short, this person has to possess what Schiller calls a 'beautiful soul'. The outward appearance of the beautiful soul is grace. Like the undulated line, it is not determined by external forces, but by its own inner law. In Schiller's attempt to unify rationality and sensuality, it is autonomy which serves as the ultimate link. Self-determination, in the Kantian definition a major quality of rationality, appears in nature as the beautiful.

This rather abstract concept becomes flesh in the gracefully moving body. Tracing the ways in which the body can actually be made graceful, and the situations in which it displays this gracefulness, *Über Anmut und Würde* encounters a complicated situation: grace is decidedly rooted in the autonomous subject, and the body can be trained to be graceful – grace is the beauty 'of those phenomena which the Person determines' (*S*, 19); at the same time, however, it has to hide its man-made character: 'Grace [...] must always be (or at least seem) natural and spontaneous, i.e., not produced by the will, and the subject himself may never appear as if he *knew of his own gracefulness*' (*S*, 26). Schiller will take pains to explain the paradoxical natural artificiality, or artificial naturalness, at the base of his definition. The paradoxical

---

5   Friedrich Schiller, *Gracefulness and Dignity*, transl. by Leon Richard Liebner (University Microfilms International, 1979), p. 4. Compare Herder's earlier claim in *Sculpture*, p. 85: '[...] so the human creature acquires grace only through movement: *grace* is nothing but *beauty in movement*, be it in lines, forms, or deeds'.

6   Hogarth's *Analysis of Beauty* (1753) was translated into German by Lessing in 1754; Hogarth writes on the English country dance: 'The lines which a number of people together form in country or figure dancing, make a delightful play upon the eye, especially when the whole figure is to be seen at one view, as at the playhouse from the gallery; the beauty of this kind of mystic dancing, as the poets term it, depends upon moving in a composed variety of lines chiefly serpentine, govern'd by the principles of intricacy, &c. The dances of barbarians are always represented without these movements, being only composed of wild skiping, jumping, and turning round, or running backward and forward, with convulsive shrugs, and distorted gestures'; William Hogarth, *The Analysis of Beauty*, ed. by Ronald Paulson (New Haven: Yale University Press, 1997), p. 111.

setting is characteristic for the neoclassicist discourse of grace that placed the notion at the intersection of nature, serendipity, morality, and art.[7] Winckelmann's *Von der Grazie in Werken der Kunst* (An Essay on Grace in Works of Art, 1765), for instance, covers all these aspects. Here, grace is not defined as beauty's appearance, but as its predisposition:

> Grace is the harmony of agent and action. It is a general idea: for whatever reasonably pleases in things and actions is gracious. Grace is a gift of heaven; though not like beauty, which must be born with the possessor: whereas nature gives only the dawn, the capability of this. Education and reflection form it by degrees, and custom may give it the sanction of nature. [...] So grace is perfect when most simple, when freed from finery and constraint, and affected wit.[8]

Schiller tries to come to terms with this dialectical tension between constraint and ease of movement. He credits the unintentional, yet morally impeccable aspects of intentional gestures with the desired quality. Although he despises the artificiality of the grace of the dancing master, Schiller openly admits the civilising process which produces the 'naturalness' of these deliberate gestures:

> The dance-instructor indisputably contributes to true gracefulness in furnishing the will with mastery over its instruments and in removing the obstacles with which *mass* and *gravity* hinder the play of life-forces. He can accomplish this in no other way than with *rules* which maintain the body in wholesome discipline and which may, as long as indolence offers resistance, be and also look *rigid*, i.e. *forced*. But when the dance-master discharges the apprentice from his school, the rules must by then have had their effect so that they *need not accompany* him into the world: in short, the work of rules must become Nature. (*S*, 27)

He refers in the continuation of this passage to the actor, which reveals the pronounced theatrical aspect of his conception. In distinguishing between the 'truth' of acting and its grace, he again finds a way to deal with the paradoxical reunion of naturalness and artificiality, this time in terms of performance techniques. The 'truth' of an actor's performance – the technical ability to refrain from one's own personality in order to incorporate a role in a convincing manner – must be totally artificial, otherwise acting would not be an art. It demands a form of body control that stems from discipline, constraint and training. Grace, in contrast, is the *je ne sais quoi* which makes the performance complete; it is the part of acting which cannot be taught (earlier he wrote: which forgot that it was achieved through training). Now, in some contradiction of the passage on the dancing-master, grace is not at all a

---

7   For a detailed investigation of the discourse of grace in the eighteenth century, see Janina Knab, *Ästhetik der Anmut: Studien zur 'Schönheit der Bewegung' im 18. Jahrhundert* (Frankfurt am Main: Peter Lang, 1996).

8   Johann Joachim Winckelmann, *An Essay on Grace in Works of Art*, in *Reflections on the Painting and Sculpture of the Greeks*, transl. by Henry Fusseli (Menston: Scolar Press, 1972), pp. 273–87 (p. 273).

matter of learning, but an expression of the actor's human culture.[9] Schiller aims at a reconciliation of opposing principles – art and nature, heteronomy and autonomy, duty and inclination, the rationality of the mind and the sensuality of the body – in order to build up his idea of progress and education on the basis of aesthetics, which he formulates in his letters *Über die ästhetische Erziehung des Menschen* (On the Aesthetic Education of Mankind, 1795).[10]

Kleist picks up on Schiller's paradoxical concept of grace. In *Über das Marionettentheater*, the synthetic thinking that is necessary to gloss over a contradictory argument culminates in the point where it turns into persiflage. He engages with Schiller not only on a thematic level, but also through the way in which he stages his essay, more precisely: through the fact that he overtly stages what could have become a theoretical treatise.[11] As will be discussed in more detail later in this chapter, *Über das Marionettentheater* at once talks of performances and is a performance itself, *une scène écrite*, as Hélène Cixous has termed it.[12] Curiously enough, Kleist finds the guidelines for his theatrical vision in the marginal popular art-form of the puppet theatre, and in dance, which also played a subordinate role in the hierarchy of the arts in Germany. Having past its first prime under Jean Georges Noverre, who had turned Stuttgart's court ballet from 1760 to 1767 into the biggest and most brilliant of Europe's companies, the quality of ballet had declined by 1800. The unorthodox choice of models must be significant. Alexander Weigel draws attention to the fact that the puppet theatre was a subject of political controversy around 1810, and that Kleist indirectly defends it as a national tradition against the Berlin theatre under the direction of August Wilhelm Iffland, who was a favourite target of the author's criticism. The ballet examples in *Über das Marionettentheater* are in Weigel's view a mere pretext for pillorying contemporary theatre and acting practices.[13] Given that the *Abendblätter* were not allowed openly to criticise the royal theatres, ballet is seen as standing in for Iffland's affected acting, and for the politics

---

9 'But now, how shall I reply to the mime artist who wonders how he is to acquire it through *study*. He should, it is my opinion, first see to it that the humanity within him should itself come to maturity, and at that time he can go and (since it also happens to be his occupation) represent it on stage'; *S*, 28.

10 Carsten Zelle points out that rather than reconciling opposites, Schiller's aesthetic sustains aporias such as the one maintained in his notion of grace; Schiller solves contradictions by introducing new ones; see Zelle, *Die doppelte Ästhetik*, p. 170.

11 See Schneider, *Deconstruction*, p. 211.

12 Hélène Cixous 'Les marionettes: lecture de Kleist – le dernier chapitre de l'histoire du monde', in *Prénoms de personne* (Paris: Seuil, 1974), pp. 127–52 (p. 127).

13 See Alexander Weigel, 'Der Schauspieler als Maschinist: Heinrich von Kleists *Über das Marionettentheater* und das "Königliche Nationaltheater"', in *Heinrich von Kleist: Studien zu Werk und Wirkung*, ed. by Dirk Grathoff (Opladen: Westdeutscher Verlag, 1988), pp. 263–80; and his 'König, Polizist, Kasperle … und Kleist: Auch ein Kapitel deutscher Theatergeschichte, nach bisher unbekannten Akten', in *Impulse: Aufsätze, Quellen, Berichte zur deutschen Klassik und Romantik*, Vol. 4, ed. by Walther Dietze and Peter Goldammer (Berlin: Aufbau, 1982), pp. 253–77.

of his theatre. Under the guise of parody, Kleist expresses his disappointment with
the director's strategy of staging ballets, and trivial farces for financial reasons,[14]
instead of mounting one of his 'unplayable' dramas (in August 1810, Iffland had
rejected *Das Käthchen von Heilbronn*). Instead of mentoring young authors, the
theatre director behaved like a good businessman: from 1806 onwards, the National
Theatre had to attract the French occupiers in order to sustain itself. Partly due to the
language barrier, but certainly also due to France's image of fostering such frivolous
pleasures as dance, the staging of popularly appealing ballets increased. Iffland
writes in 1807:

> With the arrival of the French Army, the management, having described their
> circumstances, received official instructions from those in charge at the time, who were
> under the leadership of His Excellency Prince Hazfeld, to do everything in their power to
> ensure that the foreigners would find enjoyment in the performances, and that they were
> also to put on ballet, and that if, despite their good housekeeping, they should nevertheless
> fall short, then the municipal treasury would step in to secure the theatre's survival.[15]

Thus Kleist's criticism of ballet can also be read as anti-Napoleonic allusion, and
as disapproval of Prussian collaboration. However, his vision of dance, typified in
the movement of the marionette, is seen here as more than mere counter-vision to
the styles of acting and staging at Berlin.[16] Let us now take a closer look at early
nineteenth-century dance education and ballet aesthetics which set the writer's
reflections in a specific practical context.

To what experiences and images of dance could Kleist have been referring in
his essay? He was certainly familiar with social dancing, which was part of what
was considered a polite education in his day. Moreover, the *Abendblätter* feature
two notices on theatrical dance. On 3 November 1810, Achim von Arnim reports a
'strange mistake':

---

14 As we can read in the *Abendblätter*'s ironic 'praise' of the Berlin theatre *Brief eines
redlichen Berliners, das hiesige Theater betreffend, an einen Freund im Ausland* (Letter of an
Upright Berlin Citizen on our Theatre, to a Friend Abroad), in Heinrich von Kleist, *Sämtliche
Werke und Briefe* (4 vols), ed. by Ilse-Marie Barth, Klaus Müller-Salget, Stefan Ormanns,
Hinrich C. Seeba (Frankfurt am Main: Deutscher Klassiker Verlag, 1987–1997), Vol. III,
582.

15 Landesarchiv Berlin, A Rep. 001–01, n. 178, pp. 23, 23 v, General-Direction der
Königlichen Schauspiele (A.W. Iffland) an das Comité administratif, 11. 2. 1807, quoted
in Alexander Weigel, 'Das imaginäre Theater Heinrich von Kleists: Spiegelungen des
zeitgenössischen Theaters im erzählten Dialog *Ueber das Marionettentheater*, *Beiträge zur
Kleist-Forschung*, 14 (2000), 21–114, p. 40; transl. by Chantal Wright.

16 See Erika Fischer-Lichte, 'Theatralität: Zur Frage nach Kleists Theaterkonzeption',
Kleist-Jahrbuch (2001), 25–37. In *Das imaginäre Theater*, Alexander Weigel gives a detailed
survey of the practical and political aspects of theatre in Berlin around 1810; see also Bernhard
Greiner, '"Der Weg der Seele des Tänzers": Kleists Schrift *Über das Marionettentheater*',
Neue Rundschau, 98/3 (1987), 112–32; and his *Eine Art Wahnsinn: Dichtung im Horizont
Kants – Studien zu Goethe und Kleist* (Berlin: Schmidt, 1994).

Recently, by some inexplicable act of chance, several dances from the *Opernschneider* ballet were inserted during the grand finale of a performance of the incomparable *Iphigenia in Tauris*, the only *serious* opera in the world, to the great amusement of the audience. The audience afterwards declared that it would indeed be grateful if ballets were offered for its consideration but that these things were better placed at the very end of the performance if they could not be organically introduced at any other point. Further, they would also like the dancers to replace the three or four choreographies that have been doing the rounds since Vigano, like old, threadbare decorations, with a few new ones, particularly for a heroic opera. In the first act they would also prefer, rather than the one gentleman jumping, the duo of the two warriors as it is performed in Paris, in its effect and staging [...] the most perfect thing ever produced by dance.[17]

The brief report is paradigmatic for the state of affairs in German ballet around 1800. Theatre dance oscillated between its function as a supplement to the opera, being a diverting interlude often thematically unrelated to the content of the main piece, and an autonomous discipline. However, the ballet of the National Theatre was popular. Étienne Lauchery, ballet master in Berlin from 1788 to 1813, was particularly effective as a dramatic choreographer and practitioner of the *ballet d'action*. He choreographed as well as staged *ballets entr'actes* for operas and dramas, whose story-lines were usually based on well-known classical myths, concerned with light topics of courtship and romance. As a pupil of Jean-Georges Noverre, who emphasised the pantomime aspect of dance, Lauchery's ballets must have been lively and moving.[18] Under Lauchery's direction, the ballet even gained more autonomy.

Is it possible, then, that Kleist refers in *Über das Marionettentheater* to ballets he had actually seen on stage? Louis Schneider writes in his *Geschichte der Oper und des Koeniglichen Opernhauses in Berlin* (History of the Opera and of the Royal Opera House at Berlin) on a performance of Gluck's *Alceste* in 1804 that the opera

left one unmoved, which the singers blamed on the music and the connoisseurs on the staging. Gardel's ballet '*Le Jugement de Paris*' was performed to a selection of musical pieces by *Haydn, Pleyel, Mehul* etc., and was excellently received. The liking of audiences in Berlin for independent ballets has been observed since then. One was bored during *Alceste* and amused during the ballets.[19]

---

17 *Berliner Abendblätter*, ed. by Heinrich von Kleist (Leipzig, 1925; repr. Stuttgart: Cotta, 1959), p. 121, transl. by Chantal Wright.

18 On Étienne Lauchery, see Sibylle Dahms, 'Étienne Lauchery, der Zeitgenosse Noverres', in *Mozart und Mannheim, Kongreßbericht Mannheim 1991*, ed. by Ludwig Finscher et al. (Berne: Peter Lang, 1994), pp. 145–55, and also *International Encyclopedia of Dance*, ed. by Selma Jeanne Cohen et al., 6 vols (Oxford: Oxford University Press, 1998), IV, 128–9.

19 Louis Schneider, *Geschichte der Oper und des Koeniglichen Opernhauses in Berlin* (Berlin: Dunckcr und Humblot, 1852), p. 74, transl. by Chantal Wright.

One of the ballets referred to in *Über das Marionettentheater* could certainly be Pierre Gardel's *Le jugement de Paris*, which was performed in Paris since 1793, and taken up in Berlin in the first decade of the nineteenth century (Figure 2.1); however, there is also a ballet of the same title by Lauchery, which was given three times at Berlin between 1794 and 1795. The other ballet that figures in Kleist's essay might well allude to a piece entitled *Apoll und Daphne*, which was choreographed by Lauchery to music by G.A. Schneider, and performed for the first time on 9 October 1810, two months before the essay appeared in the *Abendblätter*.[20] Lauchery, 78 years old in 1810, must have made frequent use of the same pieces, re-staging or rearranging his former ballets. A *Recueil des Ballets* of his time at the Kassel court, where he worked from 1764 to 1772, already lists two pieces entitled *Apollon et Daphne* and *Le jugement de Paris* (Figures 2.2 and 2.3).[21] The *Opernschneider* mentioned in Arnim's earlier-quoted article was also choreographed by Lauchery. The Berlin ballet was actually ruled by a dynasty of Laucherys, which included besides Étienne his son Albert, who was a soloist from 1803 onwards, a ballet teacher named 'L. Lauchery', and a 'Mad. Lauchery', who danced the role of Daphne, and may have been the model for Kleist's dancer P. Certainly not a balletomane, Kleist might have seen mediocre performers in ridiculous pieces before his inner eye when thinking of ballet in Berlin around 1810, dominated by a mafia of dance practitioners that seemed to him outdated and uninspired.[22]

A second passage on ballet in the *Abendblätter* on 12 November 1810, under the section 'news of the police', could have been a concrete background for Kleist's thoughts on dance and gravity:

At the ballet yesterday in the theatre, the union of the day [sic] with the music, Minerva and the small boy were unlucky enough to fall along with the gloriole in which she was floating 12 to 15 feet above the ground. The dancer playing the role has injured one arm and one foot, but in the opinion of the doctors who came to her aid, she will be perfectly healthy within a few weeks. The boy [...] was not injured at all. The accident was caused by the main cable that was holding up the gloriole unravelling from its hold. The stagehand responsible for the gloriole has been arrested. As a replacement for the dancer could not immediately be found, they were unable to continue the performance.[23]

---

20 Berlin theatre statistics includes both of Lauchery's ballets, see C. Schäffer and C. Hartmann, *Die Königlichen Theater in Berlin: Statistischer Rückblick 1786–1885* (Berlin: 1886), pp. 5, 86.

21 *Recueil des ballets, exécuté sur les Théâtres de Cassel, depuis l'année 1754 jusqu'à la fin de l'année 1768. Inventé et composé par Mr. Lauchery* (Cassel, 1768), held in the British Library, London.

22 See Horst Häker's commentary on the autograph of *Sonderbares Versehen*, in *Heinrich von Kleist und Achim von Arnim: Zwei Autographen aus dem Jahre 1810*, ed. by Wolfgang Barthel (Frankfurt/Oder: Kleist Gedenk- und Forschungstätte Kleist-Museum, 1995), p. 16. Writing in 1901, Reinhold Steig, moreover, detected in *Über das Marionettentheater* a satirical and critical approach to the Berlin ballet under Iffland's direction, in Steig, *Heinrich von Kleists Berliner Kämpfe* (Berlin: Spemann, 1901), p. 236.

23 Kleist, *Abendblätter*, p. 146, transl. by Chantal Wright.

Venus.

Figure 2.1 **Costume drawing *Venus*, in 'Costumes de femmes, pour le ballet du *Jugement de Paris*' (Berlin, 1803).**

The dancer, hanging by a rope high above the floor, quite literally evokes the marionette on its strings; however, the former is definitely human and bound to gravity. Yet lightness and the illusion of overcoming the forces which tie the body to the earth – whether produced by mechanical devices or by training – were expected from an accomplished dancer, and anti-gravity, the advantage of Kleist's puppet, thus the desired attribute of perfect body control. The accident must have been a tragicomic demasking of the technical means necessary in order to lend ballet performances the required note of illusionism. As Blasis puts it in his *Code of Terpsichore*:

APOLLON ET D'APHNÉ
BALLET
HEROIQUE.

De la compofition de *Mr. L'AUCHERY Lainé*,
Maitre de dance de la Cour, & des Ballets
De S. A. S. Monfeigneur Le Landgrave de Heffe.

La Mufique eft de la compofition de Mrs. RODOLPHE & DELLER, Compofiteur de la
Mufique de S. A. S. Monfieur Le Duc de Wirtemberg.

Imprimé a Caffel, chez Jean Martin Lüdicke.

Figure 2.2   Title page of *Apollon et Daphne*, in 'Recueil des ballets, exécuté
sur les Théâtres de Cassel, depuis l'année 1764 jusqu'à la fin
de l'année 1768. Inventé et composé par Mr Lauchery' (Cassel,
1768).

LE JUGEMENT
DE PARIS
BALLET
PASTORAL HEROIQUE.

De la compofition de Mr. L'AUCHERY Lainé,
Maitre de dance de la Cour, & des Ballets
De S. A. S. Monſeigneur Le Landgrave de Heſſe.

Imprimé à Caſſel, chez Jean Martin Lödicke.

Figure 2.3 Title page of *Le Jugement de Paris*, in 'Recueil des ballets, exécuté sur les Théâtres de Cassel, depuis l'année 1764 jusqu'à la fin de l'année 1768. Inventé et composé par Mr Lauchery' (Cassel, 1768).

The illusion of the scene ought to be so perfect, as to cause what is merely artificial to appear real, during the time of its representation. Neither a picture nor a ballet can be deemed excellent, unless the art used in producing it is so far kept down, that nature only is admired in it; art should do its work unseen; its greatest triumph is to conceal itself.[24]

In line with the aesthetic tone of the day, the steps, poses and facial expressions of the dancers also had to give the impression of being natural: the dancer's 'steps and movements are artificial; they are not natural, yet they are supposed to display naturalness', says the dance manual by Theodor Hentschke, who took up Blasis' precepts'.[25] However, only after exercising endless, repetitive constraints over the body was the classical dancer able to incorporate immediacy, nature and lightness. Referring to Blasis' guidelines, Hentschke writes on the professional dancer:

We have to get used to an upright posture and to the perfect balance of the body; we need to dance correctly and with precision; the timing has to be organized according to the best principles, and the execution of the *pas* has to be brilliant and graceful at all times. [...] The dancer must never show any effort; the highest achievement of art is to disguise its artfulness.[26]

The most explicitly artificial aspect of this art, the *pointe* technique, which was developed during the first decades of the nineteenth century as the ability to rise to the tips of the toes and achieve the impression of anti-gravity so crucial to the notion of grace, required particularly arduous practice of systematised exercises. E.A. Théleur's 1831 manual of technique *Letters on Dancing Reducing this Elegant and Healthful Exercise to Easy Scientific Principles* lists, for instance, the following exercise meant to meet the demand for dancing on the toes in soft, not yet blocked slippers:

To gain strength on the points of the toes, the strength of the great toes should be added to that of the ankles, keeping the joints of the toes perfectly straight from the commencement of the movement, rising gradually from the ground, then in the same manner permitting the heels to descend. By continuing this practice, strength will be obtained on the points of the toes.[27]

The difference between practitioners and thinkers becomes obvious here: while the dance-masters, who are involved in the actual production of the graceful body, do not hold back the artificiality of the idealised naturalness, Schiller's concept of grace proclaims its own staging of naturalness as 'real' nature, as if after the

---

24 Blasis, *The Code of Terpsichore*, p. 526.

25 Theodor Hentschke, *Allgemeine Tanzkunst* (Stralsund: Hauschildt, 1836; repr. Leipzig: Zentralantiquariat der DDR, 1986), p. 4.

26 Ibid., pp. 182–3.

27 E.A. Théleur, *Letters on Dancing Reducing this Elegant and Healthful Exercise to Easy Scientific Principles* (London, 1831), pp. 55–6, quoted in Sandra Noll Hammond, 'Searching for the Sylph: Documentation of Early Developments in *Pointe* Technique', *Dance Research Journal*, 19/2 (1987/1988), 27–31 (p. 28).

achievement of lightness and autonomy of movement there was no requirement for 'heteronomous' exercising, and its continuous practice. Entangling himself in a web of contradictions, Schiller may have had a vision of 'natural body control' in mind which the American choreographer Merce Cunningham brings to the point almost two centuries later:

> The daily workout, the continued keeping of the elasticity of the muscles, the constant control of the mind over the body's actions, both new and renewed is not a natural way. It is unnatural in its demands on all the sources of energy. But the final synthesis can be a natural result, natural in the sense that the mind, body and spirit function as one.[28]

The technique manuals of classical ballet, however, never tried to dissimulate the mechanical drill that was needed to turn the dancer's body into an instrument. As discussed in the first chapter, the eighteenth-century fascination with automata must have had an influence on the development of a technique as ingenious as classical dance training in producing the flawlessly functioning body: the perfection of mechanical dolls seems to have set the standard for bodily appearance and aplomb on stage.[29] It thus makes sense that Kleist's Herr C. chooses a mechanical puppet for his demonstration of the ideal dancer; and yet this choice presents the reader with nothing less than a shock. The negative judgement of the image of the machine which we find in eighteenth-century aesthetics was shared by the authors of dance treatises. Thus the dance-masters who are summoned by Schiller in order to distinguish his insistence on nature from their affectation, were in fact anxious to declare the mechanical aspects of their art a mere means to achieve the desired effects. It is important to see the distinction here between ballet as a technique and ballet as a dramatic art. When using the image of the machine or the marionette, dance manuals point out the stupidity of merely athletic virtuosity that is lacking in what makes dance into an art: the mediation of feelings and passions, embodied in vivid stories.

In his *Lettres sur la danse, et sur les ballets* (Letters on Dancing and Ballets, 1760) Jean-Georges Noverre emphasises the importance of soulful, natural expression.[30] Without denying the fact that the dancer's body has to be a machine-like tool, he states a clear difference between the 'bad' and the 'good' machine. Noverre compares the mindless dancer to an 'ill-ordered machine' and demands:

---

28 Merce Cunningham, 'Studio', <http://www.merce.org/studio.html> (accessed September 2004) (para. 1 of 2).

29 See Susan Leigh Foster, *Choreography and Narrative: Ballet's Staging of Story and Desire* (Bloomington: Indiana University Press, 1996), p. 79.

30 It is very probable that Schiller saw some of Noverre's ballets at Stuttgart, and knew his *Letters*; see Gabriele Brandstetter, '"Die Bilderschrift der Empfindungen": Jean-Georges Noverres *Lettres sur la Danse, et sur les Ballets* und Friedrich Schillers Abhandlung *Über Anmut und Würde*', in *Schiller und die höfische Welt*, ed. by Achim Aurnhammer et al. (Tübingen: Niemeyer, 1990), pp. 77–93.

Let us study then, Sir, let us cease to resemble marionettes, the movements of which are directed by clumsy strings which only amuse and deceive the common herd. If our souls determine the play and movement of our muscles and tendons, then the feet, body, features and eyes will be stirred in the right manner, and the effects resulting from this harmony and intelligence will interest equally the heart and the mind.[31]

Noverre initiated a ballet reform that shifted the emphasis away from the formal aspects of *ballet de cour*. Not least as a bourgeois response to courtly affectation, Noverre propagated a more authentic dramatic style, and stressed the narrative potential of a dance performance. The supremacy of plot is characteristic for the new genre of *ballet d'action* where gesture, movement, mime, costume, stage decoration and music all serve to tell stories, instead of celebrating absolutist power. The semiotics of dance became more complex: only in gaining the status of gesture, and not through pure, mechanical movement, could dance be deemed graceful. Not only in comparison to Schiller, then, whose grace is the expression of the soul, but also in relation to the 'proper' dance aesthetics of his time, which were still indebted to the eighteenth-century paradigms, Kleist's concept of the gracefully moving marionette stands out for its striking subversion of conventional assessments.

It is the lifelessness of his vision – the ultimate marionette is operated by a crank – which is especially remarkable. The puppet's limbs are dead, like pendulums merely following their little bit of weight, its facial expression is not even mentioned; whereas Noverre writes:

> [...] by gesture I understand the expressive movements of the arms, supported by striking and varied expressions of the features. But a dancer's arms will speak in vain if his face be unmoved. If the alteration in the features produced by the passions be not visible, if his eyes neither declare nor betray the sentiments with which he is swayed, then its expression is false, its play is mechanical and the resulting effect loses by the discord and defect of truth and verisimilitude.[32]

These facial expressions must not show any effects of the sudorific activities the dancer's legs are involved in; she or he has to gain the lightness of having mastered the technical efforts in order to be free to represent the required passions, the 'spirit' or soul of the dance:

> Every dancer whose face alters as the result of his physical efforts, and whose features are continually in a state of convulsion, is a bad dancer who disregards the first principles of his art, who concerns himself only with the mechanical side of dancing, and who has never penetrated its spirit.[33]

---

31 Jean-Georges Noverre, *Letters on Dancing and Ballets*, transl. by Cyril W. Beaumont (London: Cyril W. Beaumont, 1930), p. 108.

32 Noverre, p. 101.

33 Ibid., p. 86.

Where is the place of the soul in Kleist's argument? Noverre's dancer carries his soul in his face, while the face of the marionette is not even mentioned. Soul, in Kleist, is turned into *vis motrix*; 'the path of the dancer's soul' is the graceful line described by his centre of gravity, generated by limbs that react to the impulses of the centre of the body. Here, Kleist unfolds an intricate play on the German word for both impulse and allure, *Reiz*, which is in the eighteenth century also used synonymously with grace.[34] While *Reiz*, as allure, if too aware of an audience, bears the dangers of affectation, of Kleistian *Ziererei*, it shifts, as stimulus, towards a mechanistic template for creating this effect. In the Kleistian marionette, the interplay of impulse and reaction is the very principle of true grace. The soul as *vis motrix*, impulse, or *Reiz*, only appears in its purely external manifestation, in the effect that is pleasing to the eye.[35] Instead of Schiller's two-level model of an internal substance which is mediated through movement, the movement gains essential quality.[36] Soul takes shape in a curved line. Following the definition of grace as beauty in motion, Kleist sets out to investigate the laws of this motion, 'simple' and 'mysterious' at once (*MT*, 416). He defends a formalist approach to movement at a time where both philosophical aesthetics and dance theory valued it because of its representational quality.[37] Being appalled by the poor standard of representational dance of the Berlin ballet that could not live up to Noverre's high-flying ideas – or showed their decline – the writer is concerned with the quality of movement, rather than with dramatic content. It is arguably the originality of this position in its historical context that makes Kleist's vision so fascinating. Instead of reflecting early nineteenth-century action ballet, it foresees the twentieth century's formalist schools of classical dance, such as the one established by the choreographer George Balanchine:

---

34 In Johann Georg Sulzer's eighteenth-century encyclopaedia of art, the article on *Reiz* starts as follows: 'We are using this word to refer to the same phenomenon which various of our experts on art call grace', referring then to Winckelmann; Johann Georg Sulzer, *Allgemeine Theorie der schönen Künste*, 5 vols (Leipzig 1792–1794; repr. Hildesheim: Olms, 1967–70), IV, 98.

35 Thus Kleist's aesthetic reflections also refer to a physiological model. Philipp Sarasin shows how the understanding of the body as, in his words, *reizbare* (excitable) machine was maintained in the discourse of hygiene from the Enlightenment to the beginnings of genetics in the twentieth century. This discourse sustained *Reiz* as the body's driving force in contrast to the various claims on the soul by Catholicism, Romanticism, and Pietism; see Philipp Sarasin, *Reizbare Maschinen: Eine Geschichte des Körpers 1765–1914* (Frankfurt am Main: Suhrkamp, 2001), p. 20.

36 See Schneider, *Deconstruction*, p. 212. Nicholas Saul elaborates Kleist's 'committed exploration of surface' in 'Body, Language, and Body Language: Thresholds in Heinrich von Kleist' in *Schwellen: Germanistische Erkundungen einer Metapher* (Würzburg: Königshausen & Neumann, 1999), pp. 316–32 (p. 319).

37 August Wilhelm Schlegel's lecture on dance is an exception. Although complaining about the shallowness of the ballet, he mentions the ornamental and material aspects of dance as its true charms, in *Vorlesungen über Ästhetik I*, ed. by Ernst Behler (Paderborn: Schöningh, 1989), p. 383.

What are the elements that constitute the singular beauty of classical ballet? One might say: Among other things, certainly, a tension between weight and weightlessness. But George Balanchine was one of the first to regard this tension as the concealed essence of the ballet art, and especially as the essence of the phenomenon of grace.[38]

Rather than a victory of weightlessness over weight, it is indeed their very tension which characterises Kleistian dances. The graceful puppet not only defies her weight, her limbs also follow 'the basic law of gravity' (*MT*, 417). While anti-gravity is central to Schiller's argument, it might have been overrated in Kleist. In Schiller, physical laws represent external forces; those forces, be it the internalised gaze of the other that constitutes self-reflection, or the commands of a dancing master, by which the individual must not be determined in order to be free. He introduces his idea of beautiful freedom in the *Kallias* letters by citing gravity as an example for heteronomy, and anti-gravity as an image for autonomy. The ultimate artificiality of such a concept of beauty culminates in Kleist's marionette; even more significant, however, is Kleist's paradoxical dissolving of Schiller's binary oppositions, in devising a concept of grace that includes gravity.

Grace and Affectation in *Über das Marionettentheater*

There are numerous critical studies which attempt to follow the trickeries of Kleist's writing. Beginning with Hanna Hellmann's reading of 1911, scholarship took the *Marionettentheater* as a key text for the understanding of Kleist's *œuvre*.[39] Yet also the ironic nature of the text and its dialogic conception have often been underlined.[40] It is by now commonly agreed that the dialogue between the narrator and Herr C. is full of contradictory tensions, and that it cannot be interpreted as a theoretical disputation or logical proof of an argument. It is a poetic text, or as Paul de Man puts it, 'although *Marionettentheater* can be said to be *about* proof, it is not set up as one but as the story or trope of such a demonstration'.[41]

---

38 David Michael Levin, 'Balanchine's Formalism', in Copeland and Cohen, pp. 123–45 (p. 123).

39 Hanna Hellmann, *Heinrich von Kleist: Darstellung des Problems* (Heidelberg, 1911), pp. 13–30.

40 See, for instance, Beda Allemann, 'Sinn und Unsinn von Kleists Gespräch *Über das Marionettentheater*', *Kleist-Jahrbuch* (1981/82), 50–65; Gerhard Kurz, '"Gott befohlen": Kleists Dialog *Über das Marionettentheater* und der Mythos vom Sündenfall des Bewußtseins', *Kleist-Jahrbuch* (1981/82), 264–77; James A. Rushing, 'The Limitations of the Fencing Bear: Kleist's *Über das Marionettentheater* as Ironic Fiction', *The German Quarterly*, 61/4 (1988), 528–39.

41 Paul de Man, 'Aesthetic Formalization: Kleist's *Über das Marionettentheater*', in de Man, *The Rhetoric of Romanticism* (New York: Columbia University Press, 1984), pp. 263–90; other studies on the rhetoric of the text are, for example, Clemens Heselhaus, 'Das Kleistsche Paradox', in *Kleists Aufsatz über das Marionettentheater*, ed. by Helmut Sembdner (Berlin: Schmidt, 1967), pp. 112–31, or Brittain Smith, 'Pas de Deux: Doing the Dialogic Dance in

Despite its striking function in the dialogue, the fact that Kleist chose dance as the art form to which his two protagonists constantly refer has received comparatively little attention in the academic literature. There are, however, exceptions.[42] Müller-Farguell's *Tanz Figuren* engages most thoroughly with movement in Kleist. Concentrating on the representation of textual motion in *Marionettentheater*, he traces Kleist's attempt to find a mathematic-geometrical formula for movement, which intertwines logical thought and metaphorical use of language in order to achieve a dynamic figurality of thinking and writing.[43] However, my approach sets out from the fact that this motion is clearly marked as dance, which is concrete cultural practice, and set in a specific aesthetic and historical context. Special attention will be given to the decidedly physical examples of the text, to the fact that consciousness or grace are discussed in their bodily manifestations. The intention here is to trace these manifestations carefully since their choreography allows subtle insights into their poetic value; they also elucidate Kleist's ways of depicting the subjectivity of his figures. The rhetorical strategy of paradox becomes a guiding principle of both the physical and the narrative movement.

The body is indeed one of the pivotal agents in Kleist's *œuvre*: the powerful corporeal dimension of his writing, the literalness of his bodily metaphors or the parallels he draws between phenomena of the body and those of the soul have been widely considered as one of its outstanding characteristics.[44] In *Marionettentheater*, the body, and specifically the dancing, performing body, takes centre stage in the course of the argument. The text's examples and anecdotes demonstrate that embodiment – in the sense of being aware of one's own and the other's body – is a way of acting.[45] The preoccupation with performing in its psycho-social sense as a mode of bearing the gaze of the other, and of oneself, by oscillating between the wish for authenticity and the need for posing, often recurs in Kleist's letters and writings. The divide between the blessings of the non-conscious presence of such Kleistian figures as Käthchen, or Prince Friedrich von Homburg, and the curse of (self-)consciousness appears unbridgeable. Yet as the following sections aim to demonstrate, the metaphor of the marionette presents a complex, and in a sense counterintuitive theatrical solution to the dilemma, symbolizing a dance of the

---

Kleist's Fictitious Conversation About the Puppet Theater', in *Compendious Conversations: The Method of Dialogue in the Early Enlightenment*, ed. by Kevin L. Cope (Frankfurt am Main: Peter Lang, 1992), pp. 368–81; a deconstructive approach is given by Cynthia Chase, 'Models of Narrative: Mechanical Doll, Exploding Machine', *Oxford Literary Review*, 6/2 (1984), 57–69.

42 The dialogue has been described as a *pas de deux* of the two partners, see Smith, p. 369.

43 See Müller-Farguell, pp. 109–75. Beda Allemann also points out the metaphorical character of dance as a general poetological model, aligning the movement of the text with the movement of the body; see Allemann, p. 61.

44 See Alexander Košenina, 'Will er "auf ein Theater warten, welches da kommen soll?" Kleists Ideen zur Schauspielkunst', *Kleist-Jahrbuch* (2001), 38–54 (p. 38).

45 See Schneider, *Deconstruction*, p. 212.

self which stabilises Kleistian characters in the midst of catastrophic and agonistic scenarios.

In Kleist, absolute dancerly grace is a non-human quality. The most accomplished dance 'could take place totally in the realm of mechanical forces' (*MT*, 416): a crank figures as the superlative puppeteer. As the movements become more and more ideal, the natural conditions for dancing are disfigured. The surmounting of the organic body culminates in the bewildering praise of the prosthesis, drawing the reader's attention to the fact that flawless perfection cannot be separated from fragmentation and lifelessness. The final image of the super-marionette enacts a vision of naturalness beyond life. Its artificially constructed centres of gravity are arranged more 'naturally' than in the human body, its members merely react to the law of gravity while being at the same time held up by the master. The model of the marionette which reaches its climax in the virtuoso cripple is a distorted echo of classical dance as a cultural technique that is based on the 'taking away' of unwanted bodily features, or of inelegant views of the body through potentially painful manipulations. The 'crippling' activity, however, leads to beautifully regulated kinetic processes. Recalling the ballet dancer's movement, in Kleist, the cripple's dance is 'limited', and yet full of 'ease, lightness and grace' (*MT*, 417). The classical dancer's body can be interpreted, with Hayden White, as at once masochistic and serene.[46]

Taking into account the fact that ballet training followed the guidelines of geometry – 'geometrical forms are most useful to make the pupil understand the various poses of the body'[47] – and that a balanced posture was crucial to perform the technically demanding *pas*, Kleist's dancer's fascination with his doll becomes understandable. However, Herr C.'s less than strictly logical discourse undermines itself and thus debunks the 'science' of aesthetics; by accentuating the ultimate naturalness of the marionette's movements, moreover, he carries the paradox of Idealism's staging of naturalness to a peak where it turns into sheer absurdity.[48] The price for the puppet's extreme perfection is high: it has lost, or more precisely, never had, any humanity. Kleist comments on Schiller's denial of the constructionist aspects of gracefulness by dismantling what is suppressed in this discourse, namely the artificiality and theatricality of the Idealist notion of nature, and of 'natural gracefulness'.

If the marionette stands for a highly subverted classicist ideal, the ballet dancers, in Kleist, show the impossibility of reaching this ideal. In keeping with other Kleistian figures, and not least with the author himself, these dancers are at odds with the institution. Their main flaw is that they are affected: *sie zieren sich*, as the

---

46 See Jock Abra, 'The Dancer as Masochist', *Dance Research Journal*, 19/2 (1987/88), 33–9.

47 Hentschke, p. 181.

48 Although contributing to the aesthetic discourse himself, Sulzer takes an equally critical stance. Before proceeding with his explanation of the notion of grace, he proposes that the 'notion of grace may suffer the fate of similar metaphysical terms. Notwithstanding that no-one understands them, they are used by those who want to impress by explaining things which no other mortal can explain'; Sulzer, IV, 88.

German has it. Affectation functions as counter-notion to grace. It manifests itself in the mannerist gesture, resulting from the fact that the balanced play of impulse and gravity runs out of kilter. Affected dancers have lost their centre. Yet what is more, it also indicates the human condition at large, the fact that human beings are 'fallen'. The consequence of the Fall, the loss of spiritual grace and innocence, is represented by the loss of physical grace. Herr C.'s gaze, which had been directed at the laws behind the scenes of grace at the beginning of the text, swiftly moves to performances on stage, or meant for the eye of a beholder, performances that lack the techniques which have been investigated before. The very differences between the perfect performer and the flawed human being, affectation and weight, are shown to be the disastrous effects of post-lapsarian consciousness, and by extension of desire and shame, on the unity of bodily movement. The puppet's movements, free from desire and shame, are self-contained, centred, and closed; its body is necessarily asexual. The protagonists considered now are driven by the desire to move toward the other, to please or to resist the other. Their gestures become ill at ease and thus ex-centric; they are falling out of balance. Apollo and Daphne, Paris and Venus, Adam and Eve, the youth in the baths, the narrator and Herr C. himself: mythological, biblical, fictional figures, seen through a Kleistian eye that abstains from reproducing heroic narratives.

All of these examples deal with a quest for perfection, be it knowledge, love, beauty or superiority in fight, which can never be fulfilled. Attempts at overcoming a fundamental lack must fail: desire is punished, leads into catastrophe or remains unfulfilled. Significantly enough, Kleist places two of his parables in the realm of ballet, *the* art not only of bodily perfection, but also, from the nineteenth century onwards, of staged desire. At least in the case of Apollo and Daphne, he was presumably inspired by the actual dance piece; yet the examples tell of more than just of a concrete historical influence. Paris' desire is overshadowed by catastrophe, provoking a war for the prize of beauty. The dancer's gesture that seals this fate is thus hopelessly out of centre, in the writer's words: 'look at young F. – when, as Paris, he stands among the three goddesses and presents the apple of Venus; his soul is actually (it's frightful to see) in his elbow' (*MT*, 417). In the case of Apollo and Daphne, it is the woman whose performance lacks assurance. The dancer P. who is performing Daphne turning into a tree – one cannot help but wondering how this was staged – is compared to Bernini's sculpture of the metamorphosis. The moment when she turns her head towards her suitor accounts, in Kleist, for the mannerism of her pose: her central impulse, not any more in the balanced position necessary for graceful movement, 'is in the vertebrae of her lower back' (*MT*, 417). In contrast to the chaste and aloof mythological figure, her impersonators seem to be flirtatiously aware of being chased (Figure 2.4).[49]

---

49 The fact that Bernini is invoked might not only be caused by his sculpture on the same theme, but also by Winckelmann's judgement of Bernini, of whom he says: 'At last *Lorenzo Bernini* appeared, a man of spirit and superior talents, but whom grace had never visited even

A striking intertext here is Wieland's *Geschichte des Agathon* (The History of Agathon). Kleist greatly admired and respected Wieland, and it is likely that he knew his novel, first published in 1767. The recourse to a dance piece on the myth of Apollo and Daphne for explaining affectation might be a secret homage to the poet who was, during a few months of Kleist's life, something like a father figure. Chapter Five in the forth book of *Agathon*, entitled *Pantomimen*, figures a scene where a dancer performing the role of Daphne fails precisely in the respect that is called affectation in the *Marionettentheater*. At first, the expressiveness of the dancers is convincing: 'The whole company was delighted with the skill of the dancers, they were all life and expression, so that one would have imagined they spoke what they only acted'. When asked whether he, too, liked the performance, Agathon criticises the female dancer: 'I am of the opinion, [...] that probably, from too earnest a desire of pleasing, she has mistaken the character. Why, in her flight, does she look behind her? And with a look too, which seems to reproach her pursuer, that he is not swifter than she?'[50] In Wieland's novel, the dance is then repeated by another woman, who displays all the skills of unconscious grace accorded, in Kleist, to the marionette. A conversation on the art of dancing, the content of which is not disclosed, forms the end of the chapter. The reader only hears: 'We cannot, however, omit mentioning, that upon this occasion Agathon became eloquent, as he had before been pensive and silent; a chearful serenity enlivened his whole countenance, and his wit had never before appeared so brilliant and entertaining'.[51] *Über das Marionettentheater*, then, might stand in for Wieland's omission, inheriting its light-footedness and wit from the former scene.

The tales of catastrophe and unfulfilled erotic wishes lead back to their myth of origin, Adam and Eve, the couple implied in the mentioning of paradise and Fall. The biblical reference sets the stage for the dialectic of desire and lack; it also points up exposure and shame, two crucial aspects of Kleist's argument. The tales that build up the narrative of lost grace unfold a play of exposure and hiding, of advance and retreat. The graceful Venus, in order to convince Paris of her superior beauty, simply loosens the girdle of her tunic; whereas Adam and Eve, after becoming aware of their exposed nakedness, cover themselves with leaves. This pattern is not only the structure of attraction, flirtation, shame and fear, but also lends itself to being choreographed. *Pas de deux*, in their staging of desire, are composed of advancing and retreating figures, advances and retreats that also characterise the choreography of Kleist's dialogue itself. It seems to weave its stories not only around some core of traumatic vulnerability, but also of illicit nakedness. This is indicated by the awkwardness of the men's gestures, the repeated casting of their eyes to the ground, resulting, perhaps, from the strangeness of a chance conversation that is almost

---

in dreams', p. 285; however, in Winckelmann, the sculpture of Apollo and Daphne is the only one of Bernini's works which is deemed to come close to the ideal of grace.

50 Christoph Martin Wieland, *The History of Agathon*, transl. by John Richardson, 4 vols (London: Cadell, 1773), I, 232.

51 Ibid., p. 239.

Figure 2.4   Gian Lorenzo Bernini, *Apollo and Daphne* **(c. 1622/23).**

indecently intimate and far-reaching.[52] Moreover, Herr C.'s profession is to practise a form of expression which can escape the censorship that written performance texts were subject to. Theatrical dance is, after all, a display of the body, legitimised by the frame of art. This quality would become more and more important throughout the first half of the nineteenth century. As McCarren puts it, the dancer's body told 'stories of love and desire, the body's stories, without actually having to "tell"'.[53] Relating the body's stories under the cover of a discussion of aesthetics, Kleist's written pantomimes, and their actors, at once disguise and tell.

Kleist's desiring, affected bodies are inextricably linked to *Bewußtsein*, which is best translated by 'self-consciousness', the fact that man is constantly watching

52 On the homoerotic tension in *Marionettentheater*, see László F. Földény, 'Die Inszenierung des Erotischen: Heinrich von Kleist, *Über das Marionettentheater*', *Kleist-Jahrbuch* (2001), 135–47.

53 See McCarren, pp. 10–11.

himself – and feels watched by others – which results in ungraceful insecurity of movement and behaviour, and in alienation. The clumsy affectation of the dancers consists in their awareness of being observed, and in their observing themselves being on display for an audience, so that Herr C. concludes that if 'reflection grows dimmer and weaker, […] grace […] becomes more brilliant and powerful (*MT*, 420) As self-consciousness in *Marionettentheater* means primarily consciousness of the body, the second bite from the apple of knowledge that is summoned to bring back grace is, thus, to be understood as superior knowledge, and superior control, of the body.

In the case of the dancers, and of the youth in the baths, however, the exposed body cannot be controlled in an aesthetically satisfying way; it gives reason for embarrassment. The primal scene of this *prise de corps* as the origin of shame is Adam's and Eve's fall from grace. Yet the alliance of self-consciousness, observation, exposure and shame is most concisely spelt out in the scene with the boy taking a bath. Again, the ideal of embodied perfection plays a crucial role. The narrator recalls the story of a young man who is unable to repeat his spontaneously graceful pose once he is told to do so. Grace, here, is embedded in scenarios of explicit observation: it is discovered through the young man's gaze in the mirror, and spoilt by the fatal effects of the gaze of the other, blending with the protagonist's own way of looking at himself. The initial gracefulness of his pose consists in its similarity to a statue the boy and his companion have visited: 'A glance that he cast in a large mirror the moment he placed his foot on a stool to dry it off reminded him of it; he smiled and told me what a discovery he had made' (*MT*, 419). Following the demand of his beholder, he tries to recreate the moment, but no longer achieves his former charm. The more he tries, the more he watches himself, the less he succeeds. Despite the fact that the story is meant to prove Herr C.'s thesis that self-consciousness destroys graceful movement, it rather shows shame as a fatal hindrance to grace. It is not only – or not at all – the gaze in the mirror that costs the young man his innocence. For a moment, he is able to perceive his own gracefulness. The turning-point comes when the observer teases him because of his vanity, and thus embarrasses him. With his mockery, the beholder urges the young man to repeat the pose, which incites the latter's wishing to regain the former state of perfection, resulting in ever failing attempts. Maybe he would have had more success if he had been alone with the mirror. In ballet exercise, the mirror is indeed absolutely necessary for achieving graceful movement. Noverre writes: 'Let us consult our mirror often, it is a fine teacher which will always reveal our faults and indicate to us the means of mitigating and eradicating them, if we go before it free from self-esteem and ridiculous prejudices.'[54] Even if the parable is told to convey the idea that grace cannot be constructed: the gracefulness of the marionette is obviously a constructed one and can be explained in detail. The puppet does not watch itself; however, the mere act of self-perception and the attempt to reconstruct a certain posture, do not spoil the boy's grace either.

---

54 Noverre, p. 90.

Shame and coyness are closely connected to the failure of fulfilling the criteria of an ideal self – and an ideal body.[55] Recalling the neoclassicist heritage of Winckelmann or Herder, for the young man, this ideal body is epitomised in the graceful posture of a statue. Like the other ideal body, the puppet, a statue *cannot* be ashamed of itself; and the classical dancer, striving to achieve a marionette's ease of movement, and a sculpture's perfect shape, *must not* show any sign of embarrassment. Theodor Hentschke writes: 'If a dancer whishes to please the eye of the spectator, he must always please himself. His posture and *tournure* ought to be impeccable, the attitudes of his arms, legs and feet amiable, the positions elegant, without showing any sign of affectation.'[56] The failure of the Kleistian protagonist, therefore, is not that he acts where he should be natural, as Schiller would put it. He fails as performer: he cannot cope with his exposure on stage, or in front of a beholder.

An interesting subtext here is the cultural difficulty with the display of male gracefulness which grew more and more acute in the nineteenth century. Thanks to Winckelmann and others, the feminine gendering of grace in the shape of the tradition of the three graces had been matched, or even superseded, by its attribution to the male body in eighteenth-century aesthetic thought. Of even stronger importance was its association with a more general anthropological principle, which is also evident in Schiller: the main characteristic of grace was its mediation between the inner and the outer; gracefulness becomes the outward signature of the soul.[57] The only human being who displays a fugitive moment of grace in Kleist is a young man. While uncontested physical grace, in Kleist, is an asexual state, a state before sexuality and the frailties it engenders, his invocation of masculine grace also recalls the aristocratic tradition of the accomplished male performer, ideally the king, which stands at the origin of classical ballet. In the nineteenth century, the dancerly attribution of grace to both genders is, however, far more problematic. The male dancer's association with aristocratic power was lost, and the subtle ephebophilia of the neoclassicist aesthetic too disconcerting a discourse to be openly admitted on or off stage.

Yet the de-feminisation of grace, or, in turn, a male elegance that was perceived as effeminacy, are characteristic of classical dance. Even if dance manuals draw a distinction between masculine and feminine forms of movement – 'The male dancer has to impress by powerful, energetic *pas*, by *tours de force* and sappy, athletic positions, the female dancer by graceful and supple movements, or by an unobtrusive plenitude of attitudes'[58] – gracefulness was an overall demand, applied to both female and male dancers: 'dancers should learn [...] the real mode of displaying themselves with taste and gracefulness'.[59] In the course of the nineteenth century, especially

---

55 See Claudia Benthien, 'Gesichtverlust und Gewaltsamkeit: Zur Psychodynamik von Scham und Schuld in Kleists *Familie Schroffenstein*', *Kleist-Jahrbuch* (1999), 128–43 (p. 134).

56 Hentschke, pp. 185–6.

57 See Knab p. 14.

58 Hentschke, p. 181.

59 Blasis, p. 75.

throughout the era of the Romantic ballet, this imperative of grace became a double-bind for the male dancer; a double-bind which would also have affected someone like Herr C. If the dancer's body shape or mode of movement did not comply with the demand for grace, he was deemed too male (too brute, too inelegant) to be accepted on stage; if he danced as gracefully as a woman, he was too effeminate and equally expelled from the scene. Large theatres like the Paris Opera would thus cast women in male roles.[60] This homophobic malaise of the public with the male dancer also influences the above mentioned report of the *Abendblätter*, where the audience preferred to see instead of one male dancer's 'hopping' the 'dance of the two warriors', in its reference to battle a less ambiguous male dance piece.

A Butlerian perspective, however, casts new light on 'failed' male performances. In keeping with the aesthetic discourse, Kleist's example draws on statuary as normative matrix: through referring to its multiplication in countless copies in German museums, the narrator affirms the canonicity of the sculpture by its repeatability, that is based on one original version. Yet at the same time, the originality or authenticity of this matrix, and thus its norm-giving power, are fundamentally questioned: it is not clear whether the sculpture in Paris was the original at all. The young man may have copied a copy; and not even his initially successful pose resembles the classical 'youth drawing a splinter from his foot' (*MT*, 418), a Roman bronze which Kleist could have seen in Paris as it was on display at the Louvre between 1791 and 1815 (Figure 2.5). The youth sits on a trunk, with his one foot on the knee of the other leg, and not, like the boy, placing his foot on a stool. The *mise-en-abîme* of copies is clearly distorted even before the boy disfigures it further. The same holds true for the series of performances of the mythological Daphne. The dancer's inadequate gazing and bending resembles the inadequate gazing and bending of a sculpture that distorts what is supposed to have been, in the actual myth, mere flight. The Kleistian performances in their repetition-in-difference are situated somewhere between failure, compulsion and subversive mockery, indicating a mismatch at the core of the reiteration of cultural norms. The young man's body is at once obedient and insubordinate. By losing his gracefulness, he also loses traces of femininity, and is thus ready to assume his gendered sexual identity as a man. However, the very harbinger of his masculinity, his self-conscious vanity elicited by the 'attentions of women' (*MT*, 418), causes his unmanly failure to fulfil a set task.

Indeed, the thorn in the foot of the sculpture, suggesting a fissure within the discipline of normalisation, seems to be the central agent here. It is the motor of cultural achievement that is meant to cover up the trauma of a flawed, wilful, mutable and mortal body, a body one has to be ashamed of. Akin to Laocoon, the youth is another example of a canonical sculpture whose aesthetic effect, both depending

---

60 We will come back to this topic in more detail in the chapters on Hoffmann and Heine. The trouble with the male dancer in Romantic ballet testifies to the persistency of puritan fears of the stage as they were pronounced, for instance, a century earlier on the matter of the Italian castrati who were taken as symbols for an aristocratic emasculation of culture; see Thomas McGeary, 'Gendering Opera', *Journal of Musicological Research*, 14 (1994), 17–34.

on and concealing a wound, celebrates the achievements of culture. The scene in the baths, however, draws the fatal structure of these cultural achievements out: canonical repeatability is turned into the boy's compulsive repetitive attempts to reach an ideal; however, his efforts only bring back the impact of the traumatic loss of grace again and again while he lifts his foot a second, third, fourth, tenth time in order to resume the imitative action of extricating the thorn, which has been turned, in Kleist, into the more imposing wooden splinter.

Yet this action keeps the wound open, as it were, and thus makes its suppression or concealment impossible. The splinter becomes a traumatic force that breaks through the smooth physical boundaries of the sculpted ideal, and through the stabilising psychic boundaries of the protective economy of repression. Trauma as 'foreign body' in the psyche is visualised as a fragment of the wooden puppet being incorporated into the human body, making it strange to itself, and turning it into a dysfunctional automaton which cannot quite repeat the original move.[61] Paradoxically, both ideals – the marionette, and also the unalterable pose of the stone – are combined with the persistence of the wound, evoking Lacan's claim of the inadequacy at the heart of the stabilising identification with an image of bodily unity. This may indicate, furthermore, that it is the aesthetic law that turns the flaws of the body into traumatising forces in the first place. The text itself comes to bear testimony to the desperate experience witnessed by the narrator, and reflects upon this function in the summoning of yet another witness who could relate the event in a perfect copy 'word for word': the youth's repetitive re-enactments are displaced into the narrative.

The intrinsic irony of the demonstrations of affectation consists in the fact that the ideal of perfection and authenticity of the original is thoroughly illusionary. Grace, in turn, defeats affectation not because it is more authentic, but because it does not stumble over the obstacle of shame. The intricacy of Kleist's affectation is yet another point of distinction between *Über das Marionettentheater*'s position and Schiller's *Über Anmut und Würde*. Schiller combines the aesthetic with the moral realm, transcending mere corporeality: grace of the body is the immediate expression of the 'beautiful soul' and her flawless character. Therefore he rejects the sheer bodily quality of the grace of the dance master, which consciously tries to produce and imitate beautiful movement and results in false, affected grace. Kleist draws on the Schillerian notion of affectation while presenting, at the same time, an explicitly constructionist version of grace. The alleged 'naturalness' of the marionette's movement cannot dissimulate its origin in the technical skills of the puppeteer, or in mechanical devices. Kleistian affectation is thus not the result of having been trained to be graceful, which includes the ability to cope with the gaze of an audience, but is caused by the very lack of this ability, shame. In Schiller, shame clearly would be one of the graceful qualities of a modest girl; in Kleist, shame ruins grace: being

---

61 In 'On the Psychical Mechanism of Hysterical Phenomena', Freud compares the persistence of trauma to the impact of a *Fremdkörper* (foreign body) on the psyche, in the translation 'agent provocateur', see *StE* III, 6.

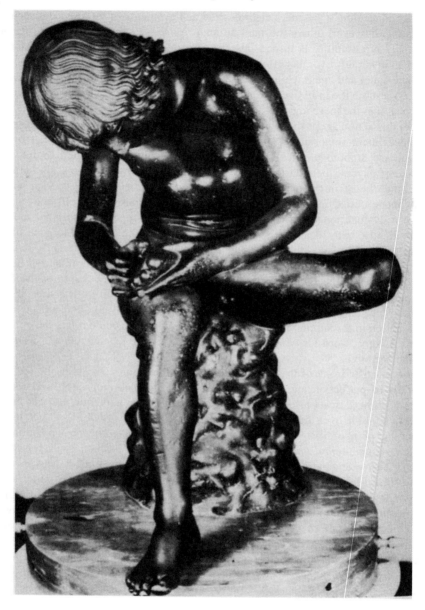

Figure 2.5   *Youth drawing a splinter from his foot*, Roman bronze, first century AD, presumably after a Greek original from the third century BC. Rome, Palazzo dei Conservatori; in Paris between 1791 and 1815.

ridiculed, the boy blushes – together with the eyes turned towards the floor, one of Kleist's often exploited signs of shame – and becomes clumsy.[62] Affectation, then, is the self-conscious, gawky posing of forced grace which tries to gloss over the embarrassment of being exposed in one's imperfection.

This danger of being too aware of an audience seems to be intrinsic to the notion of grace, for it is defined by being pleasing and amiable to the eye of the onlooker: 'one of the effects of the graces is certainly a complaisant and favourable quality, which wins over the hearts', as Sulzer has it.[63] In his *Vorlesungen über die Ästhetik* (Lectures on Aesthetics), Hegel says 'grace is an appeal to the listener or spectator'.[64] He follows Schiller by defining grace as an aesthetic quality that is flawless as long as it is exclusively concerned with the idea, or soul, it is supposed to represent. When the graceful effect turns into an end in itself, the relationship to the audience becoming more important than the idea that is to be mediated, grace declines.

Kleist's fencing bear is an even more curious version of the ideal. He does not suffer from the effects of self-consciousness or shame and therefore masters his body perfectly. His 'instinctive', 'graceful' fencing, however, is anything but natural, for he has been raised – the German *auferziehen* implies training and 'education' and also recalls the threads or the crank of the puppet – and domesticated. His centredness is clearly not the result of his primordial unity, but caused by the fact that he is chained to a post. Again, rather than lack of consciousness, Kleist's economy of the gaze is a crucial factor here for the bear's success. The inanimate marionette escapes the disastrous effects of the observing gaze; the ungainly dancers, and the youth, yield to its power. One of the most ungainly animals, in turn, comes to serve as an example for gracefulness because it is able to hold, and return, the gaze: 'As I stepped before him astonished, the bear stood on his hind feet, his back leaning up against the post to which he was fastened, his paw raised ready for battle, and looked me straight in the eye: that was his fencing pose' (*MT*, 419). Not being affected by the observational order of consciousness, then, not only means non-consciousness (as Kleist's enraptured, somnambulant, or dreaming figures Alkmene, Käthchen, or Friedrich von Homburg show), but also the capability of facing the challenge of this order by powerful, well trained activity, by being faster than reflection. While the defeat by the gaze is expressed in images of falling, the acceptance of its challenge is incorporated in the erect posture of the bear. The bear is the better fencer because he possesses visual power. He is able to read his adversary, and thus deploys his forces in an economical way, while Herr C. exhausts his resources in his repetitive lunging or falling out (*Aus-fallen*) on the animal.

---

62 For the relationship between grace and shame, see Burkhard Meyer-Sickendiek, 'Scham und Grazie: Zur Paradoxie der "schönen Seele" im achtzehnten Jahrhundert, <http://www.goethezeitportal.de/db/wiss/epoche/meyers_seele.pdf> (accessed August 2004).

63 Sulzer, IV, 88.

64 Georg Wilhelm Friedrich Hegel, *Aesthetics: Lectures on Fine Art*, transl. by T.M. Knox, 2 vols (Oxford: Clarendon, 1975), II, 617.

In Kleist, standing up to the power of the other's gaze means to fight: we might think of *Der Zweikampf* (The Duel), of 'Von der Überlegung' (Reflection. A Paradox), of the war between father and son in *Der Findling* (The Foundling), or of the ultimate battle of Penthesilea and Achill, where love articulates itself in the agonistic dynamic. This dynamic enhances the extreme vulnerability of exposed, staged or fighting bodies. The wish for perfection is turned from an aesthetic demand into a matter of life and death. The fatal pattern of winning or losing seems to be characteristic of the fact that man is subjected to self-consciousness, and therefore vulnerable. This pattern also holds for the theory of language developed in 'Über die allmähliche Verfertigung der Gedanken beim Reden' (On the Gradual Production of Thoughts Whilst Speaking). As in 'Von der Überlegung', a discussion is compared to a battle. The one who thinks too much before he talks, building up too much awareness of what he wants to say, and of the situation of exposure through talking, is unabashedly declared the loser of the communicative fight. The one who is faster in talking and more alert, by contrast, will be victorious.[65]

And yet, whether victorious or not, there is an element of compulsion in Kleistian fights. *Über das Marionettentheater*'s fencing-scene enrols Herr C. in a fatal dance of self-defensive attack that is so compulsive because he is not able to understand or to grasp the superior power of his adversary, who is, after all, 'only' an animal. Given that the essay's parables are variations on a theme, we revisit in the story of the bear, although it is supposed to be about grace, the splinter in the foot of the youth. Like the repetitive 'fight' with a primal wounding that is depicted in the incident (*Vorfall*) of the youth, Herr C.'s repetitive thrusts may also be directed against an enemy within, rather than only attacking the actual one, attempting to defend himself against the unfailing steadfastness of a suppressed traumatic condition that does not give way. Like in the futile attempts to extricate the splinter, the 'foreign body' – here of the animal – develops an imposing presence which violates not only physical but also psychic boundaries: 'the seriousness of the bear served to increase my discomfiture' (*MT*, 420). C.'s repeated 'falling out', and his identification with the *Fall* (case) of his point of reference, young Herr von G., then, build up a narrative which indirectly refers, through the figure of falling, to the persistency of a fallible body, which is, in the case of the dancer Herr C., a particularly acute wound. In Caruth's reading of Kleist, it is precisely this polysemy of key figures like falling which engenders narratives

> that in fact emerge out of the rhetorical potential and the literary resonance of theses figures, a literary dimension that cannot be reduced to the thematic content of the text [...], and that, beyond what we can know or theorize about it, stubbornly persists in bearing witness to some forgotten wound.[66]

---

65 On Kleist's agonistic view of language, see also Gabriele Kapp, *Des Gedankens Senkblei: Studien zur Sprachauffassung Heinrich von Kleists 1799–1806* (Stuttgart: Metzler, 2000), p. 406.

66 Caruth, *Unclaimed Experience*, p. 5. For another outstanding example of the key figure of falling in Kleist's *œuvre*, see the beginning of *Der Zerbrochene Krug*.

The anecdotal narrative becomes a *Fallgeschichte*, a case history recording the traumatic failure of the body. In Kleist, the necessity of repeated feints and thrusts may ultimately only lead to the lethal fall. However, his notion of grace, far from indicating the winner in a fatal game, rather seems to be a way to overcome the compulsion either to win or lose. Instead of being the opposite of affectation, and its link to the traumatic condition of man, grace is unavoidably enmeshed with the fall.

Kleist's Law of Movement

The two major templates of thought underlying *Über das Marionettentheater*, Idealist philosophy of history and Christian salvation history, are dedicated to the idea of teleological progress, be it towards the perfectibility of man through education, or the final redemption of sin in the afterlife. In the essay, however, purposeful, progressive movement is inextricably linked to failure, to the inescapability of lack and loss. Goal-oriented movement, in Kleist, leads to falling out of balance by a turn of the head, a move of the arm, or the attempt to repeat a specific posture. It is the story of the irrevocably flawed body that breaks through models of containment, installing the curse of consciousness, the awareness of this flawed body, as a traumatic condition at the base of human identity. This condition is incorporated in the literal falling of the body, in its proneness to gravity. It disturbs a system like classical dance that rests upon the idea of the perfectibility of the physical, a system that is at once a supreme cultural achievement, and a presumptuous gesture. The attempt to create machine-like bodily instruments out of human beings who are susceptible to unpredictable disruptions caused by their consciousness, by fatigue and decay, is bound to collapse at some point.[67] Adam and Eve's survival of the Fall, the idealised dance of the marionette, and also Noverre's aforementioned instructions about the use of the mirror in ballet rest upon the necessity and the capability of concealing and deleting the body's nakedness and its defects: as in the biblical punishment of desire through the cover of shame, physical exhaustion is a moment which 'allows for nothing better than to make it disappear as much as possible' (*MT*, 418). In *Marionettentheater*, this moment, the permanent presence of the splinter in the foot of the young man, and the steadfastness of the animal, is the inescapability of a body whose very 'realness' – its weight, its incalculability, its vulnerability and its desire – is a disconcerting source of shame.

The dialogue contrasts linear movement with circular movement, which gains ground in the course of the text, illustrated by the self-centred motion of the marionette. The notion of graceful dance appears for the first time in the round dance

---

67 Compare Thomas Bernhard's brilliantly concise version of the Kleistian predicament in *Ein berühmter Tänzer* (A Famous Dancer), where a dancer remains paralysed after breaking down during his dance because he has started to think about the extraordinary complexity of his movements, rather than simply and automatically enacting them; in *Der Stimmenimitator* (Frankfurt am Main: Suhrkamp, 1987), pp. 76–7.

of the puppets, a traditional image of cohesion and harmony. The circle is a symbol of perfection, embedded in a tradition of cosmological thought that relates the micro- to the macrocosm, human movement to the orbit of celestial bodies, and that finds in circular movement a paradigm of beautiful order which unites the human sphere with the sphere of the divine.[68] The marionette's limbs draw a curved line in the air, and the super-marionette is animated by the circular turning of a crank. In the dialogue's shift toward general questions of human fate, the argument comes full circle with the image of the ring-shaped world man must travel around in order to finally meet the point – of arrival and departure – where its ends meet. Herr C. proposes a poetic reconciliation of puppet and god which works by referring to the metaphors he has built up before, bending a linear scale into a circle where its two poles become adjacent, or even converging points.

The talking dancer seems to experience a state of 'circular' grace himself during the course of the conversation. Besides the agonistic potential of discussions, 'Über die allmählige Verfertigung der Gedanken beim Reden' describes a state of self-forgetful grace achieved through getting carried away by talking, by delivering oneself to the auto-poietic force of the rhetorical circle of a 'periode'. This talking bliss has the winning effect that is crucial for amiable gracefulness: 'There is a strangely enthusiastic response to the speaker in the human face before him' (*DKV* III, 536).[69] The dialogical talking indeed recalls the light-footed steps and turns of a dance. Despite presenting persuasive explanations, it is perhaps significant that the speakers never use the 'static' word 'under-stand' (*ver-stehen*); the more corporeal and dynamic 'grasp' (*begreifen*) emerges in the end, used by the dancer who supposes that his partner should now be able to appreciate his way of thinking. The two men leap from one example to the next, the conclusion floating above a metaphorical net, a rhetorical circle structure, rather than being grounded in a logical course of arguments. In 'Über die allmählige Verfertigung der Gedanken beim Reden', the generative power of spoken language is famously compared to yet another circular image, a wheel: 'Speech then is not at all an impediment; it is not, as one might say, a brake on the mind but rather a second wheel running along parallel on the same axis'.[70] A wheel, however, does not display strictly circular motion, but combines circular propelling with linear progress. This is echoed in Herr C.'s metaphor of the ring-shaped world, in his rhetorical trick that blends linear progression in time with the spatial figure of a cycle. The solution is worthy of the nimble mind of a dancer, since the combination of succession in time, and simultaneity in space is characteristic for the art of dance. August Wilhelm Schlegel illustrates the point:

---

68 See Françoise Carter, 'Celestial dance: a Search for Perfection', *Dance Research*, 5 (1987), 3–17.

69 See also the English translation of 'On the Gradual Production of Thoughts Whilst Speaking', in Heinrich von Kleist, *Selected Writings*, ed. and transl. by David Constantine (London: Dent, 1997), pp. 405–9 (p. 406).

70 Ibid., p. 408.

A short while ago we were able to categorise the arts according to whether they perform through space or through time, alongside one another or one after the other, and we were thus unable to conceive of dance, which is not simultaneous nor successive, but both of these at the same time. It is in movement that space and time connect, and where one flows into the other.[71]

The union of circularity and linearity is also at work in the straight line of the movement-generating centre that brings about curves of the limbs, and in the elliptical shape of those curves. Herder defines the ellipsis as the mediating step between the celestial circle and the straight 'line of real need':

The vessels here below, however, are not capable of *perfection* and the line of *real need* always exerts its inexorable force. In the cosmos the conflict between two forces makes the planet move in the form of an ellipse. Here a similar conflict results in the *line of beauty* that encircles the *forms of the body*; it emerges from the straight line and from roundness [...].[72]

The marionette's ellipsis, although representing an ideal, does not reach the perfection of a circle; what is more, it may be seen as pointing up the more genuine impossibility of identically repeating an absolute figure.[73] The puppet's elliptical movement is less divine than it seemed in the beginning, maybe only a few steps ahead of human one. This hints at the lesson the marionette teaches us. It is not its anti-gravity as such which makes it superior and graceful. Granted, the puppet does not fall on the floor, it does not need to achieve rest, because the force which keeps it in the air is more powerful than gravity. But at the same time, we have to imagine the movement of the limbs as a way of falling without collapsing: the limbs are not only following the forces of gravity, but also the impulses of the centre, their scope of movement is defined by the perfect balance of both. Moreover, the very principle of Kleist's formalist aesthetic of dance, the interaction of the opposing principles weight and weightlessness, mirrors his rhetorical strategy of paradox.

The second bite of the apple, likening man to the marionette, cannot be meant to cancel the Fall, but it could imply that there is a way to master the falling. Here, perhaps, lies one of the meanings of the final paradox, which attempts to solve human fate in the *falling* back into the *standing upright* of innocence (the German *Staad* means both state and standing upright): "'Consequently", I said, a little distraught, "we would have to eat again from the tree of knowledge to fall back into the state of innocence?"' (*MT*, 420). A paradox maintains its dynamic by the irreconcilable contradiction of its parts which cannot be translated into the stillness of an unambiguous meaning. This uprightness, then, is not a state, but part of a continuity of rising and falling: one is reminded of the continuous mechanical movement of a tumbling figure – or a dancer. The art of a controlled descent to the

---

71 August Wilhelm Schlegel, p. 271, transl. by Chantal Wright.

72 Herder, p. 84.

73 See Jacques Derrida, 'Ellipsis', in *Writing and Difference,* (London: Routledge, 1995), pp. 294–300.

floor without giving the impression of collapsing, which turns falling into landing, is indeed an essential element of ballet's jumping technique. Carlo Blasis' *Elementary Treatise upon the Theory and Practice of the Art of Dancing* invokes no less than Leonardo da Vinci to explain the complex elements of this technique that is meant to make the effort appear effortless:

> Leonardo da Vinci defines a man's action in jumping and the means he employs to lift himself off the ground as follows: 'When a man springs into the air his head moves three times as fast as the heel of his foot before the toes leave the ground and twice as quickly as his hips. This is because at the same time three angles are obliterated; the highest is where the torso joins the thighs in front, the second where the thighs join the legs at the back of the knee joint and the third is formed in front of the union between the leg and instep.' He then shows us how the momentum created by the raising of arms and shoulders pulls the body, already well poised upon the hips and bended knees, upward and raises it from the ground aided by the extension of the knees and elasticity of the insteps.[74]

This control of the forces of gravity is resonant with the mechanics of the marionette. The puppet thus indicates the relevance of virtuoso techniques for accomplished, natural-looking, and soulful dancing: here, the simultaneity of construction and naturalness that characterises the marionette starts to make sense. Echoing the charm of the puppet's dance, which is born out of a mechanical reaction, the mastering of movement techniques does not hinder, but enhances the enchanting effect of good ballet dancers. Given that Kleist himself was no choreographer, but a writer of dramas, it seems reasonable to extend his view on dance to theories and techniques of acting.[75] His dissatisfaction with contemporary acting practices – Goethe's artificial classicism in Weimar and Iffland's pathetic naturalism in Berlin – has been mentioned above. Alexander Košenina gives a detailed account of eighteenth-century acting theories which were a greater influence on the writer than the styles of his contemporaries. These theories concur with Noverre's *Letters*, which renewed the art of ballet by extending its scope through adding a whole new apparatus of reflection and method.[76] Košenina illustrates, for example, Diderot's use of the metaphor of the marionette for the art of well thought through, meticulously trained acting.[77] The separation of consciousness and soul in the image of the puppeteer and

---

74 Carlo Blasis, *An Elementary Treatise Upon the Theory and Practice of the Art of Dancing* (Milan, 1820; re-ed. by Mary Stewart Evans, New York: Dover, 1968), pp. 44–5.

75 Günter Blamberger sees the marionette as a model for perfectly controlled acting, in 'Agonalität und Theatralität: Kleists Gedankenfigur des Duells im Kontext der europäischen Moralistik', *Kleist-Jahrbuch* (1999), 25–40 (p. 32); see also Rüdiger Bubner, 'Philosophisches über Marionetten', *Kleist-Jahrbuch* (1980), 73–85 (p. 82).

76 See Matthias Sträßner, *Tanzmeister und Dichter: Literaturgeschichte(n) im Umkreis von Jean-Georges Noverre, Lessing, Wieland, Goethe, Schiller* (Berlin: Henschel, 1994), p. 8.

77 In 1908, Edward Gordon Craig would write the ultimate manifesto of the marionette as an ideal for the actor, in 'The Actor and the Über-Marionette', in *Gordon Craig on Movement and Dance*, ed. by Arnold Rood (London: Dance Books, 1978), pp. 37–57.

the puppet can thus be understood as a metaphor for a masterful technique where the actor is able to calculate the exterior signs of an emotion so well as to be more convincing, that is more 'natural', than if he were sincerely to experience it.[78] The inappropriateness of the actually practised modes of acting for animating Kleistian characters on stage might have been successfully replaced by a then utopian vision of the consummate dancer-actor, as later imagined by Robert Walser. He ponders the correct casting for the role of Hermann in *Die Hermannschlacht* (The Battle of Herrmann) and finds the answer in a dancerly discipline of body and soul:

> Hermann, [...], let's say a million to the one who can play him. A dark, broad manly chest and a ringing sound in his mouth, as though somebody were gracefully striking silver bells. A dancer. The actor must have had the pleasure of being instructed in dance, ritually or physically, the two are of equal value, he has to be able to juggle twelve small balls in the air with his nose.[79]

This vision of the perfect impersonator of Kleistian figures resounds with the marionette's ideal dance: gracefulness without the inhibitions produced by shame and self-awareness. Kleist must himself have experienced self-forgetfulness in the abandonment to movement in rare, cherished instances: 'Once I enjoyed dancing, because I was distracted' (*DKV* IV, 198), he writes in a letter of 1801, and in another one of the same year, 'my happiest moments are those in which I forget about myself – yet is there such thing as happiness without calmed-down self-consciousness?' (*DKV* IV, 222). Self-consciousness, however, was a constant burden. In the same letter where he writes about dancing, he tells how he suffers, at social occasions, under inexplicable states of embarrassment: 'In addition I feel an inexplicable embarrassment, which I cannot overcome as it probably stems from a physical cause' (*DKV* IV, 199). Whatever he may have meant by this cause, the idealisation of the marionette's dance in the 1810 essay – set in 1801 – seems to be rooted in personal suffering.

This dance articulates an act of psychic strength in physical terms. In Kleist's universe of complementarities between the physical and the moral world, the marionette's paradoxical combination of standing – or being held up – and falling becomes a metaphor of the inner and outer tensions that characterise Kleistian characters.[80] It is a model that works even for less perfect beings, who want to be happy in, or in spite of, their self-consciousness. It provides the structure for dealing with a traumatic condition that goes beyond the compulsive repetition of the fall,

---

78 See Košenina, p. 51; see also his *Anthropologie und Schauspielkunst: Studien zur 'eloquentia corporis' im 18. Jahrhundert* (Tübingen: Niemeyer, 1995).

79 Robert Walser in *Die Schaubühne*, Berlin, 14 March 1907; in *Heinrich von Kleists Nachruhm: Eine Wirkungsgeschichte in Dokumenten*, ed. by Helmut Sembdner (Bremen: Schünemann, 1967), p. 359, transl. by Chantal Wright.

80 See 'On the Gradual Production of Thoughts Whilst Speaking': 'We have here a remarkable congruence between the phenomena of the physical world and those of the moral world', *Selected Writings*, p. 407.

and may overcome defeat by this condition. The traumatic fall, the reference of the empirical, frail, and sexualised body, maintains a residue of unrepresentability, caused not least by matters of decorum, as the embarrassment accompanying the example of the cripple, or Kleist's telling dash that replaces the physical act in *Die Marquise von O...* show. In de Man's reading, the figure of mutilation symbolises this resistance of the body to exhaustive narration; or in other words, the physical, which is 'mutilated' by representation, in turn 'mutilates' the representational strategies of formalisation (that is, of mathematical analysis) and metaphor (for instance, the comparison of the gravitational line with the movement of the soul). Caruth further illustrates how the impact of reference – of the traumatic body – unfolds most powerfully not in straightforward representation, but in its very brittleness; this is reflected in a language which intertwines content and rhetoric in an extraordinarily dense manner, a language that becomes increasingly performative. As Kleist clears movement of its representational value by representing it in a purely formalised mode, and thus opens it up to new meaning, his performative language of the fall becomes thick with signification.[81]

The choreography of standing by, and despite, falling can thus be seen as an enactment of the rhetorical figure of paradox that indeed holds for the performance of the author's protagonists, and for the performance of the narrative discourse. Working against the persuasive thematic surface of the text which is based on the very contrast between affectation and grace, this dance of writing, and of the self, brings the two qualities together. The falling back (*Zurück-fall*) into innocence is closer to the various disturbing incidents (*Vor-fälle*) of the essay, and of other texts by the author, than it seemed. The vocabulary of traumatic shock infiltrates the celebration of the puppet, let alone its crippled double. It is, after all, the fact that the marionette's limbs are 'shaken' (or shocked) 'at random' (*MT*, 415, 'auf eine bloß zu-fällige Weise erschüttert') which causes the first rhythmic movements of the marionette. Both affectation and grace show a way of integrating the repressed into the performance: the fall – of the desiring, vulnerable body – is no longer dance's other, no longer dance's concealed wound, but paradoxically enables it. This is reflected in the series of anecdotes, or case histories, which supports (*stützt*) Herr C.'s initial idea (*Ein-fall*). The repetitive narrative performances turn Kleist's essay into a testimony that, through the distortions and displacements of the individual anecdote, gives voice to the persistent impact of trauma.

However, while the figure of the fall disturbs the thematic balance of the essay, its reiteration succeeds in overcoming the potentially destructive effects of compulsive re-enactment. The figure undergoes several creative variations which are at once parodic performances of the biblical Fall, and instances that hint at the process of working through the traumatic 'original sin' without being entirely defeated by it. For the various disguises and enactments of falling through their continuous

---

81 See also Andrew Webber's remarks on the double-talk of the term 'Zufall' in Kleist's *Der Findling*, in *The 'Doppelgänger': Double Visions in German Literature* (Oxford: Clarendon Press, 1996), p. 204.

repetition-in-difference undermine the outward closure of the text, a closure that is as consoling as it is threatening. The invocation of the 'last chapter' indicates, as it stands, not only the apparent accomplishment of the persuasive rhetorical 'periode', but also a lethal, final break. This break is challenged, ironically, by the narrative's own breaks in signification, effected through the ambivalence of the figure of the fall, which illustrates both the lack and the presence of grace. It is the text's own 'fragmented spirit' (see *MT*, 416) that questions the reliability of its oppositional structures, and disrupts the perfect dance of its argument. The graceful affectation of Kleist's writing stems from its failure to identically repeat, which enables forms of recuperation; where the stabilising force of the graceful iteration of aesthetic norms easily tumbles over into the affectation of a traumatic repetition compulsion, the inability and the refusal to repeat have a curative potential.

The potentially recuperative performances of writing and dancing might give an idea about the stabilising 'law of movement' the author sought in 1799, in his early *Aufsatz, den sichern Weg des Glücks zu finden* (Essay on the Best Path to Happiness). Here, he talks about the 'inner fermentation of forces acting upon each other' that accounts for the instability of young people like himself, and he continues:

> All of their steps and movements seem to be provoked by an invisible yet violent jolt which sweeps them along with no resistance. They are like comets roaming the cosmos in lawless circles until they finally find a path and a law of movement. (*DKV* III, 524; *CW*)

Yet given that the dance of the marionette was intended to embody such a law of movement, this law is in itself an interaction of forces, and equally results in the 'lawless circles' of elliptical curves. The expectation's only fulfilment, in 1810, was a way of life that accepted the stability of instability.

Kleistian figures are subjected to the 'violent jolt' of the rigid orders of military and juridical law, or of the catastrophic forces of fate. They develop their agency against, or under the constant discipline and danger of those forces. Their survival seems to be enabled by a technique that is built on the vulnerability of the human condition, finding its most concise image in the Würzburg arch which gains its stability precisely because each of the stones is bound to gravity. Kleist writes in a letter of November 1800:

> Why, I reflected, does the vault not collapse, given that there is *nothing holding it up*? It stands, I replied, *because all the stones desire to collapse together* – and in that thought I found an indescribably refreshing comfort that was always at my side in decisive moments, alongside the hope that I too would hold out when everything sought to bring me down. (*DKV* IV, 159; *CW*)

Rather than the passing of a threshold, it is the frail balance of the transitional structure itself that distinguishes the image of the arch.[82] It also distinguishes a dynamic pattern of movement where falling prepares for ascent and vice versa.

The ability to cope with a literal or metaphorical fall upholds such Kleistian figures as the Marquise von O...: 'Thus through this beautiful exertion coming to self-knowledge she lifted herself suddenly, as though by her own hand, clear out of the depths into which fate had flung her'.[83] In *Der Zweikampf*, Littegarde, who suffers slander, and Friedrich von Trota, who is severely injured in her defence, both rise and walk on after devastating blows of fate.[84] In *Prinz Friedrich von Homburg*, the complementarity between the stand and the fall mirrors the prince's self that is hinged between order and emotion. Here, as well as in *Das Käthchen von Heilbronn*, the trauma of the weak body is even more pronouncedly than in *Marionettentheater* correlated with this body's desire. Emotion and desire articulate themselves in countless fits and falls, in the wounding, breaking and bending of the body that is recalled in the dancer P. who 'bends as if she were about to break' (*MT*, 417). The shock of Käthchen's fall into the recognition of her desire for Count Wetter vom Strahl, which was announced to her in a dream, is immediately numbed with a fall out of consciousness that literally breaks her legs. Prince Friedrich's fall from his horse results in a wounding of his left hand, covered by a bandage which mimics the token of his desire, his beloved Natalie's left glove. In *Prinz Friedrich von Homburg*, the 'bending' of emotion encounters the power of the 'rigid will' to obey the 'sacred law of battle' (*DKV* II, 638) of a psycho-social order, as represented by the master-figure of the sovereign. It is the same unyielding law whose disciplining power rules over the rigid wooden limbs of the puppet, and the sculpted stone of idealised statuary. Like a puppeteer, the sovereign directs the prince's movements in the dream sequence, and he directs Friedrich's ultimate acceptance of Prussian law, only to release him, in the theatre he mounts at the end, into the fulfilment of his desire, which is unavoidably accompanied by a physical collapse. In these dramas, desire is a traumatising force that first and foremost exposes the vulnerability of the subject. It is inextricably linked to a loss of consciousness, or a loss of language, meant to cover and protect this exposure. The shield is only lifted in states that yet again lack conscious control, like Friedrich's and Käthchen's somnambulistic confessions. The narration, however, persistently bears testimony where the protagonists' words fail. It becomes the voice that Count Wetter vom Strahl mourns, the voice that plays 'like a beautiful dancer' through 'all the bows which enchant the soul' (*DKV* II, 285).

The bending and rising of these bows or flections complement the escape into the non-consciousness of dreams and somnambulism, and perform the unspeakable or unspoken wounds of the text. Although the fall is unavoidable in Kleist, and the ascent ambiguous, the interaction of falling and rising enables his protagonists to

---

82 See Saul, *Body, Language, and Body Language*, on Kleist's turning of the depth image of passing a threshold into the 'surface' of the transitional state, p. 319.

83 Kleist, *Selected Writings*, p. 298.

84 Ibid. , pp. 377–400.

survive, if only for a while. Some Kleistian protagonists know the art of catching themselves from falling. Their accomplishment might ultimately point towards a utopian world worthy of being looked at, where exposure gives no reason for shame; or where one has not to be ashamed of shame any more.

Chapter 3

E.T.A. Hoffmann and the
True Art of Dance

Throughout these few days (the last days of February) it was 0– to 3– fahrenheit. During the rehearsals of *Camilla* and the most implausible opera ballets which the Weimar balletmaster Uhlig puts on, in this severe cold, in an unheated theater from nine o'clock until one o'clock, I contracted rheumatic problems. (E.T.A. Hoffmann, Leipzig, 4 March 1814)

Although E.T.A. Hoffmann is seen as an icon of German Romantic writing, it was only in his later years that he started to seriously consider himself as a literary author. While having written in private from his youth onwards, he publicly established himself first as a composer and man of the theatre. He published his works anonymously until he had been acknowledged as the composer of the successfully staged opera *Undine*. Leaving no doubt as to his professional priorities, he wrote to his editor, discussing the title page of his first collection of novellas and fairytales: 'I don't want my name published, because it is to become known to the world only through a *successful* musical composition and in no other way.'[1]

The author's involvement with music as a composer, conductor and critic has been investigated in a long-standing strand of Hoffmann research.[2] His experiences in various areas of the theatrical trade, namely at the Bamberg theatre, where he worked from 1808 to 1813 as theatre manager, music director, artistic director and stage designer, have also been taken into account.[3] Hoffmann's strong interest in theatre traditions like the *commedia dell'arte*, Carlo Gozzi's fairytale comedies or Calderón's miracle plays corresponds to his practical experience. His knowledge of

---

1   20 July 1813 to Kunz; in E.T.A. Hoffmann, *Selected Letters*, ed. and transl. by Johanna C. Sahlin (Chicago: University of Chicago Press, 1977), p. 197.

2   To name only three titles that cover the various aspects of this involvement: Gerhard Allroggen, *E.T.A. Hoffmanns Kompositionen* (Regensburg: Bosse, 1970); Carl Dahlhaus, 'E.T.A. Hoffmanns Beethoven-Kritik und die Ästhetik des Erhabenen', *Archiv für Musikwissenschaft*, 38 (1981), 79–92; Wolfgang Wittkowski, 'E.T.A. Hoffmanns musikalische Musikerdichtungen *Ritter Gluck, Don Juan, Rat Krespel*', *Aurora*, 38 (1978), 54–74.

3   See Heinz Kindermann, *Theatergeschichte Europas*, VI (Salzburg: Müller, 1977), pp. 32–41; Heide Eilert, *Theater in der Erzählkunst: Eine Studie zum Werk E.T.A. Hoffmanns* (Tübingen: Niemeyer, 1977); M.M. Raraty, 'E.T.A. Hoffmann and his Theatre', *Hermathena* (1964), 53–67; Ross Chambers, 'Two Theatrical Microcosms: *Die Prinzessin Brambilla* and *Mademoiselle de Maupin*', *Comparative Literature*, 27 (1975), 34–46.

the illusionary effects of stage machinery and lighting is grounded in his hands-on work in Bamberg.

However, the author's attitudes towards ballet, and the incorporation of dance in his writings, have been widely dismissed. Although Hoffmann's interest in the *Gesamtkunstwerk* is mentioned, scholarly attention used to largely restrict itself to the writer's literary experiments on music and art. The exceptional scope of Gerhard Neumann's recent contributions on the writer in the context of a Romantic 'poetics of knowledge' may be seen as setting a new trend, however. Neumann's inclusion of dance as cultural apparatus that informs the negotiations of Romantic subjectivity complements my findings.[4] Indeed, drawing on dispersed statements in his letters, journals and critical writings, we in fact find a multifaceted picture of Hoffmann when it comes to dance. The man who passionately adores attending balls – '5.10. 1812: danced like a fool in the casino'; '26.10. 1812: wild dances in the casino'; '11.1. 1813: then late to the ball – pretty much in the mood to spin around'[5] – is the composer who hates his duty to write commissioned ballet music: 'So far I have of necessity not written but scribbled music, such as allegorical ballets and the like, which deprived me of my time and my good spirits,' he tells his friend Hitzig in a letter written in Bamberg on 25 May 1809.[6] The conductor who disapproves of 'implausible opera ballets'[7] is the critic who envisages 'the rebirth of the true art of dance' out of the dance music by composers like Reichhardt, Spontini or Gluck.[8] Hoffmann occasionally composed individual ballets himself, apparently without according much value to them; his work on operas was closer to his heart. His perhaps most elaborate ballet music is part of the musical play *Die Maske* (The Mask, 1809), the only dance piece to which he contributed the music as well as the libretto.

Yet there are two extraordinarily famous transpositions of his tales into ballets: *Der Sandmann* (The Sandman) was staged as the ballet *Coppélia*, and *Nußknacker und Mausekönig* (Nutcracker and the King of Mice) became the well-known classic *Nutcracker*.[9] The potential of the tales to serve as sources for ballets seems to

---

4   See Gerhard Neumann, 'E.T.A. Hoffmanns "Prinzessin Brambilla" als Entwurf einer Wissenspoetik: Wissenschaft – Theater – Literatur', in Gabriele Brandstetter and Gerhard Neumann, eds, *Romantische Wissenspoetik* (Würzburg: Königshausen und Neumann, 2004), pp. 15–47; and by the same author, 'Glissando und Defiguration: E.T.A. Hoffmanns Capriccio "Prinzessin Brambilla" als Wahrnehmungsexperiment', in *Manier – Manieren – Manierismen*, ed. by Erika Greber and Bettine Menke (Tübingen: Narr, 2002), pp. 63–94.

5   E.T.A. Hoffmann, *Tagebücher*, ed. by Friedrich Schnapp (Munich: Winkler, 1971), pp. 177, 180, 189.

6   Hoffmann, *Letters*, p. 154.

7   Ibid., p. 222.

8   E.T.A. Hoffmann, *Sämtliche Werke*, ed. by Wulf Segebrecht et al., 6 vols (Frankfurt am Main: Deutscher Klassiker Verlag, 1985–), V, 638.

9   *Coppélia* was first staged in Paris in 1870; the *Nutcracker* in St. Petersburg in 1892. On the transposition of the latter into the ballet, see Gabriele Brandstetter, 'Transkription im Tanz: E.T.A. Hoffmanns Märchen *Nußknacker und Mausekönig* und Marius Petipas Ballett-Szenario', in *Jugend: Ein romantisches Konzept?*, ed. by Günter Oesterle (Würzburg:

be due to their more general dramatic quality, rather than to their specific dance scenes. However, the importance of corporeality in Hoffmann's fictional writing, and its choreographic attention to bodily posture and sequential movement, must have influenced the libretto writers. Dance makes relatively infrequent, but often significant appearances in the author's *œuvre*; the following investigations focus their attention on two prominent texts, which pace out two potential scenarios of a Hoffmannesque logic of dance: *Der Sandmann* showcases the surrender to a lethal psycho-physical choreography; *Prinzessin Brambilla* (Princess Brambilla) masters instability in the creative, life-affirming enactment of dialogic dances. Both will be contextualised with an inventory of the author's thoughts on dance.

Hoffmann on Dance

Witnessing ballet after Noverre, and before Romanticism, on Germany's provincial and even not-so-provincial stages, Hoffmann was in general appalled by what he saw. Through the occasional reference to productions in his letters and journals, we are able to get a glimpse of the kind of performances that were on play. On 29 January 1811, for instance, Hoffmann records an evening with 'Cogen's funambulists' at the Bamberg theatre:

> Following the one-act comedy *The Holiday* there was a performance of 'Gymnastic exercises and dances by the Cogen Family and Madame Nante, in two parts'. [...] In the first part of the 'gymnastic exercises' Mister Cogen danced *The Pas of Zephyr*, this was followed with a dance by the younger Mister Cogen, and then an 'English solo' performed by Mme. Nante and a 'main dance' by Mister Cogen. In the second part Mme. Nante and Mister Cogen performed 'a march on the high wire' and for the finale Mister Cogen performed 'several gymnastic exercises'.[10]

Yet also high-brow entertainments at the Opera were found lacking in appeal. It must be partly due to this absence of ballet performances that matched the quality of classical music at the beginning of the nineteenth century that statements which explicitly address dance are rare in Hoffmann. On music, as is well known, the author wrote extensively. It is thus via a detour to music that one finds some hints as to what Hoffmann's understanding of dance may have been. Written under the mask of quintessential musician 'Kapellmeister Kreisler', the well-known 'Beethoven's Instrumental Music', a programmatic declaration of the association of 'Romantic' with 'absolute' in music, defines the content of such music as 'pure expression' of its own 'peculiar artistic nature', manifesting itself in a sense of 'infinity' and

---

Königshausen und Neumann, 1997), pp. 161–73. The only general investigation on Hoffmann and dance, focusing on the adaptations of his texts in nineteenth- and twentieth-century ballet, is Monika Woitas, 'Anmut im Rhythmus und Dichtung als Spiel: E.T.A. Hoffmann und das Ballet', in *Jacques Offenbachs 'Hoffmanns Erzählungen': Konzeption – Rezeption – Dokumentation*, ed. by Gabriele Brandstetter (Laaber: Laaber, 1988), pp. 389–420.

10 Hoffmann, *Tagebücher*, p. 339, transl. by Chantal Wright.

'inexpressible longing'.[11] Under the writer's pen, however, something slightly more concrete arises out of the image-producing quality of instrumental music – to be precise, dancerly movement:

> [...] within this artful edifice there is a restless alternation of the most marvelous images, in which joy and pain, melancholy and ecstasy, appear beside and within each other. Strange shapes begin a merry dance, now converging into a single point of light, now flying apart like glittering sparks, now chasing each other in infinitely varied clusters.[12]

In the mind of the listener, the immateriality of symphonic music engenders diaphanous dances of light, as incorporeal as the ones that would later emerge in the white acts of Romantic ballets which Hoffmann may have welcomed at last. More generally, images of dance most fittingly articulate the play of metamorphoses that characterises Beethoven's music.

His writing on opera elucidates the author's dancerly ideas further.[13] Praising popular composers Gaspare Spontini and Johann Friedrich Reichardt, the writer makes an even stronger case for the power of imagination. Especially when it came to the *ballets entr'actes*, he preferred listening to watching in order not to be distracted from the spectacle in front of his inner eye. In his view, the verve and rhythm of the composers' dance music were not matched by the preoccupation with virtuoso tricks that characterised the performance style of his day:

> These original pieces of music breathe the spirit of a more elevated art of dance, and one feels that that they are intended for something of more import than death-defying leaps, rigid arrow-like poses and windmill-like rotations, such as those offered by the sloppy dance of our day. For his part, the author of this essay prefers to listen to his favourite pieces [...] with his eyes closed, and willingly sacrifices the sight of those strange and unimportant gymnastic feats which only ephemeral, incorrect taste can find beautiful and delightful, and which appear over and over again in the same form, for he is then able to fully grasp the delightful magic that lies in these pieces of music. (*SW* V, 637; *CW*)

It is the eternal recurrence of the same which wearies the spectator; perhaps even more than that, disquiets him. Ballet comes to be defined, in Hoffmann, by repetitiveness; in *Nußknacker und Mausekönig*, a comical version of this alliance can be found in the 'Wire Ballet Troupe' of 'Toyland' that is unable to show anything else apart

---

11   E.T.A. Hoffmann, 'Beethoven's Instrumental Music', in *Musical Writings: Kreisleriana, the Poet and the Composer, Music Criticism*, ed. by David Charlton, transl. by Martyn Clarke (Cambridge: Cambridge University Press, 1989), pp. 96–103 (p 96).

12   Ibid., p. 102.

13 On Hoffmann's aesthetic of opera see Ricarda Schmidt, 'Klassische, romantische und postmoderne musikästhetische Paradigmen in E.T.A. Hoffmanns *Ritter Gluck*', in *'Seelenaccente' – 'Ohrenphysiognomik': Zur Musikanschauung E.T.A. Hoffmanns, Heinses und Wackenroders*, ed. by Werner Keil and Charis Goer (Hildesheim: Olms, 2000), pp. 12–61.

from the everlasting repetition of the same.[14] More often, however, the mechanical resounds with the uncanny in Hoffmann. Its typical unsettling reach emerges with the 'monstrous and abominable' music of the machine in the novella *Die Automate* (Automata).[15] In *Der Sandmann*, it indicates the protagonist's traumatic, ultimately inexplicable compulsion to re-enact a terrible experience. His dance in the doll's artificial, cold embrace embodies the relentless grasp of the fatally compulsive. It returns in a passage of *Die Automate*, which more openly spells out the disturbing overtones of Kleist's scenario:

> I suppose it would be possible, by means of certain mechanical arrangements inside them, to construct automata which would dance, and then to set them to dance with human beings, and twist and turn about in all sorts of figures; so that we should have a living man putting his arms about a lifeless partner of wood, and whirling round and round with her, or rather it. Could you look at such a sight, for an instant, without horror?[16]

Hoffmann the music writer mainly draws on the eighteenth-century musical paradigm of emotional expressiveness in order to counter the potentially eerie excrescence's of hollow bodily display. His admiration for the musical theatre of Christoph Willibald Gluck, immortalised in the novella *Ritter Gluck* (Chevalier Gluck), is a case in point. The author speaks of the composer's grandiose dances, particularly stressing the dramatic quality of Gluck's music: 'He brought to bear all the possibilities of harmony and orchestration, all the resources available to composers at that time, in order to express the extremes of dramatic intensity inflaming his fervent and fertile imagination'.[17] This statement is in keeping with the testimonies of those who knew Gluck's dances best: his two most famous choreographers, Jean-Georges Noverre and Gasparo Angiolini.

Indeed, an essential part of the composer's reformatory programme for opera was his fruitful collaboration with these ballet masters. Both artists created independent ballets as well as *entr'actes* to Gluck's music. As recorded in Noverre's *Letters*, they strove for a total integration of dance and pantomime, and for a thematical connection between the staged action and the ballets. Angiolini speaks of a gestural quality in order to put his finger on the outstanding dramatic impact of Gluck's music, which allowed for the achievement of a symbiosis between music and dance:

> Music is essential for pantomimes: it is what speaks; we only make the gestures, like those ancient actors of tragedies and comedies who had the verses of the piece declaimed, and limited themselves to gesticulation. It would be nearly impossible for us to make

---

14 E.T.A. Hoffmann, *Nutcracker and the King of Mice*, in *The Best Tales of Hoffmann*, ed. by E.F. Bleiler (New York: Dover, 1967), pp. 130–82 (p. 171).

15 E.T.A. Hoffman, *Automata*, ibid., pp. 71–103 (p. 95).

16 Ibid.

17 Hoffmann, 'Further Observations on Spontini's Opera *Olimpia*', in *Musical Writings*, pp. 431–46 (p. 436).

ourselves understood without music, and the more it is apt for what we wish to express, the more we render ourselves intelligible.[18]

Although Hoffmann thoroughly agreed with Gluck's agenda, he did not include ballets in his own major opera *Undine*; presumably, his distrust of the performance practices of his day was too profound. Despite being the most positive among his dispersed notes, Hoffmann's ironic entry on visiting dancers who executed ballets at the Dresden theatre in summer 1813 supports this view. The Viennese soloist Katharina Horschelt and her daughters are presented as nothing other than an opportunistic entertainment in view of the French occupiers:

> A Mme Horstel [*sic*] from Vienna is here with her two daughters and dances in our performances, to the greatest delight of the French. She and her daughters really are very good, and the other day the daughters, wearing the most elegant, Parisian ball gowns, danced a *gavotte* which was wildly applauded.[19]

What seems to be clear from the little theoretical or critical comments on dance which one is able to find in Hoffmann, is the scope of his distinct vision of this art: a synthesis of movement, mime and meaning – including even words, as evidenced in the literary texts. *Der Sandmann* and especially *Prinzessin Brambilla* demonstrate that written dance fulfils the same function as Hoffmann's ideal Romantic opera music: it 'springs directly from the poetry as a necessary product of it' in an intermedial experiment of 'words sounding forth' in dance.[20]

Apart from the potential of music to stimulate forms of imaginary gesture, Hoffmann draws on a second, more concrete cultural practice that provided him with ideas for movement, the *commedia dell'arte*. The Italian improvised comedy that flourished between 1550 and 1750 is indeed an altogether apposite model for Hoffmann's dealings in dance. It offers the total theatre where music, song and dance, speech, masks and acrobatics contribute to the overall effect.[21] It was a condition of employment for players that they should possess skill with musical instruments and be able to sing and dance. Hoffmann's use of this tradition is mediated by Jacques Callot's grotesque depiction of *commedia* characters in his series *Balli di Sfessania* (dances of the mad, apparently referring to a Neapolitan popular dance) etched *c.* 1620. Setting Callot's carnivalistic and provocative renderings of the theatre practice in motion at least as inspired as its model, one feels inclined to speak of a doubly carnivalistic representation of the *commedia* tradition in Hoffmann. While the writer

---

18 Gasparo Angiolini quoted in *The New Grove Dictionary of Music and Musicians*, ed. by Stanley Sadie et al., 29 vols (London: Macmillan, 2001), X, 45.

19 Letter to Kunz, Dresden, 12 August 1813, in Hoffmann, *Letters*, p. 201.

20 E.T.A. Hoffmann, *The Poet and the Composer*, in *Musical Writings*, pp. 158–209 (p. 196).

21 See Giacomo Oreglia, *The Commedia dell'Arte* (London: Methuen, 1968); for the role of dance in the *commedia*, see the article by Kenneth Richards in the *International Encyclopedia of Dance*, II, 188–93.

wished to work 'in the manner of Callot'[22] from his first publication onwards, this programme culminates in *Prinzessin Brambilla*.[23] The text is based on a selection of eight reproductions of the *Balli* which Hoffmann had commissioned for his work. The etchings that appear in illustration of the text have taken away the street scenes which are the background in Callot, and place the protagonists in front of a minimal, stage-like setting, creating a sense of enhanced theatricality which is central for the understanding of the text. They depict dances, fights and simple encounters in extraordinarily expressive poses and gestures (Figures 3.1–3.4). They give a sense of the witty and ebullient moves of the *commedia* players, in the nature of random, excited turns and leaps rather than repetitive sequences. This dancerly quality of the *commedia dell'arte* is incidentally also evident in one of Hoffmann's early ballets. His Bamberg dance piece *Arlequin*, performed in January 1809, of which only the music and a few choreographic notes are preserved, is an early nineteenth-century revival of the *harlequinade*. It was choreographed by the theatre's ballet-master Carl Macco and explicitly staged in the style of the *commedia*. As far as one can reconstruct the plot, it adumbrates several of the motifs which are fully developed in the later *Prinzessin Brambilla*, among them fights, confused lovers and a play within a play.[24]

Yet what is most central in the theatre practice of the *commedia* is its combination of typified roles and arranged constellations, of settings or clues for specific scenes (*canevaggio*), and improvisations for fleshing out the plot (*lazzi*). Hoffmann has a particular liking for this mixture of arrangement and spontaneity, a mixture that informs – and provides guidelines to read – a text like *Prinzessin Brambilla*. 'It needs to look arbitrary from the outside, yet the more artful it is underneath, the more perfect it will appear,' he writes on the sonata form, a statement which can be extended on his literary production.[25] Hoffmann's vision of theatrical movement, mediated by his theory of music and by imaginary forms of *commedia dell'arte*, is most prominently characterised, then, by two features: on the one side narrative unity, that is dancing which is wholly integrated into the plot as a physical rendering of the action. On the other side, interaction between structure and event, between virtuose bodily technique and improvisation beyond the shallow display of artistic tricks. A third aspect arises with the inclusion of the popular Italian *tarantella* in *Prinzessin Brambilla*. This dance developed experimental qualities as a favourite

---

22 As Hoffmann declares in the prefatory lines to his *Phantasiestücke* (*Fantasy-pictures*), see *Musical Writings*, p. 76.

23 *Prinzessin Brambilla* also draws on the *commedia's* refined reception in the eighteenth-century fairytale comedies by Carlo Gozzi; see Jean Starobinski, 'Ironie et Melancholie (II): la *Princesse Brambilla* de E.T.A. Hoffmann', *Critique*, 22 (1966), 438–57.

24 The author's involvement with the *commedia dell'arte* is testified to by another early composition, for it was not least the *commedia* elements in Clemens Brentano's libretto *Die lustigen Musikanten* which provoked Hoffmann to compose the musical comedy of the same title in 1804.

25 E.T.A. Hoffmann, *Schriften zur Musik*, ed. by Friedrich Schnapp (Munich: Winkler, 1977), p. 16.

bourgeois party entertainment in nineteenth-century private society. Its passionate character that transgressed traditional social dance is most vividly testified to in Nora's performance in Henrik Ibsen's play *A Doll's House*. In Hoffmann, however, another characteristic takes on even more importance: the *tarantella* still carried the connotation of compulsive dancing, due to the assumption that the dance took its name from the tarantula whose poison caused attacks of bodily convulsions.[26] A major literary embodiment of this aspect is the tarantula scene in Novalis's *Heinrich von Ofterdingen*. The third feature of Hoffmann's visionary choreographies, thus, is obsession. This darker potential of dance is at the centre of his novella *Der Sandmann*.

Performances of Trauma in *Der Sandmann*

E.T.A. Hoffmann's 'night-picture' *Der Sandmann*, published in 1816, spells out the traumatic impact of a compulsion that keeps the protagonist, a young man called Nathanael, in thrall of a disturbing event in his childhood.[27] As is well known, this event is told retrospectively – that is, as far as it is remembered – in a letter by Nathanel to his friend Lothar that opens the novella. He was hiding behind a curtain in his father's study to observe his father and a friend of the family – the lawyer Coppelius – engaging in what he thought must have been the creation of a homunculus. Even before this scene, Coppelius incorporated the boy's worst childhood fears of the punishing authority of the eye-robbing sandman. Paralysed by horror, Nathanael watches the frightful spectacle. Coppelius suddenly cries that he needed eyes for his experiment, and the boy, overcome by the violent intrusion of his imagination into actuality, falls out of his hidden auditorium. Inverting the function of a *deus ex machina* who re-establishes the divine order at the end of a play, Hoffmann's tale begins with an *ex machina* body that irreversibly destroys this order from the beginning. Pushing the Kleistian model to the edge, it is a fall that seals the loss of childhood grace by prefiguring Nathanael's future violent fall to his death. The father is able to prevent Coppelius from tearing out the son's eyes; yet another powerful scene of dismemberment takes place:

> '[...] let's examine the mechanism of his hands and feet.' And with these words he seized me so hard that my joints made a cracking noise, dislocated my hands and feet, and put

---

26 See the article on the *tarantella* in the *International Encyclopedia of Dance*, VI, 104–5.

27 My analysis of *Der Sandmann* is indebted to the wealth of readings this text has received, particularly to those that engage with Freud's path-breaking approach in 'The Uncanny', *StE* XVII, 217–56. To name but a few: Neil Hertz, 'Freud and the Sandman', in Hertz, *The End of the Line: Essays on Psychoanalysis and the Sublime* (New York: Columbia University Press, 1985), pp. 97–121; Detlef Kremer, *E.T.A. Hoffmann: Erzählungen und Romane* (Berlin: Schmidt, 1999) pp. 64–86; Gerhard Neumann, 'Der Sandmann', in *Meisterwerke der Literatur von Homer bis Musil*, ed. by Reinhard Brandt (Leipzig: Reclam, 2001), pp. 185–226; Andrew Webber, *The Doppelgänger*, pp. 121–48.

them back in various sockets. 'They don't fit properly! It was all right as it was! The Old Man knew what he was doing!' hissed and muttered Coppelius.[28]

It remains unclear whether that primal marking of the protagonist's life had occurred only in his imagination or in reality; whether the dark power which haunts Nathanael in the future is a psychological or a demonic one. He might have been merely manhandled by Coppelius rather than exploited as a source of body parts for a machine-man. Whether this first event, and the subsequent death of the father, provided a blue-print for a demonic trauma, or for the traumatic obsession with a demon, it soon becomes obvious that its effect is far more important than what exactly has happened. As the narrative continues to unfold, it shows how the childhood event leaves its traces on the protagonist's economy of desire, and his creative productivity. Coppelius will be the central figure of his writings; and he will return to the scene of Nathanael's life, enacting, as it were, the protagonist's fiction. What is more, the first dissection of the boy's body by Coppelius forecasts the lawyer's physical influence on Nathanael: Coppelius, sometimes in the shape of his double Coppola, will take on the function of master, not least dancing master, who rules over the protagonist's moves.[29] His grasp of the young man's imagination destroys the latter's engagement to Lothar's sister Clara, drives him into the arms of the automaton Olimpia, and from there into a state of increasing mental delusion that ends with his death as he throws himself off the town's central tower.

Nathanael's fateful condition manifests itself in bodily, dance-like performances. Yet rather than representing recuperative movement, the bodily performances stand for the protagonist's stasis, for his very inability to move freely – to work through, overcome and thus change his condition – due to his lethal fixation on his traumatic past. The most conventional of these performances that prepares the stage for the following ones is a dance that takes place at the house of Olimpia's 'father', Spalanzani, physicist and another expert in the creation of artificial life.[30] Enacting the passage from *Die Automate* cited above, Nathanael dances with the automaton:

> [...] he embraced the fair Olimpia and flew with her through the ranks of the dancers. Nathanael considered himself a good dancer, but the peculiar rhythmic regularity with which Olimpia danced often disconcerted him and made him realize how badly he kept time. (*HS*, 109)

In Hoffmann, the discipline that engenders perfectly regulated movement, as evidenced by Olimpia's dance, cannot be separated from its dark reverse, the discipline of a fateful psychic automatism which will paralyse its victim.

---

28 E.T.A. Hoffmann, *The Sandman*, in *The Golden Pot and Other Tales*, transl. by Ritchie Robertson (Oxford: Oxford University Press, 1992), pp. 85–118 (pp. 90–91).

29 Note Nathanael's father addressing Coppelius as 'Master', *HS*, 90.

30 Hoffmann's likely allusion to naturalist Lazzaro Spalanzani has most recently been shown by Stefani Engelstein, 'Reproductive Machines in E.T.A. Hoffmann', in Henn and Pausch, pp. 169–91.

Olimpia's fake human traits fail to charm anyone other than Nathanael; paradoxically, they do not work because they work too well. Olimpia's appearance indeed perfectly corresponds to the neoclassicist ideal of regularity and flawless contours. In an ironic move, however, Hoffmann exceeds the ideal in turning its incorporation into a hyper-classicist monster. The doll's beauty, then, is but a mask of the pronounced anti-classicist body of Coppelius, 'a big, broad-shouldered man with a massive, misshapen head, a pair of piercing, greenish, cat-like eyes sparkling from under bushy grey eyebrows, and a large beaky nose hanging over his upper lip' (*HS*, 88). Like Kleist's unoriginal 'original' sculpture, the more-than-perfect copy of a human being questions a psycho-social order which is based on the repetition of norms that are bound to entail mismatch and failure. In her impeccable subjection to aesthetic and mechanic prescription Olimpia is a parody of the 'loyal subjects' who apparently filled the salons of *Biedermeier* Germany. Echoing the *Marionettentheater's* constellation of sculpture and young man, Nathanael fails to adapt to the ideal: the doll's dance is too regular for him to catch up with its rhythm. Yet Hoffmann does not allow his protagonist to gain the sanity which might come with this failure to entirely subject himself to an alienating force. The doll's excess of control is equalled by a fatal hypercorrection on Nathanael's side, subjecting him to the discipline of a rigid psychic regime that dictates the repetitive physical automatism of his catatonic fits. The image of the machine does not represent rationality and stability, but the frightening, mercilessly destructive and radically uncanny order of a deranged mind.

The performative imitation of an idealization recurs in the ballet *Coppélia*. It deserves a brief appearance at this stage, as it encompasses *in nuce* the great distance between the ballet and its source. Here, the setting has shifted to Swanilda's (the ballet's Clara) appropriation of the puppet Coppélia's role which is the bravura passage of the piece. Swanilda poses as Coppélia in order to cure her fiancé Frantz from his infatuation with the doll, and to save him from the toy maker's experiments. We read in a review by critic Saint-Victor on the first Paris Swanilda, Giuseppina Bozzacchi: 'She must be seen playing the doll, first imitating a statue, and then darting out of this stiff envelope, like a butterfly from its chrysalis, and filling the stage with her aerial leaps.'[31] The critic's emphasis on the superiority of human over statuesque movement is significant. In *Coppélia*, the automaton is treated mockingly from the beginning. The ballet's very appeal consists in showing the human dancer to be superior to the puppet, and thus to any threat of uncanny psychic automatisms. Moreover, in making the human dancer even better than an automaton, *Coppélia* not only affirms the prowess of ballet technique, but also celebrates the nineteenth-century belief in progress, perfectibility and economic production. It thus worked against images of physical, emotional, or mental fatigue which activated the fear of a psycho-social regression that was associated with the mobilization of uncontrollable

---

31 Quoted in Ivor Guest, *Two Coppélias: A Centenary Study* (London: The Friends of Covent Garden, 1970), p. 26.

irrational and sexual impulses – impulses that are at the centre of *Der Sandmann*.[32] It is fitting that critic Elias de Rauze of the *Revue et gazette musicale de Paris* writes on Bozzacchi on 28 May 1870, shortly after the premiere of *Coppélia*: 'She dances from beginning to end without getting tired', thus commenting on the dancing as a feat of physical strength, which is rarely taken into account in the reviews of the day.[33] In *Coppélia*, the power of the puppet, and with it puppet-like compulsion, is defeated; Clara and Nathanael in the shape of Swanilda and Frantz celebrate their wedding. The third Act of the ballet, a marriage divertissement that lengthily extols controlled, procreative sexual union, can be interpreted as a bulwark against anxieties that are let loose in Hoffmann's model.

To return to the original and its protagonist's deranged mind: in short, Nathanael's life develops into a series of re-enactments of the traumatic primal scene in his father's study. In a confusing *mise-en-abîme* typical for Hoffmann's writing, his protagonist both obsessively records and re-experiences his trauma, so that the transition from the imaginary to the real is continuously blurred. His plight imprisons him in a hopeless universe where the perpetual recurrence of the same forecloses any real social interaction, most painfully visible in his relationships to his love interests Clara and Olimpia. In their presence, he finds ultimately nothing else than a reflection of his own traumatised self. This fact is most clearly articulated through the travelling of torn-out eyes in the novella. Initially a threat that was put on Nathanel himself, it returns in his composition for his fiancée: '[…] the fearsome Coppelius appears and touches Clara's lovely eyes, which leap into Nathanael's breast, burning and singeing him' (*HS*, 102), and in the horrible second re-enactment of the trauma, the fight between Spalanzani and Coppelius over the wooden doll: '[…] Olimpia's deathly pale wax face had no eyes, just black caverns where eyes should be'. A few lines further on, the cross-fading of self and other is spelt out, with Spalanzani addressing Nathanael: 'he stole *your* eyes. […] here are *her* eyes! […] Thereupon Nathanael noticed a pair of bloody eyes lying on the floor and staring at him' (*HS*, 114; my emphasis).

Both these retrospective reanimations of the primal event, and also the third and lethal re-enactment, are staged as scenes of intense physical, dancerly theatre: performances of trauma that give shape to what cannot be contained in linear discourse. They dismantle, distort and finally entirely destroy the regular social dancing at Spalanzani's ball. Nathanael is hurled 'into a circle of flames which is rotating with the speed of a whirlwind, dragging him along in its fury' (*HS*, 102); he watches Spalanzani and Coppola being engaged in a dreadful trio with their dancing figure, made up of two masters fighting for Olimpia who is stripped to her wooden

---

32 See Anson Rabinbach, *The Human Motor: Energy, Fatigue, and the Origins of Modernity* (Berkeley: University of California Press, 1990).

33 Elias de Rauze on Bozzacchi in *Coppélia*, *Revue et gazette musicale de Paris*, 28 May 1870, p. 170. On nineteenth-century ballet criticism, see Lucia Ruprecht, 'Dance Goes Public : The Romantic Ballet and its Critics', in *The Cambridge Companion to Ballet*, ed. by Marion Kant (Cambridge: Cambridge University Press, 2006).

'bones' and pulled apart as each claims her as their sole possession; crying 'spin, wooden dolly' (*HS*, 114, 117), he throws himself at Spalanzani, collapses onto the floor, executes wild leaps, flings Clara over the tower's parapet, to finally throw himself from the tower into the depths.

The narrative leitmotifs for these performances are provided at the opening of the novella. It unfolds in a sequence of scenes which are linked to each other through the repetition and variation of these motifs, most notably eyes, fire and the mutilated or dysfunctional body. Hoffmann's terrifying experiences during the battle of Dresden might represent a very concrete inspiration here. The author writes in his journal in August 1813: 'The content of many a dream became true in the most gruesome manner: mutilated, dismembered human bodies!'[34] In one of the earliest critiques of Hoffmann's tales, Ludwig Börne speaks of disruption and dismemberment as key figures of Hoffmann's writing. At the same time, his description of its unsettling quality reads like an uncanny variation on Kleist:

> If you have seen these puppet plays with dancing dolls which hurtle off their hands and arms, feet and legs, and finally their heads so that they at last bop around as horrible torsos, then you know the figures of Hoffmann's tales, only that they lose their heads first.[35]

Elizabeth Wright puts it more concisely; she characterises Nathanael's life as a 'detour to death'.[36] Combining Freud's linking of compulsive repetition to the death drive with later stages of trauma theory, Caruth glosses the traumatic experience as a person's confrontation with, and miraculous survival of, the possibility of death. In 'Beyond the Pleasure Principle', Freud explains this experience as a shocking 'breach in the shield' of the psyche that is unprepared for anxiety, and thus 'not in a good position for binding the inflowing amounts of excitation' (*StE* XVIII, 31). This lack of psychic protection is indicated by the German verb *aufreissen*: 'da ergriff mich Coppelius, [...] – riß mich auf und warf mich auf den Herd' (*SW* III, 17). While its specific ambiguity is lost in the translation – 'Coppelius seized me, [...] pulled me to my feet and hurled me on to the fireplace' (*HS*, 90), *aufreissen* denotes both the action of pulling up and of 'tearing open' the boy. It is thus a violation of physical and psychic boundaries that happens in the father's study. Moreover, as Caruth has it, the traumatised consciousness, once faced with its own extinction, 'can do nothing but repeat the destructive event over and over again'.[37] This uncanny pathological repetition arises precisely out of the impossibility of adequately representing the

---

34 Hoffmann, *Tagebücher*, p. 222.

35 Ludwig Börne, *Sämtliche Schriften*, ed. by Inge and Peter Rippmann, 5 vols (Düsseldorf: Melzer, 1964–68), II, 561. Hoffmann indeed knew Kleist's essay, see his letter of 1 July 1812 to Hitzig: 'Sincerest thanks for the most interesting *Abendblätter* (Evening Gazette). Especially outstanding is the essay on the puppet theatre. I know Kleist's tales well; they are worthy of him'; Hoffmann, *Letters*, p. 170.

36 Elizabeth Wright, *Psychoanalytic Criticism: A Reappraisal*, 2nd edn (Cambridge: Polity, 1998), p. 132.

37 Caruth, *Unclaimed Experience*, p. 63.

primal scene, for it is 'experienced too soon, too unexpectedly, to be fully known and is therefore not available to consciousness until it imposes itself again, repeatedly, in the nightmares and repetitive actions of the survivor'.[38]

As the overwhelming immediacy of the event has to be defused by numbness, it is experienced only belatedly. This initial anaesthesia is, for Nathanael, from the beginning tied to cramps, to the inability to move freely: 'but everything went black and dim before my eyes, a sudden convulsion shot through my nerves and my frame, and I felt nothing more' (*HS*, 91).[39] The belated experience, however, equally fails to reach 'what actually happened'; it is only invoked through the encoded messages of indirect reference, through distortion, substitution, displacement. Trauma, for Caruth, is the paradox of addressing an event *by not addressing it*; it is at once the repeated suffering of its impact, and the 'continual leaving of its site'.[40] The very first words of Nathanael's account of his childhood trauma articulate this paradox which will govern his every move: 'Nun fort zur Sache!' (*SW* III, 12), literally something like '*Off to* the point now!' (glossed over in the translation as 'Now, let me get on with the story!', *HS*, 86).

Hoffmann's narrativisation of trauma through ambiguity and recurring vocabulary is extraordinarily ingenious. The stiffness of his fright in his father's study ('I was rooted to the spot', *HS*, 90) matches his future erotic fixation on Olimpia, epitomised in his staring at her through the pocket spy glass ('Nathanael remained at the window, as though rooted to the spot by a spell', *HS*, 106). It also recurs more generally in his obsession with the rewriting and re-enacting of his trauma, which leads to physical fixture in catatonic fits. Nathanael's stasis embodies both his compulsive fixation on the trauma, and his inability fully to understand it: his inability to dance his way out of the trauma, as it were, a cure that will be realised in *Prinzessin Brambilla*. The repeated use of *starren* (staring) and *Starre* (rigidity, stasis) in the description of the tale's actors and events thus forms a message in code. Like the protagonist's cramps, it can be interpreted as the conversion of a traumatic experience into physical and narrative symptoms. The figures of optical fixture and fixation are complemented by those that conflate the fire that is central in the traumatising scene with images of erotic inflammation, a complementation that culminates in the blending of gaze and fire ('the amorous look that pierced his heart and set it afire, *HS*, 108). These figures bear testimony to the initial wounding and compulsively appear whenever the protagonist interacts with Coppelius, Olimpia, or his own memory of the childhood experience.

Nathanael is not only unconsciously bound to the traumatic event; through its entanglement with the economies of desire and poetic creativity, the trauma comes to be cultivated by him. The aesthetic cultivation hints at the vicarious function

---

38 Ibid., p. 4.

39 Compare Hoffmann's use of *Starrkrampf* (catalepsy) in the vampire tale of *Serapionsbrüder* (Brethren of Serapion) as pathological symptom of an uncanny spell, *SW* IV, 1130.

40 *Trauma: Explorations in Memory*, ed. by Cathy Caruth (Baltimore: Johns Hopkins University Press, 1995), p. 10.

of the games in which Hoffmann's protagonist is involved, illustrated in detail in Andrew Webber's reading of *Der Sandmann* through the parameters of the *fort-da* game that opens Freud's 'Beyond the Pleasure Principle'. While the repetitive rhythm of the game, as its replacement by creative processes, seeks to rehearse and overcome the experience of primal separation and loss, it also anticipates the final separation of death. The traumatic frame of the repetitive logic that is central to my analysis enhances the impact of death as both origin and tragic fulfilment of Nathanael's erotic and poetic preoccupations. We may talk of a lethal fetishisation of trauma in this case: Olimpia and Coppelius are being deliberately kept animate by the protagonist's burning gazes, and by the glowing colours of his writings. Nathanael's desire and his creative activity rekindle the primal inflammation over and over again. Hoffmann's protagonist is caught in the double-bind of being at once the master and the victim of his trauma, a situation that is mirrored in his inner and outer state of torment and self-division (see *HS*, 118).

Nathanael's primal fragmentation causes an alienation from his own body and a deeply disturbed identity. The metamorphosis he underwent through Coppelius's treatment has come true. The characteristics of Nathanael's bodily comportment designate the protagonist as an automaton-like being himself, mirrored in both Olimpia and Clara (whom he addresses as an 'accursed lifeless automaton' in his rage over her lack of understanding, *HS*, 103). Hoffmann effectively applies to him the frightening potential of Romantic androids that stems not least from the fear that human beings may not be very far ahead of their mechanical doubles.[41] Nathanael acts under the command of the will of his traumatic fixation, whose otherness is embodied by the master-figure Coppelius and his double Coppola. The alienating influence of trauma articulates itself in repeated attacks of sudden illness or rage, where the protagonist's body and language slip out of his control; having been called a little beast by Coppelius, Nathanael's words become, during his fits, indeed a bestial roaring.

As pointed out before, these fits manifest themselves in hallucinations of a vertiginous fire-dance. Yet rather than representing ecstatic movement, the fiery whirl completes the paralysing effect of Nathanael's fixation.[42] The protagonist's fits are not only marked by physical convulsions, but also by states of paralysis. The spinning dance of the 'fiery circle' (*HS*, 114) signifies the stasis of a consuming whirl, perpetually circling around the same traumatic core which draws its victim inside, and finally downward. Significantly, the downward spinning whirl is one of the most archaic choreographic patterns of the transition from life to death, and of the utmost regression where the body dissolves in spatial dynamics.[43] The fiery spinning dance

---

41 See Monika Schmitz-Emans, 'Eine schöne Kunstfigur? Androiden, Puppen und Maschinen als Allegorien des literarischen Werkes', *arcadia*, 30 (1995), 1–30.

42 See 'Beyond the Pleasure Principle', where Freud speaks of the paralysing character of the traumatic impact that demands all the psychic energies of the victim, *StE* XVIII, 30.

43 On the choreographic symbolism of the spiral, see Gabriele Brandstetter, *Tanz-Lektüren*, pp. 324–8.

fails to evoke circular perfection. Instead it embodies the meaninglessness of the protagonist's persistent suffering in the image of self-referential, purely formal, and ultimately lethal movement. This threatening aspect of merely formal, rather than referential, merely circling, rather than progressing movement is equally present in the telling scene with Coppola's eyeglasses. Disrobed of their function as instruments of perception, the glasses which are arranged on the table form a shimmering ornament that shoots burning gazes at Nathanael's breast. The simultaneity of at once present and absent eyes is enacted in Coppola's misnomer 'eyes-a' (*HS*, 105), in the staring out of empty eye sockets, and in the delusions of Nathanael's hallucinations. The dysfunction of the sense of sight complements the loss of kinetic control; both indicate Hoffmann's groundbreaking articulation of modern subjectivity which must fatally lack any sense of reliable self-knowledge.

To add a last twist to this analysis: through its enactment in pantomimic, dance-like performances, trauma becomes a spectacle. It culminates in the maddening fiery whirl on the tower, the last and most dangerous stage of the tale. Nathanael's lethal fall from the tower is a jump off stage, directly into the audience which watches from beneath. In *Der Sandmann*, the narrative discourse constantly challenges the positions of actor, beholder and director, echoing the protagonist's entanglement in the web of his own imagination. The events are staged as scenes where the spectator and his scopophilic pleasure, enhanced by his pocket spyglass, are drawn into the dance, where the auditorium turns into an extension of the stage and where the script writer becomes driven by the play. In a chiastic construction, the tale's end brings back its beginning; to recall the primal scene: '"Bring the eyes! Bring the eyes!" cried Coppelius in a hollow rumbling voice. Gripped by uncontrollable terror, I screamed out and dived from my hiding-place on to the floor' (*HS*, 90); and the end: 'Suddenly Nathanael paused and stood stock still; he bent down, perceived Coppelius, and, with a piercing shriek of "Beautiful eye-a! Beautiful eyes-a!" he jumped over the parapet' (*HS*, 118). While in the beginning, the bizarre events form an illicit spectacle secretly witnessed through a small gap in the curtains, the spectacle of trauma becomes the main public attraction in the end. The tower switches functions: it turns from a privileged observation post into a raised stage. Coppelius has not lost his disastrous force, and the protagonist still falls; but now the master watches, while Nathanael is the one who performs. Coppelius's ruling gaze prescribes for the last time the paralysing circles of the fire-dance executed by the protagonist. The theatrical situation where the spectator is drawn into the illusory world of the performance is ultimately reversed: driven by the suggestive power of the director Coppelius, the dancer-actor Nathanael throws himself into the audience.

As is well known, Hoffmann imprinted the circular on to the name of his major artist-figure Johannes Kreisler (the surname means 'someone who circulates'). In a passage of *Lebens-Ansichten des Katers Murr* (The Life and Opinions of the Tomcat Murr), Kreisler muses about the condition that is encompassed by his name. His thoughts can be read as a wonderful little comment on *Der Sandmann*, more precisely on the quality that could have saved its protagonist: irony. Kreisler tells his listener:

No, there's no getting away from the word *Kreis*, meaning a circle, and Heaven send that it immediately puts you in mind of those wonderful circles in which our entire existence moves and from which we cannot escape, do what we may. A Kreisler circulates in these circles, and very likely, weary of the leaps and bounds of the St Vitus's dance he is obliged to perform, and at odds with the dark, inscrutable power which delineated those circles, he often longs to break out [...]. And the deep pain of this longing may in its turn be that very irony which you, dear lady, so bitterly deplore, failing to observe that the powerful mother Irony bore a son who stepped into life like a lordly king. I mean Humour [...].[44]

Healthy mental alertness, in Hoffmann, is most often illustrated by a sense of irony, which corresponds to forms of successful physical agility, a link that will be crucial in *Prinzessin Brambilla*. Many figures thus display features of dancers or dancing masters. Most prominent is the fantastic hair-artist and puppeteer Pietro Belcampo of *Die Elixiere des Teufels* (The Devil's Elixirs). In some sense a double of both *Prinzessin Brambilla's* Giglio and Celionati, he is puppet and puppeteer, mad enough to be an actor while still working the switches from the background for his client, the monk Medardus. Above all, he is distinguished by the twists and turns of his constant mental and physical capers: 'With curious leaps and grimaces, and making queer remarks the whole time, he attended my hair'; he knows of the ballet masters and dancers Noverre and Vestris, and holds a lesson in posture and gait for Medardus.[45] Hoffmann's emphasis on the hairdresser's name, 'Peter Schönfeld' alias 'Pietro Belcampo', indicates a cheeky allusion to Pierre Beauchamp, the famous ballet-master at the court of Louis XIV. Irony as deliberate mental and bodily mobility, however, is constantly in danger of turning into the insanity that is its reverse. While the actor Giglio in *Prinzessin Brambilla* cures his unsettled, split psyche with the dancing and acting demanded by his profession, Belcampo's hyper-agility ends up in inertia and derangement.

Nathanael, who gets caught in the encirclements of his mentally and physically paralysing trauma, would have needed a dancing master and patron like Serapion, the illusionist, lunatic and saint who lends his name to the peculiar combination of fantastic and realist elements in Hoffmann's writing.[46] Serapion is convinced that he survived his martyrdom under the emperor Decius. His tortures are recalled in *Der Sandmann*: dismemberment followed by the fall from a rock. Serapion's sudden attacks of headache and rheumatic pain, however, are the only remnants of his alleged death in the third century. The Serapion brethren, the circle of friends that frames Hoffmann's collection of novellas of the same title, discuss this insanity, which is an utmost belief in the almighty power of paradox and excessive imagination. They

44 E.T.A. Hoffmann, *The Life and Opinions of the Tomcat Murr*, transl. by Antnea Bell (London: Penguin, 1999), pp. 50–51.

45 E.T.A. Hoffmann, *The Devil's Elixirs*, transl. by Ronald Taylor (London: John Calder, 1963), p. 90.

46 See Hans Mayer's fundamental article on the Serapionistic principle, 'Die Wirklichkeit E.T.A. Hoffmanns', in *Romantikforschung seit 1945*, ed. by Klaus Peter (Königstein: Hanstein, 1980), pp. 116–44.

urn the lunacy into a poetic programme, characterised as a glimpse into the most horrifying depths of nature without suffering from vertigo (*SW* IV, 37). The narrator who encompasses those depths in his fiction must have a head for heights; he must be able to keep his balance in the face of the abyss by holding on to the distancing effect of irony. Nathanael lacks these abilities. His texts and his life blur into one fateful *mise en scène* that whirls its protagonist into death.

In *Der Sandmann*, the narrator's testimony to the traumatic events echoes the protagonist's obsession with recording them. The narration develops a dynamic of its own that shows the narrator himself not being entirely free of the writerly obsession he depicts. Echoing the unresolved confusions of theatrical positions in the novella, he gives up his position of a hidden choreographer of the events, steps out from behind the wings, and starts to lose himself in the compulsive dance. The tale's thematisation of the incalculable, pathological aspects of creative activity sheds an ambiguous light on its narrator, and, by extension, on its author, whose staging of the text might gloss over the impact of his own confrontation with shocking scenes of dismemberment in Dresden. This ambiguity is enhanced by the fact that the boundaries between the protagonist's and the narrator's perspectives are shifting, and it remains doubtful whether one is dealing with primary events, their expression by the protagonist, the latter's imagination, or the subsequent modification of the action in its representation by the narrator. The pervasive repetition in Hoffmann's texts of stereotypical figures like the fixture of paralysis, or the fire of the penetrating gaze, may suggest a repressed authorial wound that indirectly manifests itself in the narratives and creates the feeling of unease so noticeable in *Der Sandmann*. The narrator's insistence on the inaccessible core of his narrative, which he can only capture in the form of a 'dim reflection in a dull mirror' (*HS*, 99), reinforces the symptomatic character of the writing. It is a narration in fits and starts, perpetually and unavailingly attempting to approach the unsayable.[47]

However, this narrator also possesses what Nathanael lacks: it is a form of irony that prevents him from being drawn into the abyss that devours the protagonist. The *mise-en-scène* of the narrative becomes a stabilising strategy in the face of the protagonist's compulsion. As has often been noticed, it is most obvious in the narrator's address to the reader that contains a discussion of how best to stage the events. Yet what is more, the narrative performance in general enacts a figurative dance that contains the traumatic. By stressing its inability to reproduce the hideous original events, the narrator's act of aesthetic repetition on one hand testifies to, and thereby affirms, a traumatic wound. Yet the mediation also introduces an element of difference and reflection into the repetitive practice and thus undermines the original trauma. Whereas Nathanael is at the mercy of repetition, the author can play with the repressed and in his turn 'cultivate' the trauma. Indeed, the subtle varieties in the tale's repetitions characterise the narration – as opposed to the plot – as a deliberate repetition-in-difference rather than as a compulsion, as a spiral

---

47 See Neumann, *Der Sandmann*, p. 204.

rather than as a circle.[48] This discursive spiral articulates a writerly technique cf movement that contains the traumatic; in *Prinzessin Brambilla*, the technique wi 1 reappear more powerfully in the form of narrative 'fireworks'. Yet we may detect the creatively spiralling movement of the discourse also in *Der Sandmann*, namely in its rich fire-imagery. It metonymically displaces the flames of the father's hearth into 'glowing colours', 'red-hot drops of [...] blood', 'red-hot arms', or a 'heart burning with desire' (*HS*, 97, 102, 108, 112). The virtually endless spiral of the narration overcomes the lethal implications of the protagonist's trauma. It gives voice to his wound where he is silenced, and moves where he is paralysed. While the protagonist's life is consumed in his repetition compulsion, the narration, by constantly renewing what it reuses, remains. In the case of *Der Sandmann*, language is the only truly able dancer of the tale.

The Dancing Self in *Prinzessin Brambilla*

Prinzessin Brambilla (1821), in turn, boasts a number of fantastic dancers, performers which are agile enough to set their identities in movement, to experiment with different roles, and so to avoid the lethal fixture of the subject to whom change is denied. While the anchorless mobility of the insane runs through the text like a dangerous undercurrent beneath a glittering surface, the mask play and dancing encounters of the carnival and the *commedia dell'arte* constitute a veritable movement cure that turns the fatal loss of self into a theatrical game of lost and regained identities. *Prinzessin Brambilla* is at once *Bildungsroman* and case history. And it is a writer's dream of physical theatre where bodily acting and dancing is at least as important as words.[49] The stage for this narrative spectacle is provided by the genre of the *capriccio*. Italian for whim or fancy, it denotes in the first instance musical pieces that celebrate the exceptional, the whimsical, the fantastic and the apparently arbitrary, indicating light-footed, but meticulously composed artefacts capturing the fanciful vaults of fantasy. As mentioned before, the more concrete setting of the *capriccio* is owed to the *balli* by Jacques Callot, transposed onto the fictional scenery of carnival in Rome. The full title thus reads *Prinzessin Brambilla: A Capriccio after Jacques Callot*.

What happens? We are introduced to the two main characters, the seamstress Giacinta Soardi and her husband (as we later find out) Giglio Fava, actor of tragedies, in a scene that triggers the duplication of their selves through Giacinta's

---

48 Roland Barthes writes on the spiral: 'it is about a return in difference, not about identical repetition', in 'Réquichot et son corps', in *Œuvres complètes*, ed. by Éric Marty, 3 vols (Paris : Seuil, 1993–95), II (1993), 1623–42 (p. 1630).

49 *Prinzessin Brambilla* received at least one staging in a 1920 production of the Moscow Chamber Theatre, directed by A. Tairov. Fully aware of the text's potential for physical theatre, this staging put special emphasis on dance and acrobatics; see Elisabeth Cheauré, *E.T.A. Hoffmann: Inszenierungen seiner Werke auf russischen Bühnen – Ein Beitrag zur Rezeptionsgeschichte* (Heidelberg: Winter, 1979).

first masquerade. Giglio enters her room while she is trying on a sumptuous costume, ordered by a certain master Bescapi, which she has just finished. Dazzled by her sight, the man mistakes his wife for a princess of whom he had dreamt the night before; Giacinta sulkily turns away from him as she feels not being loved for what she is, and Giglio leaves to join the bustle of the streets. There he witnesses a masked procession which, led by a princess called Brambilla, as he is told by the wily quick-change artist and mountebank Bastianello di Pistoja alias Ciarlatano Celionati, is looking for the princess's fiancé, prince Cornelio Chiapperi. Celionati sells Giglio a pair of glasses of allegedly magical power, which are supposed to help him find the prince and thus receive an amazing recompense by the princess. What is more, Celionati suggests that Brambilla is the very princess of Giglio's dream, and thus pushes the actor towards the possibility that he may be the longed-for prince himself.

Celionati's function as match-maker echoes to some extent that of his repulsive double, Coppola the barometer seller in *Der Sandmann*; only that here, a more light-hearted version of the delusions of love will be played out. While Giglio embarks on the quest for his ideal lover Brambilla, Giacinta seeks to forget her straying partner by looking for her ideal lover, no one other than the prince Chiapperi. Thus unfolds a play of masked encounters on the streets of the Roman carnival that leads from the alienation of a couple to their renewed mutual recognition at the end. It is interspersed with two more narrative threads, both equally in the hands of the charlatan Celionati: the latter's project of turning Giglio from a tragic actor into a skilful performer of *commedia dell'arte*, able to successfully engage with his wife who emerges as a *commedia* actress herself; and his recounting of the myth of the so-called Land of Urdar that comes to mirror the events on a metaphorical level, and feeds into their theatrical apotheosis at the conclusion of the *capriccio*.

To achieve a grasp of the elusive and intricate network of the text, my argument will follow the three variously intertwined strands of the narration.[50] This will be organised more precisely around passages where expressive gesture and mime are crucial, among them three explicitly staged as dances. They are set on the Corso, the improvised and, as it were, permeable stage of the Roman carnival, a stage which, faithful to a predilection of Hoffmann, perpetually exchanges the roles of performers

---

50 Of the substantial amount of research literature on *Prinzessin Brambilla* I found the following most useful: Detlef Kremer, *E.T.A. Hoffmann*, pp. 123–43; Claudia Liebrand, *Aporie des Kunstmythos: Die Texte E.T.A. Hoffmanns* (Freiburg: Rombach, 1996); Gerhard Neumann, 'E.T.A. Hoffmanns "Prinzessin Brambilla" als Entwurf einer Wissenspoetik: Wissenschaft – Theater – Literatur', and by the same author, 'Glissando und Defiguration: E.T.A. Hoffmanns Capriccio "Prinzessin Brambilla" als Wahrnehmungsexperiment'; Günter Saße, 'Die Karnevalisierung der Welt: Vom "chronischen Dualismus" zur "Duplizität des irdischen Seins" in Hoffmanns *Prinzessin Brambilla*', *E.T.A. Hoffmann Jahrbuch* 9 (2001), 55–69; Andrew Webber, *The Doppelgänger*, pp. 169–78; Christine Weder, 'Ein medizinisch-literarisches Symptom: Zum Schwindel bei E.T.A. Hoffmann und im Kontext des medizinischen Diskurses der Zeit', *E.T.A. Hoffmann Jahrbuch* 10 (2002), 76–95.

and beholders.[51] While the blurring of theatrical positions indicated Nathanael's pathological relation to the world, we will see that *Prinzessin Brambilla* stresses the liberating creative potential of theatricality. The first danced encounter is Giglio's confrontation with his double, Prince Cornelio Chiapperi, who is engaged in a duo with the adored Brambilla (Figure 3.1). Giglio quickly takes part in the dance that after Brambilla's disappearance turns into a rapier fight, Giglio's first grotesque antic (Figure 3.2). This ardent fight is, in the end, a solo gag that is applauded heartily by the street audience. The second dance scene, crystallising fundamental questions of the text, is Giacinta's and Giglio's danced dialogue which gives voice to their attributes, tambourine and sword (Figure 3.3). The most challenging corporeal encounter is performed in the third dance passage towards the end of the narrative where Giglio is killed by his double, now in the mask of the Capitan Pantalone, in a dance-like choreographed stage fight (Figure 3.4).

Hoffmann's *capriccio*, true to its genre, is saturated with the 'agreeable flourish'[52] of ornamental digressions and narrative pleasures, while at the same time creating a network of corresponding motifs and with it an intricately branched-out structure. Following the numerous reflections and counter-reflections that characterise the narrative strands of *Prinzessin Brambilla*, my reading of the *capriccio* will focus on its dance scenes in their reflexive function with regard to the entire text. The dances literally give flesh to what Hoffmann calls the 'governing idea drawn from some philosophical view of life' (*HB*, 119) behind the whimsical turns of the narration. They correspond to Pistoja's declaration of the winged power of fantasy, which would evaporate were it not tied to the body of humour. They incorporate the aesthetics of identity that is set out in the myth of Urdar. Most crucially, the dance and fight scenes set Callot's figures moving. In a chiastic turn, they restore the lost mobility at the origin of the images: Callot's representations are reanimated in Hoffmann's performances. In this capacity, the dance scenes double and condense the function of the *capriccio* itself. However, they do so in an ironical way. They also reflect Pistoja's – here in the function of the internal reader's – warning against the trap of the allegorical (see *HB*, 236), which would not only reduce the capricious writing to static meanings, but also diminish the pleasure of indulging in the ornament of its twists and turns. The dance scenes do not primarily explicate, but multiply the forms that give shape to Hoffmann's ideas. Yet above all, they provide the choreography for the performances of identity at work in the text. They enact a kaleidoscopic poetic strategy, experimenting with acts of self-multiplication in a spinning dance, as Hoffmann's journal of 1809 has it: 'Strange idea at the ball of the 6th I imagine my

---

51 Hoffmann obviously appreciated forms of unity between stage and audience; he writes in a letter in January 1809 about the success of a prologue he contributed to theatre festivities: 'It seemed to me as if the whole stage and house had been in a most excellent manner united in *one* action, and the awkward gap between actors and audience completely eliminated. My heart rejoiced [...]; Hoffmann, *Letters*, 141.

52 E.T.A. Hoffmann, *Princess Brambilla*, in *The Golden Pot and Other Tales*, pp. 119–238 (p. 171).

self through a caleidoscope – all the figures which move around me are selves and I am irritated by their actions etc.'[53]

Yet before Giglio is able to participate in such virtuoso dances, he needs to learn how to move. This is effectuated through his initiation in the theatre-reform, led from behind the wings by Celionati. The tragic style of acting associated with theatre director Abbate Chiari, and performed by the early Giglio before he becomes a practician of Celionati's revived *commedia dell'arte*, is ridiculed as a dysfunctional, ineffective code. Having found his way to the theatre where he must witness the fact that the former gold- and silver-laden heroes have been replaced by the masks of the Italian pantomime, Giglio overhears the following description of himself as tragic actor:

> Indeed, when Fava emerged from the wings with measured steps like a dancer, when, ignoring his fellow-actors, he squinted towards the boxes and remained in a strangely affected posture long enough to give the fair ones ample time to admire him, he really seemed to me like a young cock with gaudy plumage, proudly taking his ease in the sun. And when he declaimed his verses stumblingly and badly, rolling his eyes, sawing the air with his hands, now rising on his toes and now doubling himself up like a pocket-knife, tell me, what sensible person could have his heart truly stirred by such behaviour?

Giglio Fava's main mistake was, thus, not to bring his roles to life, but to play, and to display, merely himself with the most exaggerated affectedness, so his critics remark. He appeared as a narcissist, 'lifeless puppet, moved by artificial threads' (*HB*, 144), persistently refusing to exchange the dainty tights of a *primo amoroso* with the trousers of a Pulcinella. Hoffmann improvises on the calculated movements of his own automata, and on the theme of Kleist's *Über das Marionettentheater*. What is crucial in terms of Giglio's trajectory is the strictly monologist, and codified character of tragic acting. Abbate Chiari illustrates this acting and movement technique vividly:

> Signor Zechielli, my chief tragedian at that time, could stand with his legs wide apart, his feet planted firmly on the ground, his arms raised in the air, and gradually twist his body round until his face was looking over his back, so that his gestures and facial expressions made the audience think him a double-faced Janus. That kind of thing generally creates the most striking effect, but it has to be done every time I say 'He begins to despair!'

The described contortion undoubtedly drives an actor into despair. However, it does not convey the feeling of desperation to the audience – 'yet at every speech my hero uttered the public burst into uncontrollable laughter' (*HB*, 178). The static postures of Zechielli, and of the early Fava, recall the stasis of the real-life tragic actor Nathanael. Here, however, tragedy is distinguished as a logocentric realm of deep-rootedness and secured signification, epitomised in the firm stand and the plain one-to-one relationship between movement and meaning, which loses ground in cheerful derision that mocks any attempt at unambiguous expression.

---

53 Hoffmann, *Tagebücher*, p. 107.

The celebration of multiple identifications in the dialogue of the masks provides the counter-image to tragic acting, and the target aimed at by Celionati's intrigue. The movement and the speeches of the masks give way to a more dynamic creation of signification: possibilities of meaning and interpretation are established only to be taken back by the next turn of the events. The new vocabulary of movement is characterised by a constant exchange of words and gestures, culminating in the most extravagant leaps and turns. Whereas the tragic actor plays through a given monologue he has learned by heart, the comedians improvise. They react to each other, to the situation, and to the audience. The narrator would never escape into the realm of silent bodily expression in merely *describing* the dance scenes on the Corso. The danced encounters are performative acts of speech where the players *talk through* their dances.[54] They enact and speak their approaches to each other: 'Your coloured ribbons are waving, and, like me, you're floating on the tiptoes of your left foot, holding your tambourine high above your head; and you ask me to dispense entirely with reason and balance?' (*HB*, 205). Closely intertwined with the plot, they further the narration in a condensed, vivid way. The dances do not ask to be given a static meaning, since nothing – as Giacinta, the unknown beautiful dancer, asserts – would be more boring than to be rooted to the ground, and to be obliged to give a full explanation to every gaze and every word. The increasingly daring steps and jumps incorporate the playful character of the new theatre perfectly.

It is, however, not a display of pure naturalness and immediacy. The *commedia* masks do have a strong puppet-like quality as well. Hoffmann takes up a pattern whose pathological aspect we already encountered in *Der Sandmann*, and which he also employs in a number of other texts: without being aware of it, his protagonists execute a choreography prescribed by a master-figure. These master-figures, in Hoffmann, typically operate under cover, as charlatans or tricksters rather than figures of legitimate authority. They are doubling a certain compulsive dynamic of the text itself, sometimes leading to fatal constraints, as in *Der Sandmann*, but at other times to liberating agency. Although the disciplinary power of the master never entirely loses its ambiguity, in *Prinzessin Brambilla* its prescription is enabling rather than paralysing. In their transformation into comedy actors, the seamstress Giacinta and the tragic *amoroso* Giglio are conducted by the threads of Celionati's masterly hands; their dependence on the Ciarlatano's game is mirrored in the mythical Ruffiamonte's play with the little dolls representing Ophioch and Liris, who will later be replaced by the real couple. Celionati's galvanic purse, which is sometimes filled with 'ducats' which ring true and are 'properly minted' (*HB*, 148), sometimes with 'buttons or counters' (*HB*, 191), leads Giglio through the conspiratorial plot. It designates the theatre prince as puppet and 'plaything of unknown powers' (*HB* 145): 'Giglio reached mechanically, automatically, for his pocket and did indeed feel the little purse, filled with clinking gold pieces [...]. An electric shock seemed to shoot through all his limbs' (ibid.).

---

54 Despite the fact that Celionati praises pantomime as 'the foremost in the world, if only because it utters the profoundest truths without need for words' (*HB*, 152).

Figure 3.1   *Riciulina and Metzetin* – Giglio's double dances with Princess
Brambilla, nineteenth-century copper engraving by Carl Friedrich
Thiele after an etching of the series *Balli di Sfessania* by Jacques
Callot (*c.* 1622).

Figure 3.2   *Franca Trippa and Fritellino* – Giglio dances with his double, nineteenth-century copper engraving by Carl Friedrich Thiele after an etching of the series *Balli di Sfessania* by Jacques Callot (*c.* 1622).

The multiplied identities of the two protagonists, Giacinta and Giglio, and the labyrinthine paths they follow in their search for themselves and for each other fittingly represent the way the text fans out its meanings without indicating which one is to be viewed as decisive.[55] The dynamisation of identities in this total theatre, however, does not end up in complete fragmentation, but is playfully enacted during the carnival and on the stage of the Argentina theatre. Alienation and confusion lose their compulsive aspect when they are part of a deliberate staging and performing of identities. As long as Giglio takes the fantastic events surrounding him for real, he is declared insane. He is excluded from the theatre, and treated like a patient. His 'deviance' is accepted when the imaginary world in which he has become caught is revealed as a theatrical one. The painter Reinhold articulates this in a comment on Celionati's theatre-plot that is at the same time one of the countless confusing self-commentaries of the *capriccio* itself. It is significant that he speaks of a whirling dance in which one should take part in order not to get even dizzier; the space where such a danced upheaval can be performed is, of course, the stage of the Roman streets:

> I feel as though all sorts of figures were running in circles with ever-increasing speed, driven on by the colourful masquerade of some wild, fanciful game, until the eye can no longer recognize them or tell them apart. Let's put on masks, however, and go to the Corso! (*HB*, 226)

Hoffmann seems to follow a long-standing tradition: while being silenced and made powerless within dominant discourses, the madman is given a symbolic space in theatre, where he plays the role of masked truth.[56] In *Der Sandmann*, Olimpia and Nathanael are not granted an *official* theatrical space to perform their 'antics' which are considered insane in the real world. Moreover, the figure of the sandman is so frightening because it is not contained among the limitations of the *carnevalesque*. His grotesque physical features, in fact quite similar to the exaggerated traits of the *commedia* figures, are disconcerting because they do not belong to a masquerade. Should we thus see *Der Sandmann* as playing out the deeply subverting experience of carnival unbound – while *Prinzessin Brambilla* disarms insanity on the stages of its narration? The *capriccio* would not be the cunning text that it is if it gave so simple a solution to the questions posed by its fantastic aspects. 'But if the Devil is among the dancers, the most graceful leaps are in vain' (*HB*, 127), the reader hears already in the first chapter. Later, Giglio cuts 'wilder and wilder capers' (*HB*, 172) with his partner Cornelio Chiapperi. Only through the reaction of the audience does he recognise that the *pas de deux* was in fact a solo danced by himself, and the doubling induced, in the subtly mocking words of the narrator, by 'a kind of spiritual drunkenness' (*HB*, 171). The leaps themselves turn into some diabolic force; Giacinta

55 Jean Starobinski outlines a threefold nature of the protagonist: 'the true Giglio, a princely nature, and the most comical of the Caiptan Pantaloones'; p. 442.

56 Michel Foucault, *L'ordre du discours* (Paris: Gallimard, 1971), pp. 12–14.

teases Giglio for his unfaithfulness with a pinprick 'so that he jumped up in pain and felt compelled to cut several capers amid cries of "Damnation!"' (*HB*, 181).

The leaping dance does not only hint at the more compulsive aspects of Giglio's performances, it also becomes a metaphor for a narrative technique through which the text performs what it describes. The content of *Prinzessin Brambilla* is full of anachronisms which interrupt the linearity of the narrative chronology. Time warps abound, for instance the declaration of the Prince Bastianello that he is four hundred years old, or the assumption that situates the Abbate Chiari as an 'ancestor' of the tragedian Pietro Chiari, a contemporary of Gozzi, who, in turn, is only mentioned retrospectively. Frequent jumps from one strand of the narrative to another, abrupt breaks in the plot, or the leaping between the plot and the commentary of the narrator disrupt the coherence of the text. A 'demonic spell that is getting everything mixed up and confused' (*HB*, 209), renders clear interpretation difficult. In the *capriccio*'s play on the German homonymy of *Schwindel*, which means both vertigo and deceit, the diabolic virtuosity in treating language is perhaps most obvious. As in the maddening fiery circle of *Der Sandmann*, distinct characters are obscured in the vertiginous whirl of accelerating circles, debunking any once established identification as a deception shortly afterwards. The spheres of theatre or carnival are not as clear-cut as they appear to be. Pistoja will not reveal whether he is operating with stage effects or with magic powers; the limits between joke and seriousness are inconceivable. The theatrical sphere is neither confined to the stage of the Argentina, nor to the Corso, and any containment of the fantastic is a provisional one. This undecidability and the intricate narrative structure distinguish *Prinzessin Brambilla* as, in the much-quoted words of Heinrich Heine: 'a delicious beauty, and if her whimsicality does not make your head spin, you have none at all'.[57] A text about dizziness causes dizziness; it can only be approached by participating in the whirl of literary flexibility and poetic metamorphosis.

Reinhold, thus following the logic of inversion at work throughout the text, leaves his place in the audience and takes part in the mask-play himself. The blurring of the boundaries between spectators and performers, so important to Hoffmann, is not only one of the main characteristics of the carnival,[58] and of the highly interactive *commedia dell'arte*, it is also an intriguing principle repeated and varied constantly, and most vividly illustrated in the doubling of Giglio, who keeps on meeting, dancing and fighting with various representatives of his own self on the Corso. The shimmering ornament of the myth of Urdar, embroidered into the narrative like one of master Bescapi's fantastic costume designs, is part of another doubling. Representing an allegory of the whole plot, it is an excursion that leads directly 'to the heart of the main story' (*HB*, 159).

---

57 Heinrich Heine, *Historisch-Kritische Gesamtausgabe der Werke*, ed. by Manfred Windfuhr et al., 16 vols (Hamburg: Hoffmann und Campe, 1973–97), VI, 52.

58 See Mikhail Bakhtin, *Rabelais and His World* (Bloomington: Indiana University Press, 1984), p. 7: 'carnival does not know footlights, in the sense that it does not acknowledge any distinction between actors and spectators'.

Giglio gets a first glance at the bizarre Land of Urdar when he is watching the extravagant carnival procession to Pistoja's palace; he rediscovers it in the *commedia dell'arte* performance in the Argentina theatre. Celionati recounts the first part of the myth in front of the artists in the Caffè Greco, and Giglio listens to the sequel during his visit to the palace. In their roles as Brambilla and Chiapperi, Giacinta and Giglio fulfil the plot of the myth themselves; as we realise at the end, it provides the stage for a particularly cheerful improvisation of the two *commedia* actors. The grand finale thus celebrates the Land of Urdar as the world of theatre – and of theatrical identities. It is a *paradis artificiel* that acknowledges the imaginary performances of the self as integral part of a person's identity, and of a couple's economy of desire.

Both reason and forms of experience that allow for a more imaginative approach to the world are literally enacted in the main dance scene, the *tarantella* of the two protagonists. It offers nothing less than a physical rendering of the two concepts 'thought' and 'intuition' whose union is celebrated in the myth: 'Thought destroyed intuition, but from the prism of the crystal, formed by the fiery flood in its nuptial conflict with the malevolent poison, intuition will radiate forth new-born, itself the foetus of thought!' (*HB*, 163). The notions are part of Hoffmann's dynamic network of Romantic terminology, completed by imagination, humour and irony. The danced interaction between the woman and the man, between the tambourine and the sword, brings together immediacy and reflection, words and moves, choreography and the abandonment of any pattern in the fiery whirl of rapturous spinning (Figure 3.3). The *tarantella* has the same aerial quality as the myth told by the aerial spirit Celionati; the floating, leaping dancers, turning around each other yet permanently evading the other's grasp hardly touch the floor any more:

> She: Spin, spin harder, whirl unceasingly, mad, merry dance! Ha, how quickly everything flies past! No rest, never a pause! All manner of colorful shapes blaze up like sparks scattered by fireworks and vanish into the black night. [...] It's impossible to keep one's reason rational while dancing; so let's give it up entirely as long as our figures and *pas* go on. And so I shan't answer any of your questions, you smart, nimble fellow! See how I circle round you and slip away from you, just when you think you're about to catch me and hold me tight! [...]

> He: [...] the moment I seized you, you'd no longer be there, you'd vanish into nothingness.[59]

Hoffmann's accent on the dialectic of catching and escaping corresponds to Carlo Blasis' description of the *tarantella* in his *Notes upon Dancing*: 'The two dancers now unite, then separate, return, fly into each other's arms, again bound away, and by means of a great variety of gesticulations, they exhibit alternatingly love, hatred, indifference, disdain, coquetry and inconstancy'.[60] In the dynamic of the multiplied

---

59 *HB*, 204–5; in German: ,da *schwebst* du auf in die Lüfte'; *SW* III, 871, my emphasis.
60 Carlo Blasis, *Notes upon Dancing* (London: Delaporte, 1847), pp. 34–5.

shapes Hoffmann's dancers take on in their dance, single identities literally slip away, after having been challenged through the course of the events.

The aerial dance, however, also pays a late, subtly mocking tribute to what Friedrich Schlegel had described as Romantic writing. We read in his Athenaeum Fragment 116:

> Romantic poetry [...] can [...] hover at the midpoint between the portrayed and the portrayer, free of all real and ideal self-interest, on the wings of poetic reflection, and can raise that reflection again and again to a higher power, can multiply it in endless succession of mirrors.[61]

It is a form of writing which is neither restricted to concrete referentiality, nor are there any predetermined transcendental signifieds which it simply mediates. The binary relation between word and thought is overcome in favour of a language that is deemed a primary, productive force that always refers back to itself.[62] When Schlegel described such a notion of language as ever multiplied reflection, he hinted at early Romanticism's concept of poetic irony. Always concerned with reaching an absolute sphere above the finite utterances, the writers knew none the less that this sphere was not to be grasped.[63] Fully aware that the linguistic worldview is artificial, and statements once set down are in fact shifting, they ironically refer back to the act of producing them. The result is a poetic discourse that plays with inversions and ambiguities, states one thing only to question it immediately afterwards, and always means more than it explicitly says.[64]

Irony in the way it is used in the philosophy of early Romanticism is concerned with relativity and instability as all-encompassing principles. In language, they manifest themselves in constant ambivalence, mirrored in one of early Romanticism's master tropes, the notion of *Schweben* (to hover). The sense of floatation that characterises Schlegel's programme of Romantic poetry also indicates the post-Kantian state of subjectivity that starts reflecting itself while inquiring into the limits of reason

> The unconditioned necessity, which we need so indispensably as the ultimate sustainer of all things, is for human reason the true abyss. [...] One cannot resist the thought of it, but one also cannot bear it that a being that we represent to ourselves as the highest among all possible beings might, as it were, say to itself: 'I am from eternity to eternity, outside me is nothing except what is something merely through my will; *but whence* then am I?' Here everything gives way beneath us, and the greatest perfection as well as the smallest,

---

61 Friedrich Schlegel, *Philosophical Fragments*, transl. by Peter Firchow (Minneapolis: University of Minnesota Press, 1991), p. 32.

62 See Winfried Menninghaus, 'Die frühromantische Theorie von Zeichen und Metapher', *The German Quarterly*, 62/1 (1989), 48–58.

63 See Peter V. Zima, 'Friedrich Schlegels Romantik: Eine Dekonstruktion avant la lettre?', in Zima, *Die Dekonstruktion* (Tübingen: Francke, 1994), pp. 10–15.

64 See Manfred Frank, *Einführung in die frühromantische Ästhetik* (Frankfurt a.M.: Suhrkamp 1989), especially pp. 306, 311, 341 and 361.

hovers without support before speculative reason, for which it would cost nothing to let the one as much as the other disappear without the least obstacle.[65]

Hoffmann's specific use of irony in *Prinzessin Brambilla* is an authorial distancing gesture that consists in the narrative and physical (mock-)performance of post-Kantian positions. He weaves concepts like the unattainable realm of absolute truth into speeches of which Andrew Webber has shown how they performatively contradict themselves – with the excuse that they are spoken and, as it were, improvised dialogues: 'We had better,' replied the impresario with a smile, 'we had better not enquire too closely!'; 'You need,' replied the Ciarlatano politely, indeed almost deferentially, 'you need have no doubt, sir, that your pleasing features do indeed resemble those of that actor' (my translation; see also *HB*, 144, 220).[66] Like faltering poses that develop into dynamic movement sequences, the phrases start with small units, turn them in their performance from positive into negative, and are then built up: a stylised orality epitomising Hoffmann's playful use of language.

Hoffmann's cheeky take on early-Romanticist loftiness never lacks concreteness. The highly theatrical quality of constant reflection is enjoyed to the full when Giglio meets himself on the Corso. The dynamisation of the process of signification is staged as a dance. Scholarship has interpreted the main dance scene of the *capriccio* as an incorporation of the endless dance of self-reflexive signifiers, as the apotheosis of a self-referential, unstoppable movement.[67] It makes sense to read the dancer's slipping-away into the air, or into nothingness, as an allegory of the gliding signification in Hoffmann's texts. Dance subverts the process of signification in an excess of meaning, in *Brambilla* perhaps most notably in the play with the German homonymy of vertigo and deceit in the notion of *Schwindel*. The rapturous whirl designates the loss of control through perpetually mixed-up positions of truth and deceit. It proclaims this a state unsettling and delightful at once, both for the protagonists, and for the virtuoso ecstasy of the writing, which contains the vertiginous loss of control in the cunningly composed use of the double-edged *Schwindel*. In Schlegel's words, only 'the harmonious bores are at a loss about how they should react to this continuous self-parody, when they fluctuate endlessly between belief and disbelief until they get dizzy and take what is meant as a joke seriously and what is meant seriously as a joke'.[68]

Hoffmann seems to allude to such statements when even Giglio, far from being a bore, says 'so the most serious matters often strike me as exceedingly comical, and the most comical matters, conversely, as exceedingly serious. This [...] makes me so giddy' (*HB*, 225). However, *Prinzessin Brambilla* brings early Romanticism

---

65 Immanuel Kant, *Critique of Pure Reason*, ed. and transl. by Paul Guyer and Allen W. Wood (Cambridge: Cambridge University Press, 1998), B 641, p. 574. See also Walter Schulz, *Metaphysik des Schwebens: Untersuchungen zur Geschichte der Ästhetik* (Pfullingen: Neske, 1985), p. 311.

66 See Webber, *The Doppelgänger*, p. 178.

67 See Liebrand, pp. 276–7, and Kremer, *E.T.A. Hoffmann*, pp. 137–8.

68 Schlegel, *Philosophical Fragments*, p. 13.

down to earth: despite some metaphorical vertigo, its protagonists mainly and very concretely get dizzy from Italian wine, and from spinning around. The self-reflexive quality of their main dance scene is based on the dialogue between dance and text, on the curious combination of movement and accompanying speech. Paradoxically, the dance and the dancers enact precisely that which is denied from the start of the scene: transforming them into speech, they gloss their movements and actions, a dilemma which is at the basis of any attempt to capture dance with language. Dance which is tracked in language stops being dance. The text cunningly admits the impossibility of its undertaking in a sequence of dashes and nonetheless proceeds with it: '– – So ran, word for word, the extraordinary dance.'[69]

If language thus approaches dance, it has to assimilate its qualities. The described dance becomes a metaphor of its representation; writing strategies and thematic concerns are closely intertwined. The ever changing poses of the dancers correspond to the articulation of a perpetual chase for fulfilment that never reaches lasting satisfaction, in the words of Brambilla 'delight pursues delight and cannot catch it, and that is the very essence of delight' (*HB*, 204). This process is traced in the dynamic of figurative language. It engenders a flood of ephemeral images, which are, like the sparks of a firework, in constant metamorphosis. The female dancer calls herself a flower and a buzzing gold beetle until she finally completely melts into her clinking tambourine that replaces her voice with its own sounds, drowning out her partner's reason. The ever failing attempts of the male dancer to interpret his counterpart are embodied in his inability to grasp her shifting shapes. Each concept applied ('melancholy', 'desire', 'delight', 'rapture') is immediately succeeded by the next one in the constant turns of the dance. Giglio's attempt to maintain his reason is epitomised in his effort to preserve his position on tip-toe. He constantly tries to keep his mental balance, which manifests itself as a physical act: 'But it all depends on knowing how to observe and maintain the correct equilibrium when dancing'. Yet he cannot escape the con*fusion* of the danced harmony – with his partner, and between word and movement – which turns representation into performance, and replaces the will to understand the dance with the ability for dancing. The dance-speech is a sequence of exclamations, which are, as it were, the spoken display of skills, jumps and questions which transcribe the bodily approaches to the other. Countless dashes insert breathing into the text. At the same time, they stand for the dilemma that the passage enacts, for the speaking of the unspeakability of physical dance. Their multiplication towards the final vertigo represents the increasing performativity where words fade out in three successive dashes.

Giglio is not only involved in the vertigo of his partner's whirling dance, but also in the deceit of dissimulation surrounding her true identity. Alluding to the crystallization of 'thought' and 'intuition', which will bring about the healing well in the myth of Urdar, the mainly circular movement of the tambourine player blends with the straight poses and balances of the swordsman. They culminate in

---

69 *HB*, 206; note that the dashes have not been included in the English translation that is used here; for the German original, see *SW* III, 872.

Figure 3.3   *Fracischina and Gian Farina* – Giglio dances with the unknown beauty, nineteenth-century copper engraving by Carl Friedrich Thiele after an etching of the series *Balli di Sfessania* by Jacques Callot (*c.* 1622).

a perfect, orgasmic coordination of daring leaps and a final whirl. The spinning of the dancers, not destined to lead them anywhere, establishes a counter-realm to the economical activities of reality. It embodies the cyclical character of the aesthetic event that establishes, and refers back to, its own rules.[70] Theatre thus becomes a positive complement to the pathological condition depicted in *Der Sandmann*. The mythological tale about the power of theatre to mirror the world, and itself, is condensed in the word-for-word account of the dancing body. Hoffmann cunningly alleviates the instability of *Schweben*, the confusion of *Schwindel*, by turning them into physical enactments that are mastered by virtuoso dancers. They not only lose, but also gain their identity in the dance, as the subtitle to the chapter has it: 'How someone became a Prince while dancing' (*HB*, 204).

As mentioned before, Bastianello di Pistoja explains the notion of humour as the art of comic incorporation lifted by the wings of fantasy: 'you are imagination whose wings need humour if they are to soar aloft, but without the body of humour you would be nothing but a pair of wings and would drift away through the air, a plaything of the winds' (*HB*, 236). Humour, in the myth, is the well feeding into the Lake of Urdar in whose mirroring surface the performers truly recognise themselves, that is, recognise their mutual delight in role-play. This insight turns inevitably into cheerful laughter, a laughter that is in and of the body, that extends into dance, and that is not least the genuine element of the *commedia dell'arte*. The recognition of the lovers thus turns into the adoration of a theatre-goddess, the Princess Mystilis. She is born out of the well and bears a magician, Ruffiamonte, and a theatre director, the Prince Pistoja, alias Ciarlatano Celionati, in her crown.

Giacinta's and Giglio's back entrance to this Hoffmannesque paradise of the Land of Urdar is the stage door of the Argentina theatre, and the carnivalistic space of the Corso. It is a Garden of Eden that includes the pleasures of theatrical falls: precisely those pleasures that Nathanael ultimately lacks. Fulfilling a deathly trauma, he falls off stage into the world of physical laws where a fall from great heights is lethal. Giglio's puppet-like ability to withstand every threat to his life, in turn, recalls Kleist's marionette. Although the hyper-agility of his consciousness designates Giglio as someone who has definitely 'fallen from grace', his dancerly body control makes up for the lost innocence of anti-gravity. The traumatic impact that resounds in the figure of the fall is caught in the nets of theatricality. Each of the danced encounters, performed in front of the street audience, ends with a fall, none of them, however, serious: after his absurd solo dance, Giglio tumbles over, 'landing very ungently on his back' (*HB*, 172), only to pull himself up immediately; he sinks, succumbing to the giddiness caused by the spinning dance with Brambilla, into the arms of Celionati who miraculously happens to be right behind his back, or throws himself recklessly out of the window of the palace and runs away, 'not having suffered the slightest injury' (*HB*, 202). As we will see, even the lethal fall of Giglio's self as tragic actor is turned into the resurrection of his other self, the comedian. There is no doubt that such a skilled performer as Giglio is well versed in

---

70 See Kremer, *E.T.A. Hoffmann*, p. 141.

acrobatics, whether of the mind or of the body; in the virtuoso dance with Brambilla, he knows the underlying techniques to keep the wild *tarantella* going.

In another Kleistian reminiscence, Giglio does not displace his soul into his elbow, but his self into his left foot while dancing with his princess: 'What do you think of this caper, of this attitude, in which I entrust my entire self to the centre of gravity formed by the tiptoes of my left foot?' (*HB*, 204). Yet the attempt to analyse his and his partner's dancing, to keep the bodies in a moderate balance with his sword, the 'balancing-rod' of his mind, is a somewhat ridiculous undertaking. The actor's rational explanations are consumed in the fireworks of the whirling movement; language is drawn into the breathless rotation of mere performativity. However, the performer does not lose consciousness. He clings on to the wooden sword, to the attribute that designates the theatricality of his guise. It represents the fact that the ecstatic state is after all not an immediate, but a performed one. The ebullient dance thus moves on to the dialogue between Giglio and Celionati, who reveals that the supposed princess is an ordinary seamstress. Now there is another dance which the young man has to go through before the lady of his imagination and that of his reality melt into one.

Brambilla's and Giglio's aerial dance is a constant withdrawal of meaning, a refusal of fixed, 'standing' identities. The theatre-fight with the double, in turn, is meant to sort out the long-lasting identity trouble in favour of Giglio's comic self, represented by the mask of the Captain Pantaloon. For a last time, Giglio emerges as a tragic hero on the Corso, in his 'ballroom costume *à la* King Arthur' (*HB*, 210), to face the encounter with the wild comedian (Figure 3.4). It is the antagonistic dance of a Whitean 'divided body' whose choreography consists in grounded movement: 'Their left feet were planted solidly on the ground, while their right feet alternately advanced resolutely to the attack, or withdrew to a defensive position' (*HB*, 211). Rather than seeking to evade the other's grasp constantly, the fighters, caught in the ambiguity of aggression and desire, alternately hit and hold each other. The homoerotic overtones of the encounter, echoing something of the more explicit scenes of Callot's etchings, which Hoffmann did not include in the *Brambilla* series, are defused by the narcissistic aspect of the activity: each opponent is after all about to kill himself. They are not enthralled by the rapture of movement; they hesitate, and interrupt their steps repeatedly: 'After a hot and perilous passage of arms the combatants were obliged to rest. They looked at each other, and along with the rage of the battle they felt such mutual love that they fell into each other's arms and shed copious tears' (HB, 211). Their thrusts are well calculated and they address each other with elaborate phrases of thoroughly composed theatre speeches.

Hoffmann stages subjectivity as love-hate relationship, as encounter and fight with one's self where recognition always also implies misrecognition. This is mirrored by the typically strategic use of eyeglasses, at once enhancing and distorting sight.[71] In the fight–dance with his double, Giglio unavoidably wears his 'large pair

---

71 Here, Gerhard Neumann talks of the paradox of perception as one of the defining constituents of Romantic subjectivity, for which he finds the formula of 'masking eye glasses'

of spectacles' (*HB*, 210). A scene of a danced fight in *Meister Floh* (Master Flea), which is in some respects parallel to the encounter in *Brambilla*, pushes the grotesque scope of the setting even further. Here, the antagonists are armed with telescopes:

> Swammerdam drew a small telescope from his pocket, extended it to its full length, and assailed his enemy with a loud cry of: 'Draw, you scoundrel, if you have the courage!' Leuwenhoek promptly had a similar instrument in his hand, likewise extended it, and shouted: 'Come on, I'll fight you, and you'll soon feel my power!' The two put the telescope to their eyes and fell upon each other furiously with sharp and murderous strokes, lengthening and shortening their weapons by pulling the extensions in and out. [...] If one of them was hit, he screamed, leapt into the air, and performed the most wonderful caprioles, and the most beautiful *entrechats* and pirouettes, like the best solo dancer in the Paris ballet, until the other focused the shortened telescope on him. [...] their bloodshot eyes were protruding from their heads, and since no cause for their St Vitus dance was visible, save that they looked through the telescopes in turn, one was obliged to conclude that they were lunatics escaped from the madhouse.[72]

Hoffmann disrobes optical instruments of their proper function: devices for observation and rational control are turned into weapons engaged in the antagonistic, libidinous choreographies of madness. The power of the gaze to fixate is shown as disabling rather than enlightening. In *Der Sandmann*, it is the cruel eye contact between master and slave that brings a deathly fixation to its unavoidable fulfilment. Giglio's last dance with his double, in turn, leads into the fixture of his new identity as the *commedia* character Pantalone. In *Brambilla*, however, the dangers of fixture are resolved in perpetual mobility; a fixed identity is but a temporary state, set in the plot of one night's performance, which is going to be replaced the next night with another one. The St Vitus dance is cured by the ongoing *tarantella*.

All the gravity of the meeting between Giglio and the Pantalone is thus countered with the next capricious leap: although Giglio has been killed in the fight, he reappears shortly afterwards in the Caffè Greco to hear that the Capitan's victim was nothing but a cardboard model of a tragic hero, 'crammed with sheets from the tragedies of a certain Abbate Chiari' (*HB*, 219). The revenant, however, seems to have fully appropriated his princely self now, and is finally prepared to find the princess on the Corso. The fantastic apotheosis where the protagonists not only fuse with their mythical doubles Ophioch and Liris, but also recognise their identities as actor and actress, follows immediately. The dignified mass choreography, accompanied by 'the harmonious sounds of bells, harps, and trumpets' (*HB*, 232), recalls the grand finale of a Romantic opera and is symbolically charged with the imagery of the mythical tale.[73] The abrupt jump towards the domestic scene, set one year after the beginning of the events in the house of Giglio and Giacinta coming home from

---

('Brille als Maske'); see Neumann, *'Prinzessin Brambilla' als Wahrnehmungsexperiment*.

72 E.T.A. Hoffmann, *Master Flea*, in *The Golden Pot and Other Tales*, pp. 239–375 (p. 307).

73 Hoffmann's taste for a metaphysical apotheosis is obvious here; the final scenic arrangement of the Urdar myth recalls the apotheosis of *Undine*, see *SW* II/2, 517–18. The

their show, reveals the magical world as an annual performance on the occasion of the carnival season. Yet this explanation – too simple a solution to be faithful to the intricacies of the *capriccio* – gains a more existential dimension. Giacinta's and Giglio's new empire is as much the theatre and the *commedia dell'arte* as the land of imagination whose frontiers reach from the stage of the theatre up to a fictional Persia and India: 'It seems like a beautiful dream, the Land of Urdar – the Lake of Urdar! But no, it wasn't a dream' (*HB*, 235). The text maintains the constant tension of questioning, redoubling and reflection of its own assertions until the end. What is more, it formulates a performative aesthetics of existence where actual, imaginary and theatrical identities are of equal value, not least for a couple's mutual knowledge and understanding of each other's wishes and fantasies.

This performative aesthetics of existence declares identity to be something that does not exist beyond its various roles. It has to be enacted, danced, and incorporated in countless costumes. The attempt to grasp a face behind the mask is a movement that spirals endlessly and peters out without ever reaching its target. The dance scenes represent this mobilisation of identities in a condensed way. The bodily encounters are the corporeal and the verbal expression of a process of continuous self-creation and self-destruction. This programme is already set out in Giglio's first solo dance that started as an encounter with the armed prince. Deliberately calculated steps outline the dancing body, ecstatic jumps and turns exceed it; the self is danced into life, and it is danced to death: 'I can't understand my self, and my accursed self is attacking me with a dangerous weapon, but I'll play and dance it to death, and then I shall be my self and the Princess will be mine!' (*HB*, 172).

Hoffmann's play with the self in performance, however, possesses a deeply disturbing side. There is no real identity facing its false double, but only the paradoxical and potentially disturbing simultaneity of multiple selves, coming into being with the costumes they put on: the masquerade does not conceal an essence, but produces identities that are as essential as they are fake. There is no offstage reality to neutralise the grimaces. Behind the wings of the textual theatre are the uncanny parts of the performance. The light-footed ballet on stage masks the terrorising force of Giglio's 'chronic dualism'. This constant doubling of the self, introduced in the text through the ironical reference to a work of popular science, 'Mauchardt's *Handbook of Empirical Psychology*', indicates a more radical diagnosis in Hoffmann: a crisis of post-Kantian subjectivity around 1800 that takes shape in the literary staging of the split self. It will find its psychological formula one century later, in Freud's insistence on the forces of the unconscious that challenge the intellectual security of the self-knowing and self-mastering subject. The actor goes insane because his self is as unstable as the costumes it wears; a unique passage articulates this affliction to powerful effect. Perceiving one of his eccentric costumes lying on the floor of his room, Giglio cries:

---

goddess of the well, Mystilis, fits perfectly into Romantic ballet and opera's predilection for elementary spirits, elves or nixies.

Figure 3.4 *Taglia Cantoni and Fracasso* – Giglio fights with his double. nineteenth-century copper engraving by Carl Friedrich Thiele after an etching of the series *Balli di Sfessania* by Jacques Callot (*c.* 1622).

Yes, the spirit of madness lying there in bodily form is my self, and these princely garments were stolen by the dark demon from the feather-brain and forced upon me, so that the beautiful ladies should be deceived into mistaking me for the feather-brain! I know I'm talking nonsense; but that's all right, for I really have gone crazy, because the self has no body – ho, ho! Off we go, off we go, my dear sweet self! (*HB*, 202)

Giglio's inversed perception threatens the limits between the inner and the outer world and turns the way he experiences things upside down. This terrifies him so much that he can hardly stay on his feet (*HB*, 225). Mistaking his mirror image for his double, he almost collapses with terror, a bodily collapse that corresponds to the breakdown of the self. According to master Celionati, the main thing necessary for his cure is the 'frequent and vigorous exercise' of the actor and dancer (ibid.). The acrobatics of the *commedia* testify to a technology of the self that provides an artificial choreography as mainstay for the lost natural control over the body, and the mind. In the vertigo of the ecstatic dance, transcribed as the dissolution of language into the rhythmic beats of single words, this collapse is touched upon, yet caught in the arms of the director who initiated the scene. Hoffmann's 1819 note on camels who dance 'naturally' to avoid the painful contact with a burning floor is resonant with the profound ambiguity beneath the theatrical fantasy:

The wonderful leaps and caprioles of today's dancers very much call to mind the clever manner in which the Arabs teach their camels to dance. These camels are led around on a tin floor under which a fire has been lit. As the tin becomes hotter and hotter, the animals raise their dainty hooves higher and higher – and still higher and even more confusedly as the heat rises, until it appears as though they are floating in the air on all fours. – It is an extremely charming sight and, at the view of pure nature in the fullness of her grace and strength, many a European ballet master could be spurred on to invent totally new and strange steps. (*SW* III, 653–4; *CW*)

Resounding with the danced fight of *Meister Floh*, the classicist idealisation of the naturalness of dancerly grace is again challenged throughout in this sarcastic turning of the topic. It hints at profound fears that may motivate the dancerly preoccupation of Hoffmann's protagonists: the refuge in the theatrical suppresses an unsettling if not agonal insecurity with regard to notions of identity which otherwise would not be bearable. *Prinzessin Brambilla* cures the anxiety by equipping its protagonists with acting and dancing skills that provide their hyper-agile minds and bodies with aesthetic structures. Yet their delight in role-play is but the reverse of a pathological surrender to a schizophrenic sense of self. *Prinzessin Brambilla* resolutely abstains from establishing a reliable narrative self-commentary here. It stages a perpetual interaction between an allegorical potential, the underlying idea and the diversionary tactics of a diabolic dynamic which challenges attempts at unequivocal interpretation. The dancing Giglio becomes a mirror of the reader who tries to get hold of the text. The questioning of his dancing partner is answered teasingly by 'always the same *pas*, the same figures!' What endures is the everlasting spiral of desire for ultimate presence and identity that never comes to the close of thorough satisfaction: 'nothing

is eternal but your dance, and that is indeed the most wonderful thing about you ...'
(*HB*, 205).

Two main floor patterns can be distinguished in the choreography of Giglio's
selves. The topography that is outlined by the narrator follows circular forms, and
angular structures of labyrinths with their frequently changing directions. The oval
shape of the strange islands on which Callot's figures demonstrate their antics
reappears in the 'oval stage' (*HB*, 232) of the Argentina theatre. The plot is set in
the small, easily paced out area between the Corso, the theatre, Pistoja's palace and
the Caffè Greco. Notwithstanding this clear layout of the scenery, Giglio repeatedly
wanders through Rome for hours. He gets lost in the streets of his town; he neither
knows the way to Bescapi's house nor to Pistoja's palace. Even more than on his
walks, the protagonist loses himself 'in a labyrinth of confused and extravagant
talk' (*HB*, 140), the same confusion that the reader undergoes in the labyrinthine
discourse of the *capriccio*. The maze-like structure traditionally symbolises the
process of individuation, the initiation to one's own self. As a choreographic pattern
it emphasises disorientation, interruption and the need for new orientation, and thus
represents the self-reflection of movement.[74]

Giglio's falls, his deaths and resurrections, his perpetual articulations of what he
is doing that accompany his actions and moves, represent the erratic performative
path he follows in search of his identity. It is mirrored in the labyrinthine aspect of
the entire text. Yet even the decorative 'foliation' (*HB*, 231) of the myth, bearing
some allegorical signposts leading through the events, cannot obscure the fact
that the heart of the labyrinth only opens up the way towards the next maze. The
teleological movement is encompassed in an overall circular structure characteristic
of Hoffmann's text. However, in the positive counter-image to the fiery circle,
the sparkling fireworks, the circle becomes, recalling the fervent imagination
of Hoffmann's adored composers, a spiral of ever renewed creative energy:
'Magnificent fireworks, you can never go out' (*HB*, 205). The maddening fiery circle
of *Der Sandmann* endangers the notion of identity without a possibility of rescue;
the productive force of the fireworks enables Giglio to find healing in his performing
of different personae. The stage where this creative energy is celebrated lies as much
in the mythical space of Pistoja's palace as on the Corso, where the eternal dance is
performed, but ultimately it can be found in the unlimited inward space free from
any encirclement: 'What a magnificent world lies locked up in our bosoms! No
horizon sets bounds to it', to the 'inexhaustible diamond-mine within ourselves,
from which, in glorious radiance, shines forth the wondrous realm that is our very
own possession!' (*HB*, 170). Artistic creativity is represented in the reflecting surface
of the 'wondrous sunlit mirror of the Lake of Urdar' (*HB*, 238), the fireworks of
the whirling dancers, and the inward jewels out of which one might 'coax a more
splendid fire' (*HB*, 170). The ever-repeated circle of coercive mechanical repetition
represented by pathological automatisms, by classical ballet's sterile forms, and by

---

74 See Brandstetter, *Tanz-Lektüren*, pp. 319–24.

the calculated gestures of tragic acting, is transformed into the spiral of constant renewal animated by the spark of artistic creativity.

In *Prinzessin Brambilla*, Hoffmann replaces fatally compulsive mechanics with writing and dancing techniques which provide the self with a stabilising choreography. Hoffmann's vision of a 'more elevated art of dance' is realised in the virtuoso dance and play of the masks, and in the masterfully executed choreography of the text that stages them. The author creates modes of acting and dancing that celebrate improvisation within a finely composed dialogic structure: dancing the self, in Hoffmann, always implies the encounter with the other, whether inside or outside the subject. In a paradoxical move, these dialogic dances engender stability through motion, a form of stability that the paralysed Nathanael lacks. Yet also in *Prinzessin Brambilla*, light-footed mobility maintains the disconcerting subtext of the protagonist's mental confusion. The text transforms the mental dynamic of self-reflection and disconcertingly gliding signification into dances which, on the one hand, perform the unsettling schizophrenic state of the protagonist, and, on the other hand, provide a choreographic frame that celebrates the constant mobility of lost and renewed identity. The painful fiery circle finds its complement in the perpetual metamorphosis of the pyrotechnical fireworks, echoed in the creative spiral of the writing. The vertiginous whirl of deceitful masks upholds a spiralling rhythm that keeps the protagonists dancing.

As Hoffmann's dancers are thus always engaged in dialogic, if not antagonistic, constellations in the attempt to grasp, hold or lead their hovering counterparts, the narrator himself gets drawn into a conflictual dance when he tries to catch the whirling movement with words. Hoffmann's texts, however, demonstrate what they describe in a writing that assimilates dancerly qualities; this performativity attests to the successful interaction between text and dance, echoed in the interaction of speech and movement in the performances of Giglio and Giacinta. And yet Hoffmann's relation to dance is not free from ambiguities and might elucidate deeper creative concerns. The haunting images of dysfunctional eyes are recalled in his description of how he 'watches' dance performances in the aforementioned passage: he closes his eyes to avoid the ephemeral artefacts which repeat themselves eternally. If this avoidance is not merely caused by the poor quality of the dancing, could it mean that dance becomes a metaphor for something that troubles Hoffmann's notion of creativity? An aesthetic that prefers the act of writing to the finished work, the performance to the text, and thus mobility to fixture, is perpetually confronted with the ephemerality of its endeavours. Rather than aiming to leave durable documents, it is more likely that Hoffmann wrote his compositions and texts in order to actualise the fleeting aesthetic moment over and over again, enjoying the bliss of his writerly performance. As the analysis of *Der Sandmann* suggested, Hoffmann's own writings and their variation of similar motifs might not be free themselves from the addiction to some artistic repetition compulsion. However, they also recall the fireworks of *Prinzessin Brambilla*'s *pas de deux*, engendering a sparkling dance of repetitions-in-difference.

Chapter 4

Heinrich Heine and the
New Language of the Body

There is really nothing so repulsive to me as the ballet in the great opera in Paris. (Heinrich Heine, *Florentinische Nächte*)

In the second letter from Heine's 1822 *Briefe aus Berlin* (Letters from Berlin), we find the following passage:

A ball always has something most delightful about it in my eyes. When the drums thunder and the trumpets blare and the sweet voices of flute and violin sound invitingly in between: then I throw myself, like a wild swimmer, into the roaring, colourfully lit sea of people and dance and run and joke and tease everybody and laugh and talk about whatever comes into my head. At the last ball I was particularly joyful, I could have walked upside down, a Bacchanalian spirit had seized my entire being, and if my mortal enemy had crossed my path, I would have said to him: Tomorrow we may shoot each other, but today I want to cover you in hearty kisses. (*DHA* VI, 37; *CW*)

Resonating with the vertigo of the whirling encounters of *Prinzessin Brambilla*, it is one of the rare instances where Heine speaks of himself as a dancer. Akin to Hoffmann, the sheer dynamic corporeality of movement gains significance as a metaphor for mental mobility. In Heine, it articulates itself most distinctively in transgressions of order, in the acrobatics of writerly handstands that turn contemporary moral and aesthetic positions upside down.

Although the author rarely allows us to get a glimpse of his own delight in dancing, he is indeed a *connoisseur* when it comes to spectatorship. He arrives in Paris shortly before the first triumph of the Romantic ballet, *La Sylphide* (1832), and witnesses in the following years the successes of the celebrated ballerinas Marie Taglioni, Fanny Elssler and Carlotta Grisi, to name only three outstanding ones. The fact that Heine had the chance to experience one of the most sparkling periods in the history of dance, where ballet as we still know it today had reached its first culmination in the dramatic unity of dance technique, pantomime, choreography, libretto, music and staging, obviously resulted in a different, and more differentiated attitude towards bodily movement compared to what we find in Kleist and Hoffmann. However, even though Heine enjoyed dance theatre of the highest standard, he was critical of the ballet at the Paris Opera. In a way similar to his predecessors, he develops his own poetic vision of dance which stands in contrast to the way it was practised on stage.

While Kleist distinguishes himself as a writer with the most thought-provoking German plays of the early nineteenth century, and Hoffmann is a theatrical all-rounder, Heine's dramatic endeavours, *Almansor* (1821) and *William Ratcliff* (1823), do not establish him as a writer for the theatre. His two ballets, *Die Göttin Diana* (The Goddess Diana, 1854) and *Der Doktor Faust* (1851), were never performed. His connection to the stage was that of a knowledgeable enthusiast and critic who excelled at essayistic writing. He is a professional spectator who finds in dance, as in painting and music, a stimulus for his own poetic digressions. However, his rediscovery of the treasures of folklore provided motifs that were taken up in the Romantic ballet, the most outstanding example certainly being the myth of the vengeful Willis staged in *Giselle* (1841).

The importance of dance in Heine's work with regard to both the thematic level and that of poetic discourse has been acknowledged in scholarship.[1] The contrast between the author's bacchantic ideal of movement and classical ballet technique has been drawn repeatedly, without that the expressive complexity of this form of movement would have been explored.[2] Roger Müller-Farguell engages in a thorough investigation of the interface between language and dance in Heine. However, he takes dance exclusively in a figurative sense as a metaphor for writing strategies.[3] The aim of the following chapter is, therefore, not only a close analysis of the writer's choreographic imagination, epitomised in the dance scenes of his novella *Florentinische Nächte* (Florentine Nights, 1836). It also recognises the importance of dance as physical event and performance for Heine's work. The author approaches physical movement as a semiotic process which is inextricably, and even more emphatically than in Kleist and Hoffmann, linked to its somatic conditions. Above all, Heine engages his protagonist in an explicit discourse on the difficulty of verbalising bodily movement. Attention will be given to the ways in which dance is explored despite the lack of a clear conceptual framework, assembling hints that build up toward Heine's remarkable insights into psychosomatic expression, insights which proper aesthetic approaches of his time lacked.

In the following, the explorations of Idealist aesthetics, of the Romantic ballet of Heine's cultural theory, and of his idea of the moving body are interlinked by countless cross-references. Their main tie, however, is the reading of *Florentinische Nächte*. It is the thread that runs through the whole chapter, giving the opportunity

---

1   See, for instance, Max Niehaus, *Himmel Hölle und Trikot: Heinrich Heine und das Ballett* (Munich: Nymphenburger, 1959), and Benno von Wiese, *Signaturen: Zu Heinrich Heine und seinem Werk* (Berlin: Schmidt, 1976).

2   See Bettina Knauer, 'Heinrich Heines *Florentinische Nächte*: Form und Funktion novellistischen Erzählens und esoterischer Allegorik', in *Aufklärung und Skepsis: Internationaler Heine-Kongreß 1997 zum 200. Geburtstag*, ed. by Joseph A. Kruse et al. (Stuttgart: Metzler, 1999), pp. 833–45; and Michael Hofmann, 'Veranschaulichung von Ambivalenz in Bildern des Tanzes: Dichotomien der Aufklärung und ihre poetische Bearbeitung bei Heine und Wieland', in *Aufklärung und Skepsis*, pp. 102–17.

3   Müller-Farguell, pp. 177–261.

to refer to a number of Heine's other texts.[4] It brings together crucial subjects of this book: physical and psychic vulnerability versus physical perfection, forms of discipline that range from destabilising compulsive repetition to stabilising recurrent ritual, and the performance of identity, and not least gender, in dance.

Neoclassicism, Ballet and Heine's Cultural Theory of Dance

Florentinische Nächte is a more typical example of Heine's dance writing than the above-quoted passage. While in Hoffmann's *Prinzessin Brambilla* the characters lose and recover their identities in their dancing, here, the protagonist does not participate in the dance, but observes it. He ascertains his identity in his will to possess and to decipher the dancing other, or dance as the other. Yet his acts of carnal and intellectual cognition are challenged by the elusiveness of the dancing woman, and the indecipherability of her movement. Heine's observer hardly gives up his static position. The fragile success of a communication in which one partner dances her contributions is only realised in rare instances of concurrence where two monologues, the emotional experience of the spectator, and the physical expressivity of the dancer meet. However, the dance of *Florentinische Nächte* is not only paradigmatic for the incompatibilities of embodiment and description; it also condenses and reflects upon the difficulty of representing and communicating psychic pain, and the complex displacements engendered by this desire for expression.

Notwithstanding these depths, Heine successfully wrote a popular and amusing novella. He avoided obvious allusions to political or religious issues after a number of his previous publications underwent substantial modifications following the guidelines of the increasingly strict Prussian censorship of the 1830s. Yet *Florentinische Nächte* bears delicacies of its own kind. Trivial and at the same time parodic, daring and psychologically charged, it is not surprising that it still suffered under the infringements of German censorship.[5]

The two parts – in fact, two nights – of *Florentinische Nächte* are structured by the switching back and forth between a frame and an internal narrative. In the frame narrative, Max, the protagonist and narrator, gives his erotic confessions to a bedridden woman, Maria. The couple has a special, yet evidently platonic relationship whose consummation is thwarted by her contagious state and thus replaced by, or indeed displaced into, the diversions of Max's suggestive stories. Maria's liminal

---

4   Heine's two ballets shall only be mentioned in passing; however, the outline of the author's cultural theory that influences his ideas about ballet, and about free and unbound movement, could easily be adapted to an analysis of the libretti. Both ballets are examples of Heine's choreographic imagination that is examined in detail in the analysis of *Florentinische Nächte*.

5   For the censorial practices in France and Germany, see the notes on *Florentinische Nächte* in *DHA* V, 854–83. The changes that were forced upon the text before it was published, for instance in Cotta's *Morgenblatt für Gebildete Stände* (Morning News for the Educated Public), mainly concerned the bedroom scene in the second night.

state on the verge of death sets the pitch of the entire text; the women who are introduced one after the other in the internal narratives, Max's memories of past loves, are, in some way, variations of her. These narratives, encompassing reports of the life in Paris salons, and vividly describing musical encounters with the composer Bellini, and the violinist Paganini, thus build up a digressive declaration of love. They are meant to entertain the patient, and to keep her in a state of passive listening in order to avoid her moving or talking, which would endanger her life even further. Max confesses his exclusive predilection for inanimate, physically inaccessible women: a statue, a Madonna, a dead girl reanimated in the lover's imagination and a visionary incorporation of what he calls 'a soul' in a dream. With more than a hint of Gothic irony, they allude to necrophilia as a hands-on version of the disembodied ideal of Romantic love. Yet these past passions culminated in the encounter with a real woman, the street dancer Laurence. Laurence, however, is equally close to the uncanny regime of death: she re-enacts in her dance her mysterious origin as a 'Death Child', a child from a mother who was buried alive and died immediately after giving birth to her daughter.

The initial spark that triggered Max's libidinal conditioning, however, was a statue. Fallen down from its pedestal in the neglected garden of his mother's deserted childhood home, it became the first object of lust for him as a boy. Eerily immobile, in a state between sleep and death, it prefigured the future fascination with beautiful 'corpses': 'There in the green grass lay the beautiful goddess, as immovable as all around; but her lovely limbs seemed to be fettered, not by petrifying death, but by quiet slumber'.[6] As is well known, the Pygmalionic heritage of the marble statue is an aesthetic-erotic topos in Heine. It at once reproduces, and radically reassesses, the image of the sculpted body in eighteenth-century aesthetics. Both the neoclassicist admiration for Greek sculpture, and Hegel's idealization of it in the nineteenth century, negotiates beauty as something that is born out of control over the sensual. Herder, overlooking the erotic undercurrents in Winckelmann's writing, points out that classical sculpture as it is seen through the Idealist perspective represents a body before, or rather entirely beyond the Fall:

> A statue stands in its *entirety*, under the open sky, in paradise, so to speak. It is a likeness of one of God's beautiful creatures, surrounded by innocence. *Winckelmann* rightly observed that the Spaniard must have been a beast who lusted after the statue of virtue in Rome, which is now modestly covered. The pure and beautiful forms of sculpture may well awaken friendship, love, and daily conversation, but only in a beast can they stimulate desire.[7]

In order to ground the newly established discipline of aesthetics on the subjective category of taste, an exclusively aesthetic form of pleasure had to be identified.

---

6   Heinrich Heine, *Florentine Nights*, in *The Sword and the Flame: Selections from Heinrich Heine's Prose*, ed. by Alfred Werner (New York: Thomas Yoseloff, 1960), pp. 101–51 (p. 104).

7   Herder, 52.

Kant's formulation of disinterestedness as the reaction that distinguishes the truly beautiful is the most concise expression of this endeavour. In his *Vorlesungen über die Ästhetik*, Hegel also aims at avoiding any ambiguity: the physical beauty of the sculpted body is Idea revealed – 'the beautiful is characterized as the pure appearance of the Idea to sense', form imbued with meaning.[8] When Hegel stresses the sensuousness of works of art, he makes clear that it is not meant to address the senses, but the mind; or to put it differently, to reach the mind, the level of the conceptual, through the senses. Sensuousness is the appearance of something higher than itself; in the philosopher's words:

> sensuous shapes and sounds appear in art not merely for the sake of themselves and their immediate shape, but with the aim, in this shape, of affording satisfaction to higher spiritual interests [...]. In this way the sensuous aspect of art is *spiritualized*, since the spirit appears in art as made *sensuous*.[9]

In Heine, the sculpted body has a more open erotic appeal. Although the fallen goddess in *Florentinische Nächte* turns the boy's love for her inevitably into a largely spiritual experience, Max does not approach her disinterestedly. And his response to the work of art is not a theoretical one. It is emotional, sensual and kinetic:

> At last I kissed the beautiful goddess with a passion, a tenderness, and a desperation such as I never felt in my life from any kiss. Nor can I ever forget the grimly sweet emotion which ran through all my soul as the comforting, blessing coldness of those marble lips touched mine [...] (*FN*, 104).

The enactment of the sensual indeed reveals a spiritual dimension; ambiguous as it is, the pleasure induced by the touch of the cold marble lips is of the body, and at the same time of the soul. Yet what is more, Heine addresses sculpture, the epitome of the symbolic body, as material reality that turns the aesthetic experience into a psycho-physical one. He abstains from Idealist attempts to recreate the body as an aesthetic abstraction that dismisses every aspect of bodiliness that could potentially be abject, or traumatic. In the novella, this need to cover the organic becomes a parodic display of half-hearted, failed or excess veiling. In a moment of passion, Max covers Maria with her shawl, in place of doing exactly the opposite. Maria's white muslin dress, in turn, is a cover that reveals. The marble nudity of the sculptures, finally, is an exposure that covers: the smoothly carved skin glosses over every orifice and every wrinkle of the body. In some mocking act of hypercorrection which recalls Hoffmann's strategies, the nudity receives even more protection: 'I remember a Diana whose nether limbs were overgrown with dark ivy in a comical fashion' (*FN*, 103). The neutral realm of aesthetic pleasure becomes the playground of a refined eroticism and its toying with displacements. Deferral, renunciation and imagination are part of the erotic game. Inaccessibility is celebrated not to avoid, but to enhance

---

8   Hegel, I, 111.
9   Ibid., p. 39.

desire; it is not even the non-existent orifice of the mouth, but the closed surface of its corner that provokes the boy's fantasy: 'Tomorrow I will kiss thee, thou beautiful marble face; kiss thee on the lovely corner of the mouth were the lips melt into such a charming dimple!' (*FN*, 104). The erotic practice of disclosing while disguising, and hiding behind the apparently revealed, not only hints at aesthetic censorship, but also at the political censorship that Heine had experienced immediately before writing *Florentinische Nächte*.[10]

Forms of animation are at the heart of Heine's fascination with sculpture: 'by a changing illumination, we can to a certain degree realise motion in forms, and the torches which light them from without appear to inspire real life within'.[11] Departing from the eighteenth-century practice of simulating life through the illumination of statuary, it is Heine's writing which becomes the most powerful torch. His *Die Göttin Diana* is the most explicit example of the enticing relation between sculpture and movement, which has a long-standing tradition in the history of ballet, ranging from Marie Sallé's *Pigmalion* of 1734 to such variations on the theme as *Coppélia*. Heine's ballet opens with the view of a marble Diana, soon replaced by a living dancer who introduces a human suitor to her spheres.[12] The goddess Diana has a predecessor in Signora Francesca, the so-called masterwork of *Die Bäder von Lucca* (The Baths of Lucca), whose divine Greek profile has nothing to do with the virtue, nor with the virtuality of the aesthetic ideal. The narrator's emphasis on the essential role of movement in her beautiful appearance, making it difficult to cast an image of her, resounds with Schiller's discussion of grace as beauty in motion: 'what avails the dead copy of mere outline in forms whose divinest charm consists of living movement' (*BL*, 377).

The animation of the marble body, however, makes stone susceptible to physical and psychic afflictions. We do not know if Laurence, 'this love of a rather doubtful substance' (*FN*, 109) is dubious because of some relation to the deadly coldness of carved stone, to the realm of ghosts, or to that of the *demi-monde* and its venereal dangers. When Max meets her in a Paris salon, the purity of her skin is not entirely preserved: 'A closely observant eye could detect on brow and cheeks faint traces as of small-pox, which exactly resembled the weather-marks which one sees on statues which have been for some time exposed to the rain' (*FN*, 140). As we will see, the dancer is not able to live up to any preconceived notions of unity and wholeness of bodily movement, of narrative, or of identity. The violations of, and breaks in, her

---

10 On the topic of censorship in more detail, see Lucia Ruprecht, 'Heinrich Heine's *Florentinische Nächte*: A Tale of Transgression', in *Field Studies: German Language, Media and Culture*, ed. by Holger Briehl and Carol Fehringer (Oxford: Peter Lang, 2005), pp. 139–56.

11 Heinrich Heine, *The Baths of Lucca*, in *The Sword and the Flame*, pp. 356–424 (p. 377).

12 Heine's vision of ballet challenged contemporary staging practices. The content of the libretto was considered too complex, the choreographic ideas too daring. For more details about the reasons why the ballet was never staged, see *DHA* IX, 629–38.

body and mind echo the cracked and fallen sculptures and the crippled trees in the decrepit paradisal garden of Max's childhood.

In keeping with the diagnostic tendency of nineteenth-century cultural criticism, a figure like Laurence transgresses the personal to represent the illness of a civilization. In Heine, however, pathological is not the return of the repressed in the shape of the ghostly suffering body, but the repressive structure of the Judeo-Christian tradition that expelled this body in the first place. As many of his predecessors, the writer thus seeks refuge in classical antiquity. Yet he does not follow the path prescribed by the aesthetic thinkers, but undermines, moulds and animates the ideal according to his taste. He takes the celebrated superhuman calm of the sculptures as a sign of mortification.[13] Their amputated marble bodies indicate their powerlessness in the modern world, as the desperate author, marked by his own illness that was soon to tie him to his bed, recounts. In 'Nachwort zum *Romanzero*' (Afterword to *Romanzero*, 1851), he writes about his last visit to the Louvre:

> [...] I was almost beside myself when I entered that sublime room where the most blessed goddess of beauty, our dear lady of Milo, stands on her pedestal. I lay at her feet for a long time and I cried with such emotion that a stone would have taken pity on me. The goddess looked down on me sympathetically, and yet with so little comfort as though she were trying to say: Do you not see that I have no arms and therefore can be of no help? (*DHA* III/1, 181; *CW*)

It is not composure and harmony he is looking for in his work, but radical re-animation. The utopian goal may be an enlightened, embodied pantheism which is aware of its own ambivalences.

Time and again, however, we will encounter the traces of suffering entailed by the more realistic dominance of what Heine terms spiritualist values over sensualist ones, of the mind over the body.[14] There is, for instance, the medieval custom of raising a new building only after having sacrificed a child or an animal, and grounding the foundations on their blood to assure its solidity; even more gruesome are the sacrifices enacted by the Christian Institution, epitomised in Heine's reading of the architectural programme of a cathedral in 'Die Romantische Schule' (the Romantic School):

> When we now enter a Gothic cathedral, [...] we realise an elevation of feeling and mortification of the flesh. The interior is a hollow cross, and we wander among the instruments of martyrdom itself; the variegated windows cast on us red and green light, like blood and corruption; funeral songs wail around; under our feet are mortuary tablets and decay, and the soul soars with the colossal columns to a giddy height, tearing itself with pain from the body, which falls like a weary worn-out garment to the ground. But when we behold the exteriors of these cathedrals, these enormous buildings which are worked so aerially, so finely, delicately, transparently, cut as it were into open work, that

---

13 See Dolf Sternberger, *Heinrich Heine und die Abschaffung der Sünde* (Hamburg: Claassen, 1972).

14 For Heine's definition of 'Sensualismus' and 'Spiritualismus', see *DHA* VIII/1, 49.

one might take them for Brabant lace in marble, then we feel truly the power of that age which could master stone itself that it seems spectrally transfused with spiritual life, and thus even the hardest material declares Christian spiritualism.[15]

In its attention to the dialectic of discipline and mutilation, of cultural achievement and its shortcomings, the example resounds with Kleist's image of the graceful cripple. With an acute sense of the satisfying potential of masochistic pleasures, Heine paints the picture of a culture that revels in the 'most thrilling chain' of 'luxury of pain'.[16]

The classical gods have therefore no other chance to show themselves in the age of Christian Romanticism than by assimilating this culture's sweet horror, reflecting the writer's ironical strategy of appropriating a discourse while simultaneously taking up distance from it. In travesties whose parodic appearances are born out of a serious concern, Heine takes his share in Gothic delights. The spirit's murder of the body is rendered palpable when Venus appears as 'corpse-like goddess', the glorious rulers of antiquity turn into 'Faded, night-wandering shadows […] in death-throes, […] sorrow-transfigured', as the poem *Die Götter Griechenlands* (The Gods of Greece) has it. The pathological deformation of classical mythology mirrors the consciousness of modern man more adequately than the neoclassicist exhumations of a censored version of antiquity.[17] Paleness becomes the author's ideal of beauty, for it recalls the lost age, and carries the promise of its reanimation, induced, not least, by the poet's compelling words:

> Thus I exclaimed. And the bright flush of shame
> Sped o'er the pallid shapes in the cloud-land.[18]

The constantly rosy cheeks of health, however, cause dislike, as becomes obvious in the description of Bellini in *Florentinische Nächte*: 'Bellini's face, like his whole physique, had that physical freshness, that blooming sensuousness, that rose-color which makes on *me* a disagreeable impression – on me, I say, because I like much better that which is death-like and of marble' (*FN*, 113–14).

Pygmalionic animation blurs here with the neoclassicist ideal of beauty, and with the nineteenth-century disguises and pitfalls of desire. Sander Gilman showed in his study of the rise of aesthetic surgery during the nineteenth century how qualities like delicacy or paleness often ascribed to the ill became a variation on the beautiful; how beauty, covering its dangers and diseases with the veil of sublime

---

15 Heinrich Heine, 'The Romantic School', in *The Works of Heinrich Heine*, transl. by Charles Godfrey Leland, Vol. 5 (London: Heinemann, 1892), pp. 227–384 (p. 254).

16 Ibid., p. 240.

17 See Norbert Altenhofer, 'Die exilierte Natur: Kulturtheoretische Reflexion im Werk Heines', in Altenhofer, *Die verlorene Augensprache*, ed. by Volker Bohn (Frankfurt am Main: Insel, 1993), pp. 174–206 (p. 203).

18 Heinrich Heine, *The Gods of Greece*, in *Poetical Works*, transl. by Margaret Armour, 4 vols (London: Heinemann, 1917), I, 264–7.

appearance, became increasingly ambivalent, and how desire and illness entered a public alliance.[19] Healthy people, in Heine, seem to be insensitive to the pathologies and pleasures of their age, and even comfortable with its psychosexual repressions, whereas the writer's fictional mistresses reflect the time's undeniable sickness in their faces. They forget about it in moments of carnal fulfilment – or they act it out in their dance.

How are these cultural discourses, and Heine's contribution to them, linked to the author's thought on dance? How are they reflected in, and influenced by, the cultural practice of ballet? Although Heine is critical of the dance technique that was shown on the official stages, he embraces the cultural practice of dance, whether social or theatrical, as a significant discourse. For the writer, the 'arch-pagan' art of dance has the potential to revive a primordial approach to the body that did not restrain its desires. Yet this potential is not realised in the classical ballet as practised in the *Académie Royale de Musique*. Ballet, in Heine's eyes, is the result of the Christianisation of a formerly Dionysian expression of ecstasy, turning it into an artificial arrangement of meticulously calculated steps and affected prudishness. However, Heine sees a double game at work to compensate for moral restrictions. He writes in *Lutetia*: 'Indeed, French ballet is chaste by form and nature, but the eyes of the danseuses add depraved commentaries to their demure *pas*, and their smile is contradicting their feet' (*DHA* XIII/1, 155). Akin to Kleist and Hoffmann, Heine turns his back on the big stages and looks for inspiration in popular culture. It is the cancan that catches his eye: a dance that appeals through energy and openly staged erotic display. The cancan provides the writer with the stimulating impulses he seeks. In his fictional dances, he explores them further than the actual parameters for physical activity measured out by society allowed.

For even the cancan, although probably the most ecstatic dance of Heine's time, partakes in the economy of repression and excess that is characteristic of the author's critical account of nineteenth-century culture. As in classical ballet, it is not so much the daring and explicit poses and steps of the dance, but the duplicity of the setting that appals the beholder. In Heine's description, the cancan is a *carnivalesque* orgy which responds to the restrictive gaze of policemen, meant to maintain the order on the dance floor, with the mockery of everything that is supposed to be held holy. Excessive repression is countered with excessive compensation, with the sad ridiculing of sexual relationships, enthusiasm, patriotism, heroism, and the divine, testifying to the failure of a bourgeois society to preserve the high aspirations of the revolution.[20] The potentially straightforward eroticism of the cancan is distorted in

---

19 Sander L. Gilman, *Creating Beauty to Cure the Soul: Race and Psychology in the Shaping of Aesthetic Surgery* (Durham: Duke University Press, 1998), p. 47.

20 Heine's strongly moralising description of the cancan might have been written in view of a German audience. Moreover, Siegfried Kracauer suggests that Heine did not see the light-heartedness of the parodic spectacle, stemming from 'a truly French' inclination for persiflage; in Kracauer, *Jacques Offenbach und das Paris seiner Zeit* (Frankfurt am Main: Suhrkamp, 1976), p. 46.

the allusive gestures of the dancers. They stage a cheap strategy to undermine the censorship placed upon their pleasures; a strategy to counter the law that has nothing to do with Heine's cultic veneration of the sensual:

> This Gallic carelessness performs its most enjoyable leaps precisely when it finds itself in a straitjacket, and though the beady eye of the police prevents the cancan from being danced in its cynical nature, the dancers have learned to reveal their scandalous thoughts in a variety of ironic entrechats and exaggeratedly moral gestures, so that concealment comes to appear even more indecent than nudity (*DHA* XIII/1, 157; *CW*).

However, the potential of the cancan in the way it was intended, that is as a physical response to the rebellious spirit and the social unrest of the 1830s, did attract Heine. It set its exuberance against the more rigid disciplines of respected social and theatrical dance.[21] Rather than the flawless performance of chorus line girls that it was to become around 1900, the original cancan or *chahut* was a social dance based entirely on improvisation. The students, working-class girls and professional dancers who frequented the dance halls of Paris expanded the steps of the then-popular polka, 'making them larger and much more grandiose, incorporating kicks, leaps, and even acrobatics, to make it more interesting'.[22] Disdaining the well-rehearsed execution of theatrical dance, Heine values the immediacy and spontaneity of the cancan, which intrigues by its capacity to represent the otherwise censored. Although the writer is taken aback by the practices the cancan is forced into, he liberates it in his fictions, where it provides the ecstatic bacchanals of antiquity with a distinct style of movement. In a curious mixture of classical and Gothic references that is significant for Heine's personal mythical universe, *Die Götter im Exil* (The Gods in Exile) stages a bacchanal as a dance of the dead, as a last rising up of the agonising Greek gods:

> this assembly of delightful phantoms, risen from the sarcophagi of their monuments or their lairs in ruined temples, to again renew their ancient gay and festive rites, to once more celebrate with games and dance the triumph of the divine liberator, of the savior of sensuality, to revive the joyous dance of heathendom, the cancan of the merry world of

---

21 To illustrate the way that the cancan was practised during the Second Empire, David Price notes what an American observer said about the girls in the dance hall *Bal Mabille*: 'Deliberately gathering up their long skirts, they threw them over their shoulders and thus left themselves unencumbered and exposed to the public view from their waists to their feet. In this condition they executed all manner of capers, with the utmost ease and coolness. One of the spectators venturing to thrust his face too close, the younger girl suddenly threw up her leg and with her foot sent his hat rolling into the circle amidst the yells and laughters of the lookers-on, and without pausing went hopping around the circle with her foot higher than her head'; in David Price, *Cancan!* (New Jersey: Farleigh Dickenson University Press, 1998), p. 42.

22 Renée Camus, 'Cancan: Blurring the Line Between Social Dance and Stage Performance', in *Proceedings of the Twenty-Fourth Annual Conference of the Society for Dance History Scholars* (Stoughton: The Printing House, 2001), pp. 6–10 (p. 7).

yore, without any of the policemen of spiritual morality to hinder – all revelling, rioting, hurrahing, Evoe Bacche![23]

The popular and the erudite, the erotic and the morbid are fused to create choreographies of excess that could only be performed on the literary stage; and even here, some cunning was necessary to avoid the restrictions of censorship. The official stages presented Romantic dreams in white that found different, less transgressive solutions to combine the classicist heritage with sensual titillation.

As Gautier used to state, ballet was first and foremost the art of displaying limbs to best advantage. Thus beauty, modelled after the Greek ideal, was the most important quality of a dancer. Gautier thus compares the stage to a 'gallery of living statues'.[24] The critic's description of the decoration for the ballet *La filleule des fées* (The Goddaughter of the Fairies, 1849) is a direct reflection of this aesthetic fantasy: 'the light that just now was shining white on the marble breasts of the statues turns pink, and the sculpted nymphs seem to come to life at the touch of the fountain like so many Galatheas.'[25] *La fille de marbre* (The Marble Girl), mounted in 1847 by Arthur St Léon to introduce the young Fanny Cerrito to Paris, is another case in point. The ballet stages the fate of a marble maiden who is allowed to live and to move as long as she does not fall in love; once this happens, she is to turn back into a statue. The piece takes up themes which will be discussed in more detail in the analysis of *Giselle* later in this chapter. It negotiates female sensuality and the pleasure of dancing as transgressions that endanger woman's state as a commodity exchanged among men; thus her excessive energy has to be contained.[26] Taking the metaphor of the dancer's statue-like body literally, the commodification of woman displayed in the libretto of *La fille de marbre* was quickly extended to the female artists who represented the contents of such libretti in their dance. Small statuettes of the famous ballerinas were highly fashionable in the traffic of souvenirs surrounding the Romantic ballet.[27] Moreover, departing from Manet's infamous painting *Olympia*, T.J. Clark points out that the term 'fille de marbre' was, by the 1860s, one of the established names of the *femmes publiques*.[28]

---

23 Heinrich Heine, *The Gods in Exile*, in *The Sword and the Flame*, pp. 541–84.

24 Gautier, *Gautier on Dance*, ed. by Ivor Guest (London: Dance Books, 1986), p. 7.

25 Ibid., p. 220.

26 On danced adaptations of the theme of Pygmalion, among them *La fille de marbre*, see Susan Leigh Foster, 'Pygmalion's No-Body and the Body of Dance', in *Performance and Cultural Politics*, ed. by Elin Diamond (London: Routledge, 1996), pp. 131–54; see also Ivor Guest, *The Ballet of the Second Empire 1847–1858* (London: Black, 1955), pp. 29–33, and Gautier, *Gautier on Dance*, pp. 182–8.

27 See 'The Statuette of Fanny Elssler', in Gautier, *Gautier on Dance*, pp. 3–4. See also Deborah Jowitt, *Time and the Dancing Image* (Berkeley: University of California Press, 1988), pp. 44–5.

28 T.J. Clark, *The Painter of Modern Life: Paris in Art of Manet and his Followers* (Princeton: Princeton University Press, 1984), p. 109.

Yet around 1800, the purity of the white body was still applied to reduce the erotic appeal of ballet dancers. It is not without irony that in 1798 the dancer's costumes for a ballet entitled *Bacchus and Ariadne* at the King's Theatre in London were criticised as being offensive, and the flesh-coloured tights meant to be in tune with the Greek-style costumes were replaced with white ones to make the impression less carnal.[29] In the Romantic period, the colour white had become ambivalent in itself. Its thrill consisted in the combination of innocence with seduction, epitomised in the translucent whiteness of the dresses seen against the stage lights which made the outline of the body visible. In *La Fanfarlo*, Charles Baudelaire even thinks that this visibility went too far to be still erotic, talking of 'those insipid gauzes which reveal everything and leave nothing to the imagination'.[30] The costume issue perfectly echoes the aesthetic discussions of nudity in statues. If they were depicted wearing tunics, their garments were not supposed to conceal, but to enhance the contours of the body, emphasising its idealised nudity in the same way it was emphasised when protected only by the flawlessly modelled skin.[31] As in sculpture, it was the imagined body in dance, and not the real one, that was of interest to the spectator, ballet's creation of nudity, and not nakedness, that attracted the gaze. By the 1830s, the use of flesh-coloured tights was uncontested. The tights revealed, and at the same time covered, the dancer's legs, smoothing out the skin into a sculpted surface and thus turning the body into a work of art. The Romantic ballet was meant to be an artifice – an artifice whose strategies were immensely successful.

Although Heine admires particular dancers, especially Carlotta Grisi, whom he cheekily singles out as 'an orange among potatoes' (*DHA* XIII/1, 154), he does not simply succumb to the general tendency in nineteenth-century dance criticism to perpetuate and expand the staged illusion. Ludwig Börne, for instance, indulges n his own projections while watching Marie Taglioni in *Flore et Zéphire* (1831): 'She fluttered about, flower and butterfly at once. In fact, she did not move; she did not rise, nor did she drop; she was drawn up and down, air and earth fought for her possession.'[32] Heine, however, takes the calculation behind the staging into account,

---

29 See the full account of this scandal in Mary Grace Swift, *A Loftier Flight: The Life and Accomplishments of Charles-Louis Didelot, Balletmaster* (Connecticut: Wesleyan University Press, 1974), pp. 68–73; I would like to thank Judith Chazin-Benahum for bringing this reference to my attention.

30 Charles Baudelaire, *La Fanfarlo,* in Baudelaire, *The Poems in Prose*, 2 vols, ed. and transl. by Francis Scarfe (London: Anvil Press, 1989), II, pp. 214–63 (p. 247).

31 See Winckelmann, p. 24: 'This Contour reigns in Greek figures, even when covered with drapery, as the chief aim of the artist; the beautiful frame pierces the marble like a transparent Coan cloth.'

32 Börne, III, 241; see also the ironical doubling of the Romantic discourse of dance by Albert Smith, who writes in his *Natural History of the Ballet Girl*: 'Let us hope in the Ballet-girl we may now take up a more agreeable subject – The Butterflies', in *The Natural History of the Ballet Girl* (London: Dance Books, 1996), p. 8.

and writes about 'dancers who rely on the poetic effects of their thighs';[33] what is more, his dance criticism does not restrict itself to reporting the enthralments of the visual. In a curious passage in his letters *Über die Französische Bühne* (On the French Theatre, 1837), he turns to an unspeakable subject that remains untouched in all the idealisations of woman in Romantic ballet. The author addresses neither poetry nor eroticism, but something that very concretely affects the dancer's working life: her menstrual cycle. The attention shifts from how she appears to what she experiences; dance is acknowledged as a physical profession, an athletic effort that is affected by the physiological rhythms of the body. However, the turn toward what Heine names indirectly yet unmistakably 'dancing cold' (*DHA* XII/1, 286), alluding to the ailments that prevent singers from performing, is meant to attack the politics of the Paris Opera. Louis Véron, Director of the Opera between 1831 and 1835, and preoccupied with his own financial situation, invented ingenious devices to keep his cultural enterprise running smoothly: Véron allegedly introduced the intriguing 'red book'. Here the director kept track of the dancers' monthly afflictions in order to avoid economic losses due to last-minute changes of the scheduled performances. Hence not only the twisted aesthetics of Christianised art, but also what Heine calls the 'god of materialism' presided over the Paris Opera, a fact that attracts the writer's relentless scorn.

The *ballet blanc*, the second act that gives Romantic ballets like *La Sylphide* or *Giselle* their characteristic partition between a worldly and an otherworldly sphere, most impressively displays the mechanics of stage illusion. The dancers' bodies, cold, pale and smooth like animated stone, moving with an ethereal lightness that makes them appear as if evaporating into the air, link whiteness to the pallor, and to the transfiguring force of death. The *ballet blanc* is a realm of revenants. The ornaments and floor patterns created by the identically dressed, identically moving *corps* echo Heine's metaphor for the intricately carved design of Gothic cathedrals, stone that appears 'spectrally transfused with spiritual life'. The sacrifice of blood on which the danced architecture rests may be the bleeding toes caused by *pointe* work, one of the very real fatigues and pains caused by a physical technique that breaks the rules of human anatomy. Apart from the ethereal impression produced by the *pointe* technique that reduced the contact with the floor to a minimum, the ghost-like floating of the dancers was, of course, a stage effect. A late nineteenth-century compendium on the machinery of illusionary effects in the theatre mentions laconically:

> In ballets the dancers are frequently represented as floating in the air. This movement may be produced by means of a common see-saw. In aërial ballets and in the appearances of angels, etc., special devices are provided in up-to-date theatres, the mechanism usually being in the form of a trolley.[34]

---

33 Heinrich Heine, *Ideas: The Book of Le Grand*, in *Selected Prose*, ed. and transl. by Ritchie Robertson (London: Penguin, 1993), pp. 89–143 (p. 121).

34 Albert Hopkins, *Magic: Stage Illusions and Scientific Diversions including Trick Photography* (New York: Arno, 1977), pp. 321–2.

The second act of the ballet *Giselle* is one of the most striking versions of the *ballet blanc*, inspired by Heine's account of the popular myth of the Willis, brides that died before marriage. Denoting the dangerous liminality of the ghostly sisterhood who inhabits the no-man's-land between father and husband, and between life and death, whiteness unfolds its treacherous potential. The refined pleasures promised by the translucent cover of the chaste muslin have to be paid for with one's life. In *Florentinische Nächte*, Max tells how 'the madness of the Parisiennes' reminds him 'of the legend of the dead dancing-girls who are called by us the Willis':

> These are young brides who died before the wedding-day, but who still have the unsatisfied mania for dancing so deeply in their hearts, that they rise by night from their graves and meet in crowds on the highways, where they at midnight abandon themselves to the wildest dances. In their bridal dresses, with wreaths of flowers on their heads, sparkling rings on their pale white hands, laughing fearfully, irresistibly beautiful, the Willis dance in the moonshine, and they dance the more impetuously and wildly the more they feel that the hour allowed them for dancing is drawing to an end, and they must again descend to the icy cold of the grave. (*FN*, 139)

As is well known, the girls are doomed to take revenge for having been jilted by faithless lovers.[35] Their compulsive dancing thus replaces an excess of unsatisfied sexual energy. It bears a decidedly autoerotic aspect – they dance themselves into ecstasy – and it incorporates the fundamental anxiety of lethal lust, being a dance of vengeance that drives the man to death. In the ballet, the young village girl to whom the ballet owes its name defuses the image of the dangerous woman by preventing her lover from being killed. Giselle's short liaison with count Albrecht who courts her in disguise ends with her death from a broken heart when she finds out about his engagement to a noble lady. In spite of her metamorphosis into one of the vengeful spirits, her love for Albrecht is stronger than the fatal dance-compulsion. Against the orders of Myrtha, queen of the Willis, Giselle manages to keep Albrecht alive until dawn when the revenants have to return to their graves. Her last wish is that he may find the happiness, which she herself cannot give him any more, with his fiancée. Like her biblical model Mary Magdalene, or her literary model Margarethe, the seducing yet repenting Willi reconciles sensuality with piety.[36]

Much has been written on the fact that it was a largely male fantasy which conceived of this aesthetic of femininity which came to characterise the Romantic ballet as a genre. The *ballet blanc* is the culmination of the idealization of woman in the display of femininity as a mythological, non-individual concept, its glorification.

---

35 Cyril W. Beaumont, *The Ballet Called Giselle* (London: the author, 1944), p. 19.

36 See Gautier, who writes on Grisi as Giselle 'Goethe must have imagined Margarete exactly like that, walking with Faust in Martha's garden', in *Giselle ou les Wilis* (Paris: Librairie de l'Opéra, 1841), p. 8; and also the Magdalene-motif in Heine's last poem in the sequel of poems on the dancer Pomare: 'God has ended now your story; / He had pity, you are dead. / As your mother here, your Father / Showed you mercy from above. / This He did, I think the rather / That you too did greatly love'; *Poetical Works*, III, 126.

and demonisation. The topos of the white woman proliferated in the nineteenth century not least because of its extraordinary ambiguity: it ranges from 'a "little maid" in white, a fierce virgin in white, a nun in white, a bride in white, a madwoman in white, a dead woman in white, and a ghost in white', and of course the sick woman in her white nightgown.[37] Whiteness, however, always implies an idea of purity, of transcending the organic reality of the body. The white-robed, carved-out body of the ballerina is not only an erotically charged artifice; it also de-realises itself by merging with the ornament of the dance.

Elisabeth Bronfen has shown that the beautiful corpse in art can be read as the index of a cultural repression of the reality of death, linked, in the image of woman, to the threatening potential of female sexuality. Artistic representations of the dead woman are the traces of this process, as well as of its failure; they become symptoms of something that is too powerful to be suppressed. The highly ambivalent symptom results from the attempt to maintain order while at the same time pointing out what threatens it. It covers and simultaneously highlights the danger by replacing it with a substitute.[38] It is the ultimate unrepresentability of death that asks for this substitution; as Edgar Allan Poe famously thought, 'the death [...] of a beautiful woman is, unquestionably, the most poetical topic in the world'.[39] Cross-references between the morbid, the erotic, the aesthetic, and the religious abound in mid nineteenth-century ballet, and in *Florentinische Nächte*. What these realms have in common is that they provide experiences at the limit of reason, and of representability, and thus, due to their very evasiveness, provoke ceaseless artistic approaches to representation. Bronfen undoubtedly offers a striking model for reading the beautifully dancing revenants of the Romantic ballet. Sick, dying and dead women were almost *de rigueur* in nineteenth-century ballet and opera; Heine's *Der Doktor Faust* ironically comments on this necrophilia by staging a grotesque scene of dancing female skeletons. While the inexhaustible Gautier, stressing the homosocial triangle of author, librettist and *connoisseur*, plainly writes, after having explained the first act of *Giselle* to Heine: 'That, my dear Heine, is the story that M. de Saint-Georges conceived to give us the pretty young corpse we need.'[40] Men wrote the libretti and the reviews; men were, to a large extent, responsible for the choreography and the staging. The ballerina is a symptom that expresses, in a codified, displaced and condensed form the fears and desires of a patriarchal culture. The thrills and threats of her femininity are placed out of reach, in a safe distance, banned to the theatrical.

Although Heine participates in creating images of the white woman, he unsettles their implications. His expressive dancers enhance their physicality. As we have seen

---

37 Sandra M. Gilbert and Susan Gubar, *The Madwoman in the Attic: the Woman Writer and the Nineteenth-century Literary Imagination* (New Haven: Yale University Press, 1979), pp. 621–2.

38 Elisabeth Bronfen, *Over Her Dead Body: Death, Femininity and the Aesthetic* (Manchester: Manchester University Press, 1992).

39 Edgar Allan Poe, 'The Philosophy of Composition', in Poe, *Essays and Reviews* (New York: The Library of America, 1984), pp. 13–25 (p. 19).

40 Gautier, *Gautier on Dance*, p. 98.

in the remarkable passage on the red book, even the aerial whiteness of the ballerina is weighed down by the most physical of matter, blood. The highly substantial, and at the same time highly metaphorical life-force breaks through the white varnish of cultural achievement, and civilised human beings. As the blushing of pale faces, it speaks of sexual awareness; it soils the skirts of the dancers, and resonates in the red glow of the stained glass windows of the cathedrals.[41] Blood is reminiscent of the inescapability of the body as matter, it tells of vulnerability and mortality and their traumatic impact on human life. Yet it also becomes the harbinger of a cultural process of healing, as the author writes in 'Zur Geschichte der Religion und Philosophie in Deutschland' (On the History of Religion and Philosophy in Germany, 1834):

> Our immediate task is to become healthy; for we still feel very weak and faint. The holy vampires of the Middle Ages have sucked out so much of our life-blood. And then great expiatory sacrifices must be performed in deference to matter, so that it may forgive the old insults. It would even be advisable to organize festivals and pay extraordinary honours to matter as compensation for the past.[42]

In *Die Göttin Diana*, the protagonist attempts suicide as the ultimate transfigurative surrender to matter that leads to a new life in Dionysian bliss. The ballet opens with the knight's wish to sacrifice himself on the altar of the goddess to declare his devotion: 'he remembers that the goddess once loved human sacrifice, and full of drunken passion he seizes knife and bowl – he is ready to offer the goddess the libation of his heart's blood' (*DHA* IX, 69).

In nineteenth-century dance criticism, however, the appeal of unstained whiteness persisted. The non-colour white was most intriguing in its capacity to predicate woman as the not-yet-marked, as the blank page that simultaneously incorporates the dream of unrestricted signification, and offers itself to be inscribed by the male writer's projections. When Gautier writes to Heine after the first performance of *Giselle*, he reports how, after having read *De l'Allemagne*, he merged the writer's vision of 'white-robed elfs' with the whiteness of the dancing chorus, and of the blank page while conceiving the ballet: 'I said to myself, "What a lovely ballet that would make!" In a burst of enthusiasm I even took up a large sheet of fine white paper and wrote at the top, in superb rounded characters, "*Les Wilis*, a ballet".'[43] The superb rounded characters of Gautier's title might not only indicate the tracing of a

---

41 Compare the bloody patch on the dress of another sexually aware dancer, Hoffmann's Giacinta in *Prinzessin Brambilla*, *HB*, 122.

42 Heinrich Heine, 'On the History of Religion and Philosophy in Germany', in *Selected Prose*, pp. 197–294 (p. 248).

43 Gautier, *Gautier on Dance*, p. 94; in the beginning, Gautier thought of a first act that would be the mimed version of Victor Hugo's poem *Fantômes*, where a girl dies of catching a cold after having danced too much at a ball. Yet he confided the definitive version of the libretto to the stage writer Vernoy de Saint-Georges, who decided in favour of the more dramatic version of the broken heart; see Beaumont, pp. 20–21, and Gautier, *Gautier on Dance*, p. 98.

female body; they also hint at an identification of writing with dancing, of the writer with the dancer.

This identification suggests that the gender perceptions of the Romantic ballet are less clear-cut than it seems at first sight. While the plots convey patriarchal motifs like heterosexual coupling, exchange of women and the male mastery over women and story, the performing of these plots bears ambiguities. In a curious reversal of gender constellations, the Romantic ballet defines masculine looks and modes of movement as the inadequate other of the feminine ideal, the male in relation, and contradistinction, to the female dancer. Jules Janin's tirade is representative of the opinion of contemporary commentators: the *danseur* is: 'a frightful danseuse of the masculine sex, come to pirouette front and centre, while the pretty girls stand off respectfully at a distance, this was surely impossible, intolerable, and thus we have done well to erase such great artists from our pleasures'.[44] However, Janin finds words of praise for Jules Perrot, Carlotta Grisi's teacher, partner and patron. In accordance with the common taste, he lauds nothing specifically masculine in Perrot, but his feminine qualities, especially his extraordinary lightness, and his beautiful legs. Yet recalling the Kleistian double-bind of male grace, the only achievement that made a male dancer acceptable in the Romantic era, his potential to be 'a male Taglioni', at the same time accounted for his rejection when termed as 'the foolish affectation of French male dancers'.[45] Scholarship has enquired into the historicity of gender perceptions in classical dance. The feminisation of the male dancer is obviously at its acutest in the Romantic period when ballet is declared female, stressing the divide between gazed-at feminine object and gazing masculine subject.[46] The homophobic refusal to gaze at the male dancer at all, however, existed side by side with a homoerotic component which found curious performative disguises.

Corresponding to the feminisation of the male dancer, the female dancer took on masculine attributes. Resonant with the androgyny of statues, her idealised femininity indeed embraced a good deal of hermaphroditism. The more useless the male dancer was in the eyes of the spectator, the more phallic and powerful the female dancer became. The perception of her body as hermaphrodite, whether in male costume or not, made a dandyesque identification with the female dancer possible; and it provoked a blurring of hetero- and homosexual fantasies, subverting the display of outright homophobia that expelled men from the stage.[47] Let us turn to Gautier again to illustrate this point. He writes of Fanny Elssler:

---

44 Quoted in McCarren, p. 85; for a more detailed account of the gender trouble on the Romantic stage, see pp. 84–92.

45 Gautier, *Gautier on Dance*, p. 6.

46 See Ramsay Burt, *The Male Dancer: Bodies, Spectacle, Sexualities* (New York: Routledge, 1995), pp. 10, 14; see also Thomas Simonis, 'Zwischen (Ohn)macht und Begehren: Männlichkeitsinszenierungen im populären Tanzfilm', *Jahrbuch Tanzforschung*, 12 (2002), pp. 273–87.

47 See Clark, *Bodies at the Opéra*.

If Mlle Elssler resembles anyone aside from herself, it must be the son of Hermes and Aphrodite, the hermaphrodite of antiquity, that ravishing chimera of Greek art. [...] There is a supple, vivacious quality in their [her arms'] contours that conjures up the image of a marvellously beautiful and somewhat effeminate young man such as the Indian Bacchus, Antinoüs or the Apollo Belvedere. The same relationship extends to every other part of her beauty, which is rendered all the more attractive and piquant by this delightful ambiguity. Her movements too are impressed with this duality. Beneath the amorous languor, the intoxicating sensuality that yields to the heat of passion, and the feminine sweetness and all the gentle fascination of a ballerina, can be sensed the agility, the sudden speed and the steely muscles of a young athlete. Also, Mlle Elssler appeals to everybody, even to women who cannot endure ballerinas.[48]

Although this physical prowess was not considered as something genuinely feminine, muscular strength and vigour were imperative for a female dancer, and noticeable for the beholder. Heine's Mephistophela of *Der Doktor Faust* is another example of a mighty, non-traditionally feminine female dancer. The author goes as far as inverting the relationship between male master and female *élève*. In a scene bearing great choreographic comedy, the stereotypical constellation of the Pygmalion-pattern is reversed; the rejuvenated Faust is decidedly *her* creation:

Mephistophela now gives Faust a lesson in dancing and shows him all the handy, or rather footy, tricks of the trade or game. The awkwardness and stiffness of the sage, who attempts to perform the dainty and graceful *pas* of his teacher, form the most amusing effects and contrasts. [...] by the power of love and of the magic wand, with which his rebellious limbs are constantly being touched, the pupil in choreography at last attains perfect dexterity.[49]

As we will see, both *Florentinische Nächte* and *Giselle* talk of this potential of dance to represent resistance, even if their plots seek to contain the danger of confident femininity.[50]

Dances of Mourning: Laurence and Giselle

Laurence's dance in *Florentinische Nächte* breaks with the code of movement set by classical ballet technique. At the same time, it reproduces Romantic topoi. It transgresses and reiterates stereotypes, building up a complex network of references which raises issues of representation, communication and agency that reflect upon, and challenge, the patriarchal economies of authorship and desire. It is the opposite of what Heine was able to see at the Opera:

---

48 Gautier, *Gautier on Dance*, p. 32.

49 Heinrich Heine, *Doctor Faust: A Ballet Poem*, in *The Sword and the Flame*, pp. 503–40 (p. 509).

50 See Marion Kant, 'Wo getanzt wird, da ist der Teufel', in *Giselle*, ed. by Staatsoper unter den Linden Berlin (Frankfurt am Main: Insel, 2001), pp. 36–75 (especially pp. 62–3).

It was not the classic dancing such as we still see in great ballets, where, as in classic tragedy, only sprawling unities and artificial effects flourish. It was not those footed Alexandrines, those declamatory leaps, those antithetic *entrechats*, that noble passion which whirls in pirouettes so distractingly down on one foot that one sees nothing but heaven and *stockinette* – nothing but ideality and lies! [...] Mademoiselle Laurence was no great *danseuse*, her toes were not very supple, her legs were not practised in all possible contortions; she understood nothing of the art of dancing as Vestris teaches it, but she danced as Nature teaches; her whole soul was in time with her steps; not only did her feet dance, but her whole form and face. (*FN*, 132)

However, even if here, Heine writes an anti-classicist aesthetics of dance in contradistinction to the way ballet was practised in his day, there are instances where ballet itself breaks its own code. A few years after *Florentinische Nächte* was written, Giselle's dance of madness at the end of the first act bears striking similarities to Heine's fiction. It is a short scene where the outrageous movement and mime is justified for dramatic reasons. Yet Giselle's excessive gestures and steps are more than a dramatic rendering of the plot. While mime was an integral part of the Romantic ballet, these moments of rupture are unique in their reflexive function. They are moments where ballet as body technique and cultural practice reconsiders its own charged history of representation, disciplinisation and display. In the following, the dances of Laurence and Giselle will be compared in order to point out cross-references and differences between them that will help to distinguish Heine's ideas about dance.

Whereas Laurence's dance only exists on paper, Giselle's madness scene has been performed time and again on stage, which makes it more heterogeneous and harder to explore. Here, we will refer to the original libretto and to some reconstructions. The following comparative analysis, however, bears the fundamental difference between the two dances in mind. It is indeed central to my argument that two scenes which resemble each other on the level of movement each carry a distinctive signifying potential due to their different frameworks. Let us consider Laurence's performance first: 'She often became pale, almost deadly pale; her eyes opened spectrally wide, yearning and pain convulsed her lips' (*FN*, 132). The spectator assumes that the dancer's face and body talk about something terribly painful. Max continues to trace the movements in more detail:

Was it some national dance of the South of France or of Spain? These were recalled by the irrepressible energy with which the dancer threw her body to and fro, and the wildness with which she often threw her head backwards in the mad manner of the bold Bacchantae whom we see with amazement on the reliefs of antique vases. Her dance had in it something of intoxicated unwillfulness, something gloomily inevitable or fatalistic, for she danced like destiny itself. Or was it a fragment of some primevally ancient, forgotten pantomime? Or a secret tale of life, set to motion? Very often the girl bent to earth, with listening ear, as if she heard a voice calling up to her. Then she trembled like an aspen leaf, sprang quickly to the other side and there indulged in her maddest gambols. Then she inclined her ear again to the earth, listened more anxiously than before, nodded with her head, grew sad and pale, shuddered, stood awhile straight as a taper, as if frozen, and finally made a motion *as if washing her hands*! Was it blood which she so carefully, with such terrible anxiety, washed away? (*FN*, 133)

While Laurence's dance turns out to be a ritual that is performed over and over again, Giselle's madness scene is performed once, and leads into death. It takes place immediately after she has discovered Albrecht's betrayal. The English version of the original libretto gives the following opening of Giselle's agony: 'The deepest horror is depicted on the unfortunate's girl's features; her brain begins to reel, a horrible and sombre delirium seizes her as she sees herself jilted, lost, dishonoured.'[51] She swoons at her mother's feet, who loosens her daughter's hair. Several times Giselle flings up her head and arms only to collapse again. When she finally rises, 'it is clear from her vacant gaze that her mind has given way. She lives in the past, believes herself to be dancing once more with her beloved Loys' (Loys being the name of Albrecht's fake identity as a peasant). Beaumont's investigation of the original version continues as follows: 'Giselle [...] wanders slowly in a circle to her L.[oys], then, coming down centre, she pauses, placing first one hand then the other over her eyes in a gesture of bewilderment. She then makes a vague, appealing gesture first with one hand, then with the other.[52] Giselle takes up Albrecht's sword and, with a sudden movement, forces the sword point into her breast.[53] With her last strength, she believes herself still dancing with Albrecht, while the music repeats the characteristic melody of the dance of their happiness. Giselle enacts it slowly and jerkily. "Suddenly her limbs refuse their office. She resembles a grotesque clockwork toy, the mainspring of which has snapped".[54] Her movements become weaker, "she places her hands to her breast, then clasps her cheeks and strokes her hands. Alarmed by the icy coldness that is stealing over her, she stumbles along the fringe of frightened onlookers, looking for someone to help her. She staggers towards her mother and falls at her feet."'[55]

The dances of Laurence and Giselle display remarkable similarities. They most vividly perform horror and pain through facial expression, mime and movement. Both break with the classical code: like Laurence, Giselle dances and moves on flat foot, abandoning the *pointe*, and the tightly fixed chignon of the ballerina that represents discipline and control. Both dances include some sort of collapse that defies one of the most basic hierarchies of classical ballet technique, and of culture in general, which values the vertical over the horizontal, that which is further away from the earth over that which is close to it. Giselle's last dance as a village girl starts and ends with a fall; moreover, her moves and poses show that she is hardly able to hold herself upright. Although the dancer is only acting as if she was on the brink

---

51 Beaumont, p. 44.

52 Ibid., p. 101.

53 Scholarship tries to reconstruct if Giselle was meant to die of her broken heart, or because of the injury that she inflicted upon herself; see for instance Marian Smith, 'What killed Giselle?', *Dance Chronicle: Studies in Dance and the Related Arts*, 13/1 (1990), 68–81.

54 Beaumont, p. 107.

55 Ibid., pp. 101–2.

of collapse, this display of physical weakness and tiredness disrupts the illusion of superhuman lightness and energy at the heart of the classical school. Giselle's painful, slow repetition of the formerly exuberant steps of her love-duet with Loys reveals the amount of vigour that normally stays hidden behind the graceful surface, and that now suddenly becomes evident due to its absence. Laurence's dance, not bound to end in death, is more energetic, yet one of its characteristic movements is a repeated bending toward the earth, bringing her ear close to the floor. However, even if the two performances of psychic pain resemble each other on a physical level, they differ in their signification.

Both dances are yet again 'failed' performances, or more succinctly, transgressions of the disciplinary order, which is here, in the first place, the 'proper' code of movement prescribed by classical ballet technique. In the case of Giselle, this aesthetic transgression reflects the plot: her *mésalliance* with Albrecht, and her exaggerated love of dancing are but two sides of the same coin. Giselle's abundant lust for life soon provokes the doom-laden evocation of the reign of the Willis by Berthe, her mother, who warns her daughter that her delight may turn into a compulsion. In one of the most famous mime scenes in the history of the Romantic ballet, Berthe's gestures 'speak' as follows: 'You will always dance then [...] night and day [...] it's an absolute passion [...] and this, instead of working in the vineyards or doing housework.'[56] Giselle's inappropriately excessive behaviour threatens patriarchal values. Her broken heart, becoming identical with madness and death, is the logical result of a 'madness' that started long before. It is significant that the final outbreak of this madness cannot be fitted into ballet's system of perfection. Indeed, her insanity is conveyed by the breakdown of the order of balletic movement.

The complementarity of the outrageous pleasure of dancing, and the dancing compulsion as a form of punishment by dance, which underlies Giselle's story, recalls the fairytale motif of the red shoes. They too invoke blood as a marker of the essence of life, but also as an indicator of death, here illustrated by excessive dancing as a person's consummation and consumption. Epitomised in Hans Christian Andersen's *The Red Shoes*, an extreme passion for dancing undergoes its own castigation in the compulsive need to move, however exhausting and painful this may be. Heine's poem *Rothe Pantoffeln* (Red Slippers) is a variation on the theme: 'A young and white little high-born mouse' is incautious enough to get lured into buying red slippers from a cat, which results in her wearing the desired shoes only for her death dance at the last judgement.[57] We can conclude from these popular versions of the topic that the metonymically overcharged pleasure of physical movement challenges cultural norms, and must be subjected to a control that invests this movement with

---

56 Ibid., pp. 40–41.

57 'and when from the tomb / You are called, by the awful trump of doom, / To the last great dance, you'll wake, white mouse, / And rise from the grave, your deep, dark house: / Like everyone else you'll leave your bed, / And then you will draw on your slippers red'; *Poetical Works*, IV, 104.

pain, or death.[58] Gilbert and Gubar refer to the motif in their interpretation of *Snow White*, where the stepmother's lethal dance in red-hot metal shoes is related to the fact that women who are too powerful, or too productive, take on a sickening, and a potentially self-destructive role in a patriarchal society that punishes their transgression with 'a "hidden" but crucial tradition of uncontrollable madness'.[59]

Laurence's dance displays indeed a powerful transgressive potential in more than only one sense. For a start, it has nothing to do with the academic school of ballet and its rhetoric. Most scenes of *Giselle* display a vocabulary of mime that was, for the knowledgeable ballet-goer, relatively easy to decipher. Gestures clearly correspond to concepts or activities, for instance Berthe's above-mentioned rendering of compulsive dancing that is destined to end lethally for her daughter, and for the potential prey of the Willis: Berthe refers to dancing by gradually extending and raising her arms vertically upwards above her head, wreathing one hand about the other. As Giannandrea Poesio's investigation of the version by Tamara Karsavina has it, this is followed by a gesture 'indicating either "death" – crossing the fists in front of the lower part of the torso – or "falling to the ground" – extending the arms downwards, with palms facing the audience at the side of each thigh'.[60] Laurence's gestures are equally evocative, yet, as we will see, they cannot be related to a stable meaning. However, although Laurence's dance might be unsettling, she is not declared mad, and she does not have to die. In a work like *Giselle*, which celebrates the status quo of the Romantic ballet, the transgression of the aesthetic order denotes abnormal behaviour. Giselle's deviance has to be contained; she is turned into the beautiful corpse that glosses over the anxieties of a civilization which has to keep up its functionality. In a text by a writer as progressive as Heine, the same transgression indicates a new aesthetic of movement.

Laurence's nightly performance is not as pleasant a sight as the one of the floating Willi. Yet although it quotes the Romantic aestheticisation of the sculpture-like inanimate woman, it is a ritual that more openly displays the pains and terrors of a mind and body locked in a pathological form of mourning their traumatised past. It is telling that Laurence is accompanied by the decomposing corpses of her now ghostly stepfamily. Akin to Hoffmann, we find that Heine contrasts neoclassicist body images with their repressed other. His passionate veneration of the beautiful classical shape never seems to be unaware of the fragility of perfection. He does not depict the mutilation of the ideal body; yet he tells, brimming with irony, of its grotesque, distorted, or rotten escorts. Thus Bacchus, 'a young man of extraordinary beauty' is followed by a 'companion' with a 'mighty paunch',[61] and the Greek beauty

---

58 See Gabriele Brandstetter, 'Nachwort', in *Aufforderung zum Tanz: Geschichten und Gedichte*, ed. by Gabriele Brandstetter (Stuttgart: Reclam, 1992), pp. 401–24 (pp. 408–9).

59 Gilbert and Gubar, p. 56.

60 Giannandrea Poesio, 'Narrative Gesture & Speaking Music', *About the House*, 1/3 (2001), 40–43 (p. 43).

61 Heine, *The Gods in Exile*, p. 568.

Francesca lives next door to Signora Laetizia whose appearance is drastically marked by the traces of age and gluttony.

In order to understand better what Heine could have had in mind by envisaging a dance as extraordinary as Laurence's, his thoughts on painting in his account of the Paris Salon of 1831, *Französische Maler* (French Painters), provide some hints. Here Heine gives voice to his belief that art represents the often conflicting and disparate tendencies of its time. It should not cling on to reactionary currents, but place itself at the edge of cultural renewal. The writer's wishful formulation of a new art recalls Laurence's dance:

> The new age will also give birth to a new art form which will co-exist with it in enthusiastic harmony; it will not need to borrow its symbolism from the fading past and it will bring forth a new technique which will differ from that which has gone before. (*DHA* XI/1, 47; *CW*)

Heine finds his vision confirmed in the dynamic of bodily movement in paintings by Alexandre Gabriel Decamps, or in the impression of burgeoning, guilt-free sensuality in Leopold Robert's work (Figure 4.1). In Heine's reading, Decamps's painting *Patrouille à Smyrne* (Turkish Patrol) displays the same almost grotesque aesthetic of movement as Laurence's dance (Figure 4.2):

> The strange shadows thrown by the humans' and horses' thin legs amplify the Baroque magical effect. The men perform such comical caprioles and unheard of leaps, even the horse throws its legs around at such a wild speed that it appears to be half crawling on its stomach and half flying. (*DHA* XII/1, 23; *CW*)

Laurence's gracelessness – and graceless she is indeed, if grace is defined by the prescriptions of ballet, emphasising anti-gravity and *équilibre* – is thus programmatic. Giselle's enacting of madness, in contrast, is a slip out of a code that is restored immediately afterwards. If not graceful, how is Laurence's movement described? It is wild, unbound, reckless, enraptured, modelled after poses that can be seen in depictions of the dances of the Greek maenads.[62] In nineteenth-century Paris, critics rediscovered them in the outrageous moves of the cancan dancer. Siegfried Kracauer quotes Ludwig Rellstab's description of the cancan at a masked ball: 'in this dance the speed of the music grows ever faster and finally one sees the female masks, like galloping Maenads, with dark, glowing cheeks, breasts heaving for breath, thirsting lips, streaming, half-wild hair, running circles around the room at stormy speed [...]'.[63] The sensual goings that increase in speed in order to reach a point of culmination and utmost exhaustion were all-too-readily linked to a thinly disguised abandonment to sexual madness. In the neoclassicist tradition, the frenzied rites of the bacchantes were outrightly scorned. The unbound female bodies of

---

62 On the body image of the maenad in contrast to other body images of antiquity, see Brandstetter, *Tanz-Lektüren*, p. 187.

63 Kracauer, p. 40; transl. by Chantal Wright.

Figure 4.1   Leopold Robert, *Arrival of the Harvesters in the Pontine Marshes* (1830).

course challenged the cherished Greece of calmness and serenity. The account of a bacchanal in Wieland's *Geschichte des Agathon* is representative of the rejection of an abject rite:

> The loose and flowing hair of these Thracian votaries, the rolling eyes, the foaming lips, the bloated cheeks, wildness of their looks, and the wanton postures by which they expressed their licentious mirth, shaking their thyrsi entwined with serpents, and striking together their cymbals, or stammering out, in faultering accents, their unconnected dithyrambics; all these exertions of a frantic rage [...] were so far from having any attractive influence, that they excited in him a disgust for charms, which, in losing their decency, had lost their power.[64]

As is well known, the characteristic arching backwards of the maenad would be most successfully pathologised in the iconography of hysteria in the second half of the century; reinvested with an emancipatory potential, it then became one of the celebrated signature moves of modern dance.[65]

---

64 Wieland, I, 7–8.

65 See McCarren, *Dance Pathologies*, for a detailed exploration of the transfer between dance and pathology; see also Brandstetter, *Tanz-Lektüren*, pp. 182–207, and by the same author, 'Psychologie des Ausdrucks und Ausdruckstanz: Aspekte der Wechselwirkung am Beispiel der Traumtänzerin Madeleine G.', in *Ausdruckstanz: Eine mitteleuropäische*

Figure 4.2   Alexandre-Gabriel Decamps, *Turkish Patrol* (*c.* 1828).

German literature presents us with one of the most intriguing representations of the cannibalistic maenad in the shape of Kleist's Amazon Penthesilea, who is compelled to bind carnal love to carnal destruction. In more Gothic approaches to the topic, the literary imagination mingles the image of the carnivorous woman with that of the blood-sucking female vampire, bearing such curious examples as the matrilineal vampirism in Hoffmann's novella *Vampyrismus*, a text that in fact relates a case of necrophagy. Both Giselle and Laurence are called vampires. The Willis are 'vampires of dance'; Gautier revels in the description of their nightly feast: 'The willis, cannibals of the waltz, have scented a fresh dancer; they hastily assemble to take part in the feast.'[66] The 'Death Child' Laurence, in turn, is born with the primordial sin of having sucked all the life force out of her mother's body. Laurence's hand-washing gesture looks as if she had to get rid of bloody stains; fictional stains which might remind her of some repressed, or at least never fully acknowledged, feeling of guilt that works its way through her body rather than through her mind. In her hand-washing, and in her blushing, the theme of whiteness soiled by blood recurs. Again it belongs to a tale about female impurity, but also about a very individual wounding.

Bewegung der ersten Hälfte des 20. Jahrhunderts, ed. By Gunhild Oberzaucher-Schüller (Wilhelmshaven: Noetzel, 1992), pp. 199–211.

66 Gautier, *Giselle ou les Wilis*, p. 20; see also Beaumont, p. 19, on the etymology of 'Willi': 'the legend is of Slavonic origin is doubtless correct, for there is a Slav word *vila*, meaning a vampire, the plural is *vile*, and probably *wilis* is a Teutonic form of *vile*'.

The blood obviously hints at adult female sexuality, bringing back the secrets of the 'red book'. Like the autoerotic aspect of the dance of the Willis, Laurence's performance of terror displays orgasmic traits: her shivering, her will-less drunkenness, the way she releases herself in the most boisterous jumps. Her ecstasy is clearly indebted to the reverse of the cultural paradigm of the masochistic pleasure of martyrdom or lustful pain: it performs painful lust, reflecting the above-discussed patriarchal fears that stigmatise uncontrolled, here literally unaccompanied, female sexuality as one of the primary threats of the social and domestic order of things. We are still in the realm of a gender-troubling vampiristic, non-fertile sexuality that does not impregnate, but drains out. Hence it is to be punished, or purified, as the hand-washing gesture suggests. However, what are we to make of the mysterious anamnesic quality of her behaviour? Laurence tries to reconstruct her birth by what she has been told by her stepfather, a ventriloquist, who reported that her real father, a cruel nobleman, had mistreated her pregnant mother, buried her alive, and that she herself was found by desecrators of the grave and thus saved from imminent death. Imitating the mother's voice coming out of the earth, the ventriloquist used to scare the girl with stories about her mother's bitter fate. Laurence, however, assures Max that she has forgotten all of these stories, and that the only way to remember them is her dancing, during which she feels as if she is losing herself to become an entirely different person. When invited to the dance floor at social occasions, she therefore replies that *she could not* dance. Her nightly performances again take up the haunting image of blindness, lack of, or distorted sight, so powerful in its representation of the subject that must lack secure self-knowledge: they are enacted in a state of somnambulism, eyes closed. Dancing, Laurence slips into a state between sleeping and being awake, between life and death, surrounded by the remnants of her step-family; a state that is part of the economy of her psyche, yet remains foreclosed from her waking life. The nightly spectacles are indeed a ghostly dance of the return of the expelled, mixing the polluted corpses of the grotesque musicians with the equally uncanny body of the 'pure' white woman, moving like a statue animated by a will that is not her own. The woman's sculpture-like appearance is reinforced through the moments of transfixion that are part of her performance.

The overdetermined blood-gesture thus also refers to a sacrificial structure underlying Laurence's dance, telling of the replacement of conscious memory with unconscious re-enactment, of understanding with repetition, of the need to cover up traumatic experiences that persistently seep through the protective shield. Laurence turns into her own revenant, telling about her life that was marked by death from the beginning. Her performance opens a liminal space cut out by a bleeding wound which violates the border between the inside of the body and its outside. The dancer is unsealed not only because she is sexually available. Entering a physical process based on the repression, and return, of a traumatic condition, her dance connects her innermost feelings to the surface of her body in movement, apparently without making the detour through her mind.

Both the dances of Giselle and Laurence are placed on an imaginary stage confined by their memories. Giselle re-enacts her happy times with Albrecht, while Laurence's body leads her back to what she has been told about her origin. In Laurence's case, this theatre of memory is repeated ritually over and over again. The fact that it is performed seems at least as important as the content it refers to. This content is far from being clear, as it is doubtful whether the term 'memory' really applies to what Laurence is enacting, since the evidence about her past is inextricably blurred with the fictions she has been told, and which she declares she has forgotten. The pain that causes her strange behaviour is twofold: not only the repression of the terrible details about her mother's fate, but also the experience of a primordial loss, here literally incorporated in her motherlessness, keep Laurence in a state of melancholia. Her dance becomes an uncanny anamnesis of the 'forgotten' that should have stayed hidden and is now displaced into the eloquent yet ambiguous silence of physical movement, hence the ultimately undecipherable character of the bodily hieroglyphs produced by this symptomatic act. The recurring hand-washing gesture, then, might also be representative of the ineffective hygiene of Laurence's economy of repression, attesting to the persistent, if disguised, return of the expelled.

Suggesting a Lady Macbeth-like feeling of guilt, it may more specifically indicate the wish to overcome the pain of the loss of her mother. The assumption that this loss is at the heart of Laurence's trouble is reinforced by her metamorphosis into another person while dancing. The slipping into a different identity, presumably that of her mother, prefigures what Freud would describe as hysteric or melancholic identification, both part of a process of pathological mourning.[67] Laurence's identification with her lost object of love can then be seen as a way to deny, and momentarily overcome, the loss. Presenting a different form of Giglio's suffering under 'chronic dualism', the only way to perform 'her' identity is a self-alienating identification, caught in a matrilineal genealogy of melancholia.[68]

Heine indeed formulates stunning insights that foresee the psychical economy of hysteria as it was explored increasingly from the second half of the nineteenth century onwards. Referring to Freud's early assumptions about the aetiology of hysteria, recent research stresses the link between the hysterical symptoms and a traumatic wounding, instead of necessarily and exclusively connecting them to the discontents of female sexuality.[69] This strand of thought about hysteria not only reinforces a non-gendered view of the phenomenon, it also underlines the inextricable interplay between real suffering, hysterical performance, and the ongoing enmeshment of cure and illness. Parallel to Laurence's 'forgetting' of the stories about her origin and their disguised and enigmatic articulation in her dance, the primal wounding

---

67 See Freud, 'Mourning and Melancholia', *StE* XIV, 237–60, and Renate Schlesier, *Mythos und Weiblichkeit bei Sigmund Freud: Zum Problem von Entmythologisierung und Remythologisierung in der psychoanalytischen Theorie* (Frankfurt am Main: Europäische Verlagsanstalt, 1981), p. 46.

68 On similar settings of corpse-like, melancholic mothers and their mourning offspring in Hoffmann, see Susan E. Gustafson, 'The Cadaverous Bodies of Vampiric Mothers and the Genealogy of Pathology in E.T.A. Hoffmann's Tales', *German Life and Letters*, 52/2 (1999), 238–54.

69 See Bronfen, *The Knotted Subject*.

of the hysteric can never entirely and unequivocally be contained in representation. Physical articulation becomes a way to express something without actually having to tell. Dramatic hands and bodies take over the narrative, as many of Freud's analyses illustrate: bodies suffer under 'fainting fits and spasms', faces display 'every sign of horror', hands 'are tightly clasped', or rubbed together 'as though [...] in a rage' (*StE* II, 49–50, 78). However, despite being like a spell that haunts the dancer, the physical enactment does create an experience of presence, of Laurence's dissolving into what she is performing. During this momentary and enraptured self-forgetfulness, Laurence seems to recover from her pain through dancing.[70] Yet the occurrence of presence unavoidably results in the suffering of renewed loss, provoking the never-ending need for re-enactment.

It is significant that Laurence's dance is a form of improvisation. While the performance of a choreography consists in the memorising, and the execution, of fixed movements, the act of improvising is characterised by techniques that enable the very forgetting, or expanding of preconceived elements and rules. Laurence's freedom from any prescribed choreography, and from the code of ballet, guides her into the submission to an 'improvisation' that is dictated by the compulsive discipline of her own psyche. Her performing of a traumatic condition in a transgressive dance is at once expression and exposure, challenging the category of a sovereign subject that masters the creative act, and strongly pointing toward a loss of control at the heart of any transgressive experience.[71] Laurence's dance might suggest that this exposure implies an encounter with her own finitude, with the reality of her own death which she only escaped by coincidence.

Although her performance carries all the symptoms of a hysterical performance, it is most significant that Heine does not declare her mad. In accordance with the author's logic in which a repressive culture must result in suffering, her illness seems to be a sign of health; we may also think of Freud's clear distinction between pathological symptoms and dancing in the famous case of Anna O., where her regained bodily mobility indicates her recovery from hysteria.[72] For Laurence, dancing is both psychic compulsion and ritual which gives form to her anxiety. The narrative stages her performance in the liminal space between the real and the fantastic, the conscious and the unconscious. Repetitively performative, and at the same time referential, it is, and is not, the other of language. The dancing is part of the symbolic order of representation – Heine is interested in the meaning of movement, and not merely in the ornament of 'footed Alexandrines', as he terms classical steps – yet it is nourished by pre-verbal experiences. It is said to be the most natural physical expression; however, although it does not reproduce the

---

70 Compare Wiese, p. 86.

71 See Michel Foucault on transgression, eroticism and death with reference to Bataille, in 'Preface to Transgression', in *Language, Counter-Memory, Practice: Selected Essays by Michel Foucault*, ed. by Donald F. Bouchard (New York: Cornell University Press, 1977), pp. 29–52 (p. 51).

72 See also Phelan, *Mourning Sex*.

official aesthetic of dance and its images of gender, it nevertheless reiterates pre-existent representational frames of movement: the pale transfixion of the sculpture, the arching of the maenad, and the boisterous jumps of the contemporary cancan dancer. As a performance, it is set in pre-given discursive fields, and at the same time alludes to experiences that exceed the beholder's knowledge.[73] Performing, the dancer re-enacts, and simultaneously reinvents conventions of gender and bodily display. Laurence is erotic object and expressive subject at once. She does not simply perform woman, nor does she succumb to disorganised physical convulsions, but rather stages her own complex subjectivity in a mixture of mime and free dance movements that both uses and expands given codes. A strong emphasis is placed on the rendering of her distinctive story. Max is intrigued by what she has to tell, and how she communicates it in the reciprocity of inner impulse and kinetic power. His spectatorship does not only indulge in the spectacle. It is challenged by the 'foolish' wish to slip into Laurence's skin in order to understand what she wants to say: 'What was the meaning of this woman? What significance lurked under the symbolism of this beautiful form?' (*FN*, 149).

We find the same idea of inverted perspectives even more fully developed in a dream that Heine relates in 'Ludwig Börne' (1840). He is obviously complaining about the political passivity that is forced upon him; however, the situation he chooses as an illustration is revealing in our context:

> Yes, to my own amazement I am dressed in a pink ensemble, in a so-called flesh coloured outfit, as the lateness of the season and also the climate do not allow total nudity as they do in Greece at Thermopylae [...] I am dressed like Leonidas in the David painting, when I sit in my dreams on the cornerstone, on the Rue Lafitte, where the cursed coaches [...] spray dirt on my leggings [...]. (*DHA* II, 117; *CW*)

Here, the author literally slips into the flesh-coloured leotard, the second skin of a dancer, exchanging the visual power of his observing gaze with the tactile experience of this gaze's passive object, sitting bespattered amidst the bustle of a busy street.

If we remind ourselves again of Laurence's persistent amnesia which safely keeps the insights into her situation locked in her unconscious, Max's desperate effort to decipher her movements recalls the process of a psychoanalytic cure. His failed attempt to construct a consistent reading of her dance forecasts Freud's treatment of hysterical patients. Freud initially assumed that a coherent narrative, filling the gap in memory and retrieving the primal scene of traumatic impact that led to the symptoms, would make the production of these symptoms redundant. He

---

73 Susan Manning talks of the 'double move of subverting the voyeuristic gaze while projecting essentialized notions of identity', a strategy and a practice to which Laurence's dance can undoubtedly be compared; see Manning, 'The Female Dancer and the Male Gaze: Feminist Critiques of Early Modern Dance', in *Meaning in Motion*, ed. by Jane C. Desmond (Durham: Duke University Press, 1997), pp. 153–66 (p. 154).

soon encountered the limits of this assumption.[74] An affliction like hysteria does not distinguish clearly between illness and cure: in view of the extreme cruelty of Laurence's story, the protective performance of her symptomatic act seems to be a 'defensive measure' that enables, rather than hinders, her coping with her traumatic wounding (*StE* II, 123). Its destructive force is contained in the impossibility of its ultimate disclosure.

In Heine, we revisit the success of a 'failed' performance that turns cultural and personal wounds into dance's incitement, rather than into dance's negation. This time, the failure explicitly pronounces a new aesthetic. Precisely the fact that Laurence 'does not know how to dance', and her loss of control while moving, bear the potential of new and other movement.[75] Ambiguous and haunted as it is, Laurence's dance might not fully represent what Heine envisages. Yet it does give a foretaste of physical revolutions to come, standing perhaps for 'the eerie premonition of rebirth, the pregnant breeze of a new spring' (*DHA* XII/1, 48), as Heine writes with regard to contemporary art in *Französische Maler*. Dancers of the future like Isadora Duncan will proclaim a cultic dimension of transgressive bodily movement: 'Isadora danced the shivering holiness of the temples, where incense ascends to the gods, she danced the bacchantic delight of Dionysian feasts. She danced the majestic pace of tragedy. Then she raved again like a maenad.'[76] Such dancers will indeed formulate a programme that overcomes the fixed positions of the fallen body and the transcending mind, meant to direct the gaze onto 'a constantly affirmed world [...] without that serpentine "no" that bites into fruits and lodges their contradictions at their core'.[77]

That which in *Giselle* remains a momentary negation of established ballet technique turns in *Florentinische Nächte* into an exploration of the unknown, of the repressed Gothic underside of the classical surfaces of a code of movement, and of the perfect, sculpture-like appearance of a woman in white. The dancing Laurence thus embodies Heine's very particular approach to the neoclassicist reception of the Greek heritage, a reception that favoured the Olympian aspects and denied the demonic ones. Heine takes the threatening sides on board. It is not Laurence's sensuality that is demonic, however, but her tortured psyche and its repressive structure. The settings of this exploration, the streets of London or the bedroom, are significant: in 1836, Heine's new aesthetic of movement did not have a place on the official stages.

It is a blending of the sensual with the sacred that Laurence's ritualised dance could lead to, and which Leopold Robert's painting *Arrivée des moissonneurs dans*

---

74 See Freud, 'The Aetiologie of Hysteria', *StE* III, 189–221; see also Bronfen, *The Knotted Subject*, p. 38.

75 See Gabriele Brandstetter on fall and improvisation, in 'Choreography as a Cenotaph. The Memory of Movement', in *ReMembering the Body*, ed. by Gabriele Brandstetter and Hortensia Völckers (Ostfildern-Ruit: Cantz, 2000), pp. 102–35 (p. 126).

76 Helene von Nostitz, quoted in Brandstetter, *Tanz-Lektüren*, p. 196.

77 Foucault, *Preface to Transgression*, p. 37.

les marais Pontins (Arrival of the Harvesters in the Pontine Marches) successfully conveys (Figure 4.1):

> Robert's harvesters are [...] not only without sin, they know no sin either, their daily labour on earth is prayer [...] they are blessed without heaven, reconciled without victim, pure without constant washing, perfectly holy. Thus, where only the heads, as the seat of the spirit, are graced with a gloriole to symbolise spirituality in Catholic images, by contrast, in the Robert paintings, matter is sanctified, in that here the whole person, the body as well as the head, is surrounded by heavenly lights, as though from a halo. (*DHA* XII/1, 34; *CW*)

However, Laurence is more than a harbinger of the revalorization of the body. She is an expressive dancer who is compelled to tell her story by other means than those provided by verbal language. In the following, the challenge of 'speaking' her performance will be investigated to round off this analysis.

Speaking Dancing

Heine's protagonist Max describes a dance that is a painful, enacted funeral monument for Laurence's dead mother. Yet his words, in turn, are also like epitaphs: epitaphs for the death of the dance itself. Language memorises, mourns, and replaces the moving body which cannot remain present. Max tries to keep what cannot be kept; he tries to understand what evades his grasp. Thus it is not only Laurence who 'remembers', but also he who describes her dance, and reports it retrospectively. Like the distortions and displacements at work in the woman's bodily memory, Max has to deal with the distortions and displacements implied in the translation of dance into speech. Language becomes the metaphor through which the spectator attempts to understand what he sees: 'It was a dance which did not attempt to amuse by outward phases of motion, but by phases which seemed to be words of a strange language which would say strange things. But what did the dance say? I could not understand it, however passionately it pleaded' (*FN*, 132).

The challenge is twofold: firstly, we have the overdetermined movement that cannot be fitted into contemporary aesthetic conventions; secondly, the beholder's eagerness to comprehend what he sees is no less uncommon. While Gautier extols dance as the one 'universal language', Heine's protagonist puts this Romantic stereotype to the test.[78] Max's account of the dance is not primarily an act of successful interpretation or understanding, but rather a description.[79] The narration thus echoes the economy of the dance that replaces comprehension with re-enactment: the woman's stories

---

78 Gautier, *Gautier on Dance*, p. 215.

79 The autograph manuscript of *Florentinische Nächte* shows how demanding a mere description of the dancing body is. The passage on Laurence's dance is one of the most heavily corrected in the whole text; Heine played through a number of versions, see Susan J. Ringler, 'Heine's *Florentinische Nächte*: The Autograph Manuscript', *Heine-Jahrbuch*, 25 (1986), 42–60 (p. 55).

of her childhood at once explain and do not explain her eerie obsession; knowledge does not help to still the voice of pain. The beholder's interpretation is equally locked in a circle throughout the course of the events; he repeats a shorter version of his initial description twice in a very similar way. Max admits his lack of understanding by remarking that in this case, his talent for deciphering the signature of all things failed him completely.

Scholarship has discussed Heine's notion of signature extensively. Benno von Wiese explored the 'signature of dance' in Heine's work as a term that articulates the increasing difficulty of reading and understanding the world. The most significant re-definition of signature with regard to dance can be found in Müller-Farguell's *Tanzfiguren*.[80] Drawing on Derrida's 'Signature Évènement Contexte', he proposes to understand dance as lettering, as the trace left behind by the dancers that constitutes a readable, though ephemeral sign. Müller-Farguell's intention is obviously not to approach dance as a physical event; he is interested in textual movement, movement in and of texts as a function of their figurality.

While Müller-Farguell's study unquestionably helps to make sense of the writer's textual dance, the attention here is directed toward Heine's own approach to movement, as formulated in the musings of Max. The narrator is confronted with an embodied event whose interpretation does not fail because it is an unreadable text; it fails because dance is not a written text at all, and can never be analysed as if it was one. The notion of signature as readable or unreadable lettering reduces dance to the process of its literary reflection.[81] 'Reading' dance is merely metaphorical, and used because one lacks a better metaphor for the reception of bodily movement.[82] With regard to both dancing and understanding dance the aspect of signature that refers to impression, to the distinctive and distinguishing mark which clearly relates to some underlying concept is particularly problematic. Following Derrida, Müller-Farguell's argument thus strongly accentuates a dynamisation of the primarily static notion. In Laurence's case, the idea of a danced signature is indeed constantly confronted with the evasiveness of its signified, thus turning in fact into an extremely polysemous mark, as in the example of the hand-washing gesture. The writer's account of the

---

80 Müller-Farguell, pp. 177–261.

81 To apply 'signature' as a hermeneutical tool also perpetuates the indeterminacy that is already at the core of Heine's use of the word. The imprecision of the term has not prevented Benno von Wiese or Wolfgang Preisendanz from employing it as a key to Heine's texts. However, I agree with Markus Winkler that one should not overemphasise the notion of signature in a methodological approach to Heine; see Wolfgang Preisendanz, *Heinrich Heine* (Munich: Fink, 1983), pp. 43–4, 49, 53, 56, and Markus Winkler, *Mythisches Denken zwischen Romantik und Realismus: Zur Erfahrung kultureller Fremdheit im Werk Heinrich Heines* (Tübingen: Niemeyer, 1995), for instance p. 68.

82 On the notion of readability in the novella, see also Sigrid Weigel, 'Zum Phantasma der Lesbarkeit: Heines *Florentinische Nächte* als literarische Urszene eines kulturwissenschaftlichen Theorems', in *Lesbarkeit der Kultur: Literaturwissenschaften zwischen Kulturtechnik und Ethnographie*, ed. by Gerhard Neumann and Sigrid Weigel (Munich: Fink, 2000), pp. 245–57.

1843 Salon raises a similar problem; his attempts to single out a characteristic trait behind the heterogeneous productions are unsuccessful: 'It is to no end that I force my mind to impose order on this chaos and to discover in it the thoughts of the age, or even the common element which announces these paintings as products of our present time' (*DHA* XIV/1, 85; *CW*).

In spite of the lack of a conceptual framework, Heine does give some hints as to what the actual experience of 'watching' dance could be. In the encounter with Francesca in *Reisebilder*, the narrator describes an emotional-kinetic response, an imaginary movement performed simultaneously by the empathising beholder to participate in the presence of the dance:

> The lady [...] leaped joyfully up to the centre of the room, and pirouetted around on one foot. I felt strangely that my heart in my bosom spun around also, until it was well nigh dizzy [...]. And my heart danced ever with her, executing the most difficult pas and exhibiting a capacity for terpsichorean accomplishments which I had never suspected. (*BL*, 377)

Clearly the dancing heart indicates its readiness to fall in love. Yet the passage also alludes to a way of experiencing dance beyond the terms of language, hinting at a proprioceptive sense that is activated in the mere watching of movement. The articulation of this process shifts from a description of the dancing to the expression of what the beholder experiences. As Müller-Farguell points out, dance in Heine is often more of an interaction between dancer and beholder than an individual act. The poem *Pomare* makes this transfer between dancer and spectator strikingly clear. Again we find the idea of 'changing skins'. Here, the one who watches wants to leave his skin, and with it the immobile position of the observer, in order to slip into the dancer's 'skin', her movement. Watching dance ends in the transitive fusion of dancer and spectator – 'she dances me':

> She dances. How her body sways!
> Her dainty limbs a thousand ways
> Flutter and flit and leap and spin;
> I'll soon have jumped from out my skin! [...]
> She'll dance me crazy! Woman, take
> Whatever gift is mine to make.[83]

There is no single passage where Heine describes his dancers as if they were writing movement, or arranging their dance according to given notations. It is mere acrobatics, or the acrobatic, calculated sides of dance that are depicted by metaphors referring to the rhetoric of written poetry. This 'metrics of movement', as Heine says in *Die Bäder von Lucca*, is contrasted with 'real' dance, which is far closer to the realm of orality: movement becomes enacted speech – it becomes quite literally a 'speech act' that performs, and produces that which it names. The dancer Francesca

---

83 Heine, *Poetical Works*, III, 123–4 (translation slightly changed by myself in order to render the German more accurately).

may serve again as an example. Her intermingling of dance and speech recalls the danced communications in *Prinzessin Brambilla*: 'She often leaped up, dancing as she spoke, and it is possible that dancing was her most natural language' (*BL*, 377). In contrast to Laurence's gestures, Francesca's performances plainly and parodically enact what they refer to: '"I am now so old – guess how old?" But without waiting for my answer, she sprang up and cried, "Eighteen years!" and spun round eighteen times on one foot' (*BL*, 378).

Could it be that in Heine, the notion of speech leads us further than the notion of writing when it comes to dance? The voice, as the bedridden writer says in 'Nachwort zum Romanzero', is the last mainstay of the physical: 'My body has deteriorated so much that it only left my voice behind' (*DHA* III/1, 177). The spoken word replaces the acts that have become impossible for the frail body. What is more, speech is a genuinely evasive, equivocal form of communication in Heine. Although the oral resounds with the genuine and with the immediacy of inspiration in a long-standing strand of cultural thought going back to the bible and Plato, Heine turns to speech's pitfalls. He stresses the double talk at work in utterances whose materiality undermines and outweighs their content or their speaker. Bellini's French is described as outrageously distorted – 'I will not say that he spoke it *badly*, for the word *bad* would here be entirely too good. One must say outrageously, incestuously, world-destroyingly' (*FN*, 113) – and builds the utmost contradiction to his rather shy character, and his beautiful music. Heine's description of spoken English is equally drastic. Again it is the pronunciation, in this case the extraordinarily organic qualities of the sounds, which overshadows the content completely: 'They take a dozen monosyllables in the mouth, chew them, crush them, and spit them out, and call that talking' (*FN*, 126). Moreover, speech does not present the beholder with a secure author position. The ventriloquist, Laurence's fake father, uses the origin of 'his' voice at his will: 'as he was of great skill in his calling, he could so modulate his voice as to make any one think that it came from the ground, and so he would make me believe that is was the voice of my dead mother who related her story' (*FN*, 148). The dancing Laurence herself, oblivious about her identity, turns into this voice which she listens to, and which she ventriloquises through her dance, telling in a distorted form about experiences that are kept away from conscious recognition. In a more serious rendering of the 'bloody' poor quality of Bellini's pronunciation of French, Laurence's less-than-graceful dance-speech is soiled with the bloody traces of a wounded life.

Dance, however, also comes to incorporate the one universal speech act, the *doing* that typifies Heine's idea of creative activity in general: 'Thought wants to become deed, word wants to become flesh' (*DHA* VIII/1, 79). Dancers like Francesca and Laurence incorporate the writer's performative power of the word. It pronounces the neoclassicist heritage, the static marble body, and its Romantic echo, the ballerina, into movement, producing an alternative and new vision of the art of embodiment. This embodiment may be disarmingly plain and clear-cut, as evidenced by Francesca's performances, or it may resist secure signification. However, it does not defy communication; it is rather a mode of communication beyond the discursive that is predominant in a rational culture. Heine conceived of Laurence's dance as a semiotic event in its own right, engendering a somatic code that may lead back to language's very origins, instead of defying it. Freud's thoughts on the primordial quality of the hysterical conversion provide an apposite view here:

> It is my opinion, however, that when a hysteric creates a somatic expression for an emotionally-coloured idea by symbolization, this depends less than one would imagine on personal or voluntary factors. In taking a verbal expression literally and in feeling the 'stab in the heart' or the 'slap in the face' after some slighting remark as a real event, the hysteric is not taking liberties with words, but is simply reviving once more the sensations to which the verbal expression owes its justification. [...] Indeed, it is perhaps wrong to say that hysteria creates these sensations by symbolization. It may be that it does not take linguistic usage as its model at all, but that both hysteria and linguistic usage draw their material from a common source. (*StE* II, 180–81)

A passage in 'Die Romantische Schule' exemplifies how Heine aligns mind with body, investing the latter with better cognitive capacities: 'Indeed, the body seems to be more reasonable than the mind, and man thinks often better with his back and stomach, than with his head' (*DHA* VIII/1, 185). In this sense, Laurence's dance only condenses communicative processes which are at play in the eye and body language running through the entire text. The ventriloquist sequence showed that it is the physical side of speech, the sound of the voice, which communicates at least as effectively as the words that are actually uttered. A more positive example of the power of sound is Max's soft voice, coming directly out of his sore heart, that makes Maria take her medicine (*DHA* V, 224).

In Heine's ideas on music, this power of sound leads, as is well known, to a genuine aesthetic concept in the shape of *Klangfigur* (acoustic figure). Examples of *Klangfigur* recur several times in Heine's work.[84] It is marvellously illustrated in the passage on the violinist Paganini, in the first part of the novella. While Hoffmann listens to dance, Heine's protagonist watches music: recalling a concert in Hamburg, the narrator explains how the act of listening to Paganini's music turned into a visual spectacle. Paganini's introduction to the text is significant in this respect: Max recounts that the only person who was ever able to draw a successful portrait of the virtuoso was a deaf painter named Leyser, who 'hit off with a few pencil strokes the head of Paganini so well that one laughs and is frightened at the truth of the portrait'. Remembering the deaf man's love for music, and his ability to read it in the visible effects it has on the faces of the musicians, Max continues to defy the strangeness of this constellation: 'What is there wonderful in that? The deaf painter could, in the visible signature of the playing, *see the tones*. Are there not men to whom tones

---

84 See, for instance, the passage on Liszt's piano playing in 'Über die französische Bühne' (On French Theatre), *DHA* XII/1, 287–9, and the scene with Francesca in the church in *Die Stadt Lukka* (The Town of Lucca), *Selected Prose*, p. 161. Jocelyne Kolb describes Heine's non-aural mode of appreciating music in more detail in 'Heine and Music: Let it Sound No More', *Heine-Jahrbuch*, 23 (1984), 90–113.

themselves are only invisible signatures in which they hear colors and forms?' (*FN*, 116). Of course, Max is one of them, possessing what he calls his 'musical second sight', the 'gift of seeing with every note [...] its corresponding figure of sound'; and thus, he claims, Paganini brought 'visible forms and facts' before his eyes 'with every stroke of his bow'. We are offered a form of 'musical picture-writing' that tells 'all kinds of startling stories' (*FN*, 118–19).

If acoustic imagination thus turns sound into something physical, it seems to provide a conceptual tool to approach dance through music. *Klangfigur* indeed grasps the aspect of performed speech which is central in Heine's conception of dance; yet the latter poses far more hermeneutical problems. The sound-figures merely illustrate the meaning carried by the music. Laurence's dance, by contrast, carries and illustrates its own meaning, a meaning that is thwarted, rather than evoked, by the accompanying music (*FN*, 132). However, the main challenge of dance, as opposed to visual music, is the fact that it does not originate in the beholder's mind. It confronts the spectator with an otherness that disinvests him of his authorial power to name and to judge appropriately. This is reflected in the narrative structure of *Florentinische Nächte*.

While Max's position as the narrator – or rather 'talker' (*FN*, 101) – is uncontested throughout the main part of the text, his narration moves toward, and ends in, a scene where he is divested of his capacity to tell and to understand. Let us take the narrator at his word here, although we face, of course, the fundamental paradox of someone who *tells about* how he *stopped telling*. In the internal narrative, a body takes over; a body that speaks otherwise than Max used to speak. To stress the correlation between Laurence's dance and a hysteric performance once more, both the dancer and the hysteric patient have the potential to unsettle those toward whom their discourses are directed. They challenge narrative authority: the 'trauma' at the heart of hysteria, and we could equally insert 'Laurence's dance', 'uses the body as the material for its impression, encrypts the disturbing experience psychosomatically rather than encoding it into a story, and such marks the limit of narrative'.[85]

The regimes of power negotiated in Laurence's performance are thus not only the prescriptive conventions of bodily display. Even if Max tries to catch it in words, the dance also inverts the relationship between the eloquent male narrator and his silent female object. Laurence's performance tells something, rather than being something to be told about. This is mirrored in the setting: in the frame narrative, Max is the one who talks and moves, in the sense of both the freedom to move around and the ability to 'move' his listener, Maria, who is confined to the bed. In the internal narrative, he himself stays in bed, while the woman paces out the space in her room. The correspondence between Maria and Laurence is further enforced by the fact that Maria is in a state between sleeping and waking herself when Max talks about Laurence's somnambular trance. However, the changed agency is not a mere reversal of roles. While she dances, Laurence does not possess the authorial

---

85 From an unpublished manuscript by Aleida Assmann, quoted in Bronfen, *The Knotted Subject*, p. 36.

power over what she says, and there is no libretto; her movements are an effect of feelings and experiences transposed into bodily motion. Thus the narrative authority of the 'word' is challenged at a deeper level: it gives way to new and other, to bodily modes of speaking.

The truly unsettling potential of these performative reversals becomes clear when we take a brief look at the next stage of this process, the display of the male body in the novella. Paganini boasts the same 'drolly unpleasant' (*FN*, 113) aspect as the composer Bellini. Disrobed of the arts they excel in, both men attract nothing but mockery, pity, or even terror: 'convulsive, maddening desire to laugh' (*FN*, 113) and 'shuddering pity' (*FN*, 118). The depiction of the rose-skinned, virgin-like Bellini is reminiscent of the ambiguous stance towards the male dancer on stage; the jerky bows of Paganini are no less ridiculous than the boastful fencing gestures of the dwarf Türlütü, or the unimpressive fairground giants in their pink tricots and fake beards. While the exhibition of hyperbolic masculinity by an athlete does not have to be considered objectifying, here, the useless, clumsy or preposterous physical spectacle transgresses what was supposed to be legitimately masculine, coming far too close to a feminine mode of bodily display.[86] Max, recounting these antics, seems to take pains to keep up the patriarchal setting, a setting which enables him, not least, to unfold his narrative domination over Maria. Patriarchy allows for masculine body practices as long as they are a demonstration of power, representing and consolidating male dominance.[87] Hence the male virtuoso does not pose a problem; the 'athletic' aspect of technical brilliance assures the masculinity of the artist. As soon as Paganini begins his virtuoso playing, he loses his ludicrous aspect. This phenomenon appears to include even an art like pantomime, as the enthusiastic reaction to the mime-actor Mazurier in Ludwig Börne's *Schilderungen aus Paris* (Reports from Paris) shows. Mazurier's acrobatic talent and his extraordinary suppleness caused a sensation.[88] Max's refusal to engage with male beauty or even with male physicality, if not in the safe context of painting or sculpture, is only the reverse side of the extreme emotional response mentioned above. The gender-bending performance evades critical categories. The powerful ambivalent reactions it evokes – obsessive laughter, but also horror and terror – liken it to the other, unusual modes of speaking in Laurence's dance.

While being characteristic of rhetorical modes of speech in general, 'speaking otherwise' is traditionally the field of allegory. Given that Heine's work features practices that recall allegorical writing and reading techniques, allegory is perhaps also a better term than signature, or *Klangfigur*, to explore Heine's ways of thinking dance.[89] Rather than the description of a clearly defined subject or concept under the

---

86 See Simonis, p. 284.

87 See ibid., p. 280.

88 'In short, Mazurier is a miracle, and the fact that fluency of the feet is an innate talent of all Neapolitans does not diminish his fame'; see Börne, II, 66–7.

89 For a general study of the allegorical dimension of Heine's work, see Norbert Altenhofer, 'Chiffre, Hieroglyphe, Palimpsest: Vorformen tiefenhermeneutischer und

guise of another subject – a definition of allegory that is stigmatised in *Prinzessin Brambilla* – my use of the notion in Heine stresses its basic meaning, disguised speech. It is a speech that talks of the indefinable otherness of its reference. Allegorical descriptions, depictions or enactments cannot be explained through a conventional relationship between the signifiers and their content. The allegorical passage on the diplomatic meaning of the steps by the Berlin dancer Hoguet in *Harzreise* (The Harz Journey) is thus full of irony against both the art of ballet and the anti-liberal political writer Buchholz, if one knows that the pre-Romantic ballet in Berlin was everything else but political:

> I was at pains to point out that there is more political skill in Hoguet's feet than in Buchholz's head, that all his steps signify diplomatic negotiations, and that each of his movements has a reference to politics. For example, when he leans forward yearningly and spreads out his arms, he means our Cabinet; when he spins round a hundred times on one foot, without moving from the spot, he means the Federal Diet; when he minces about as though his feet were bound, he has the petty princes in mind; when he sways to an fro like a drunkard, he is signifying the European balance of power [...].[90]

This passage, a parodic counterpart to Laurence's dance, does not question the importance of movement's meaningful aspects. Yet the attempt to decipher dance like a code which functions by way of a referential relationship between sign and meaning, an attempt already playfully exposed in Francesca's 'speech acts', becomes here the target of plain mockery.

Although Benjamin's explanation of allegory in *Ursprung des deutschen Trauerspiels* (The Origin of German Tragic Drama) refers to the allegorical ingenuity of the Baroque, its theoretical nature gives some hints for exploring Heine's understanding of the language of dance.[91] In Benjamin, allegorical representation provides a key to a realm of secret knowledge, of past knowledge, a fragmentary region whose limits are never fixed. Prone to transpositions and deformations, it is a complex cluster of historical layers that work their way through iconological or poetic traditions. In spite of being a frozen monument of the past, the allegorical representation is always polysemous, and thus dynamic, for it is dependent on the reader or beholder who attempts to make sense out of it. Its imagery is not the figurative expression or interpretation of a stable, abstract linguistic content, or an underlying story, but a language of its own, an abstraction of its own. In this sense, allegory is performative; it is not primarily a 'sign of something', but a 'sign for someone'.

Detailed readings of *Florentinische Nächte* that understand the text as a more concrete allegory exist. The attempt to provide an unequivocal meaning does

---

intertextueller Interpretation im Werk Heines', in Altenhofer, pp. 104–53.

90 Heinrich Heine, *The Harz Journey*, in *Selected Prose*, pp. 32–87 (p. 72).

91 Walter Benjamin, *The Origin of German Tragic Drama*, transl. by John Osborne (London: NLB, 1977).

sometimes indeed evoke the ironical explanation of ballet in *Die Harzreise*.[92] When the young Heine says 'I believe a novel is not supposed to be an allegory' (*DHA* VI, 52), he seems to allude to the pedestrian aspect of a schematic production and reception of works of art. Let us here concentrate on how the text rethinks allegorical expression as a complex, evasive artistic practice that blends discursive and non-discursive means, and on the ways in which it links allegorical representation to bodily expression. Bearing in mind that the novella was written in the aftermath of severe censorial infringements on Heine's work, this artistic practice certainly can be seen as a strategy of resistance. The motif of the veil as see-through cover which we encountered several times in the reading of Heine's work resonates in the eloquent silence of Laurence's dance.

By describing how a complex message works its way through the guise of a bacchantic performance, Heine cunningly turns dance as one of the least politicised arts of his time into a political statement. Not only does he give voice to the body as the site where the shortcomings of a repressive culture are most obvious. Revaluating attractively non-discursive yet highly expressive ways of communication, he implicitly questions given distinctions between a harmlessly entertaining, and a dangerously operative art, distinctions that are vital for a practice like censorship. Heine's artfully sparkling writings always bear a message; yet they are also always more than their message. The author's dislike for a merely operative art that cannot dance any more found its unmistakable expression in the clumsy bear Atta Troll, whose lack of grace is matched by his lack of wit.

Laurence, however, indeed 'speaks in disguise', incorporating all the aspects implied in the veils of allegory. The dance talks of a past knowledge that is preserved in the moving body rather than in the mind. It is an enacted monument that ritually performs the same sequence over and over again; its elements re-actualise historical patterns of movement, and they 'give body' to the historicity of an individual biography. The dance neither illustrates music or language, nor does it relate a coherent story. Laurence's body speaks for itself, acting out its intrinsic pleasures and pains. The historical patterns thus gain a new, personal signification. This signification is constituted between the dancer and the spectator; it is partly explained in the background information, but also lies in Max's reaction to what he sees. He has an emotional, almost visceral reaction. The dance evokes enchantment, terror, and leads to an uncanny tenderness: without being able to grasp her, Max holds Laurence in his arms. In Heine, the dancing body not only seeks to perform pain, but also love, translating emotion into motion. Physical movement, emotional movement and mental movement are interlinked in countless ways, not least by their 'foolishness': Laurence dances in 'maddest gambols', Max tells 'fanciful stories' to

---

92 See for instance Ralph Martin, *Die Wiederkehr der Götter Griechenlands: Zur Entstehung des 'Hellenismus'-Gedankens bei Heinrich Heine* (Sigmaringen: Thorbecke, 1999), who reads the Laurence-plot as a political allegory; see also Elvira Grözinger, 'Die doppelte Buchhaltung': Einige Bemerkungen zu Heines Verstellungsstrategie in den *Florentinischen Nächten*', *Heine-Jahrbuch*, 18 (1979), 65–83.

distract Maria with 'movement [...] of a mental nature' (*FN*, 133, 101), and when in love, man behaves "like a fool; he dances on rocks and hills, believing that the whole world dances with him"' (*BL*, 382), as the narrator writes about his infatuation with Francesca in *Die Bäder von Lucca*.

In Heine, dance as the voice of that which can hardly be uttered in any other way points up a civilisation's discontents. It is as much a symptom for the age's ill health as it is a remedy. Laurence's re-enactment of her pain is a sign of her suffering, yet it is also a cure. It is an ongoing process of finding physical images, a process where clear-sighted creativity plays a major part in both detecting and dealing with the pain. It gives room to a ritualised allegorical practice of mourning that is glossed over in more official social or aesthetic practices, as typified in the ethereal corpses of the Romantic ballet. Dance as remedy and symptom is caught in a paradoxical interdependence with the censorial practice of the culture that it tries to unsettle. When we think of the political context of *Florentinische Nächte*, or recall the example of the cathedral in 'Die Romantische Schule', we realise that Heine views artistic creativity as a practice of repression and sublimation, distortion and articulation, which originates in or at least defines itself by its relation to some internal or external censorship. Art as transgression needs limits that can be overstepped; limitations and censorship engender complex creativity. Heine's Laurence shows how dance can turn into a metaphor for such creative resistance. The body, although assimilating ideals of physical beauty, and codes of proper comportment, also becomes the source from which the unconscious persistently articulates itself. It questions the safely-sealed neoclassicist shapes, and the self-transcending bodies of the Romantic ballerinas, and sets its own expressiveness against the authority of the word.

Heine's writings testify to an acute and painful perception of the porosity of the culture he was living in. His discontent is at once caused and alleviated by a sharp and perspicuous irony. The dancer who specialises in the more ironical performances of the author's *œuvre* is Francesca; her dances are hardly as uncanny as Laurence's, but no less original, as for instance the following little spectacle in which she remembers her love for the seminarist Cecco through mime and movement:

> During this description she indulged in the most delicate pantomime, pressing one over the other the points of her fingers on her heart, then seemed with cup-like hand to be scooping out the tenderest emotions, cast herself finally with heaving breasts on the sofa, hid her face in the cushions, raised her feet high in the air, and played with them as if they were puppets in a show. The blue foot represented the Abbate Cecco and the red his poor Francesca; and while she parodied her own story, she made the two loving feet part from each other, and it was touchingly ludicrous to see them kiss with their tips, saying the tenderest things; and the wild girl wept delightful tittering tears, which, however, came at time unconsciously from the soul with more depth than the part required. (*BL*, 377–8)

Heine, slipping into Francesca's skin, called his own writings indeed 'the puppet plays of my humour' (*DHA* III/1, 178), meant to entertain his audience. However, they also bear testimony to an acute sense of vulnerability that found its most powerful choreographic expression in Laurence's dance.

Conclusion

The chapters on Kleist, Hoffmann and Heine have shown that the writers' answer to the artful classical tradition of ballet is indeed itself an artful, and insightful, performance. Heine's cultural theory of classical dance is representative of the perception of these writers: he most acutely diagnoses a repressive economy on which the discipline of ballet relies, and points up the cracks in the classicist surface. The dances designed by him, and by Kleist and Hoffmann, become the symptomatic expression of the cultural trauma of physical and psychic vulnerability, which is covered up, or stigmatised as madness, in the official aesthetic of dance. The stabilising aspect of a framework of aesthetic and psycho-social norms, and the affirmative quality of their repetition, is driven to the deeply unsettling extreme of the repetition compulsion. Instances of failed or parodic repetition, in turn, defy the fatal power of psychic automatisms; yet they also endanger the containing agency of idealising norms which define the shape of the body, styles of movement, and gendered attributes and behaviour. The failure to repeat is caused by the very features that characterise a person's embodied being in the world: desire, loss and the confrontation with death, evoked, in the literary texts, by the relentless presence of figures that indicate a lack of control through failed, excessive, or transgressive movement. What is more, these figures mirror the texts' own breaks and leakages, showing at once the necessity of articulation and the resistance to it. Rather than on a representational level, they are most powerful in their performative dimension. Metaphorical uses and literal bases of words mutually reactivate each other to tell the body's stories, most obvious in the writings of Kleist, where the realm of falling is shown to entail a textual agency that indicates the breaks in the utopian scenario of anti-gravity and weightlessness. In Hoffmann, spinning becomes a metaphor for the obsessive circling around a traumatic event. In Heine, the persistently recurring trope of blood invokes a never-closing wound that seeps out, as it were, over the white stone of perfect sculptures.

However, the writers create dances that at once reject and respect discipline in the form of bodily techniques; and they turn the disruptive and destabilising figures into elements of the physical performance. While automatic repetitiveness comes to denote lethal fixture, repetition-in-difference and unorthodox dances provide degrees of stability through figurative and corporeal choreographies. In figuratively speaking about dance, literature displays its own rhetorical strategies. Kleist's virtuoso use of the paradox echoes his formalist view of graceful movement that is engendered by the interaction of opposing forces. Hoffmann's embodied response to Romantic irony unfolds its charms in dialogic dances in which identity is lost and regained. Heine's allegorical writing techniques are typified in a new and expressive form of dance. These dances of the self that we have found in the texts are based on the fragile balance between mobility and malady. They pace out possibilities of movement between floating and falling, between the creatively spinning spiral and the downward spinning whirl, between the secure stance of the stone sculpture and the blood that leaks through its fissures. They break the isolation of the body and the mind which are sealed too safely in the bulwarks of consciousness, as in Kleist, of a traumatic monologue, as in Hoffmann, or in the inaccessible stone body of cultural prescriptions, as in Heine. In spite of developing new steps and poses, the transgression of a given vocabulary, however, is as unsettling as it is liberating. The new movement proposed by the writers is thus always linked to the disturbing forces of sexuality, of instability of identity, and of death that threaten any sense of security.

All three authors therefore sustain an ongoing dialectic between autonomous and heteronomous movement. Echoing both the fixation on, and the overcoming of, psychic wounding, dance is shown as compulsive repetitive act or as possibility to move freely. This dual potential may indicate the limits of the comparison with Foucault's concept of self-care. By developing technologies, Foucault's subject aims to achieve the best possible economy of pleasures through perfect self-regulation and self-modification: the goal is the machine *en miniature*. My use of dances of the self, in contrast, addresses subjects which never attain to the full mastery of their bodies and minds;[1] indeed, the written dance is seen as specific apparatus that negotiates modern subjectivity as a condition marked by lack. Kleist's, Hoffmann's and Heine's figures are never entirely self-possessing; and the transforming power of their dances is limited. It implies an inherent dynamic which stabilises not through the realisation of a static state, but through continuous activity. Dancing the self means that the forming of subjectivity is a process which has to be repeated and renewed. The embodied, choreographed and enacted subject is in the paradoxical 'state' of becoming, toppling over either to pathological instability, or to artfully sustained, pleasurable movement. By engaging with the cultural discourse of dance, the authors thus show post-Kantian subjectivity in a crisis both unsettling and productive: a crisis that would enter the public stages, many decades later, through modern dance's groundbreaking revolution on the dance floor.

The two main discourses of this book, literature and dance also confronted us with a transgression of given vocabularies in the encounter between self and other. Literature and dance entered into a dialogue where each of the partners evades, but also enriches its opposite. As was stated in the introduction, language shows dance as much as hiding it. Yet although the texts bear witness to the insurmountable paradox of the encounter between words and physical movement, they also demonstrate literature's potential to create, and perform, unique dances which could hardly be transposed onto real bodies and real stages. While one can argue that the

---

1   Compare Sarasin's critique of Foucault's understanding of the technologies of the self in *Reizbare Maschinen*, p. 465.

physical life and grace that literature must traumatically lack remains its haunting wound, and the wish to recreate it one of the texts' motors, the literary text, and the representational power of verbal language, in turn, may become the 'trauma' of dance. The relationship between Laurence and Max in particular illustrated the difficulties of communication in a dialogue of distinct partners where, despite reciprocal fascination, understanding is severely challenged. In their mutual contemplation and influence, writing and dancing achieve as much – perhaps even more – knowledge of themselves, as of the other.

This book is deliberately selective; it explores three segments of a history and theory of the dancing body in literature. One of the outstanding female voices of dance, who would deserve the attention of another book, can provide a concluding illustration of both the eye-opening overstepping of borders between two media and the turning back onto the specificities of each. Bettine von Arnim writes her dance before Goethe, returning his display of eloquence in her performative élan: 'My gentle steps draw magical circles that are catching your eye, you must follow me wherever I go, and I feel the triumph of success; through my dance I show you all those things which you can hardly imagine, and you marvel at my danced wisdom.'[2]

In their encounter with, and distinction from, each other, writing and dancing see their own relative blindness; yet they also celebrate the triumph and the wisdom of their unique performances.

---

2 Bettine von Arnim, *Werke und Briefe*, ed. by Gustav Konrad, 5 vols (Cologne: Bartmann, 1959–63), III, 75.

Bibliography

Primary Sources

Arnim, Bettine von, *Werke und Briefe*, ed. by Gustav Konrad, 5 vols (Cologne: Bartmann, 1959–63).

Baudelaire, Charles, *La Fanfarlo* in Baudelaire, *The Poems in Prose*, 2 vols, ed. and transl. by Francis Scarfe (London: Anvil Press, 1989), II, pp. 214–63.

Bernhard, Thomas, 'Ein berühmter Tänzer', in *Der Stimmenimitator* (Frankfurt am Main: Suhrkamp, 1987), pp. 76–7.

Blasis, Carlo, *Notes upon Dancing* (London: Delaporte, 1847).

——, *The Code of Terpsichore: The Art of Dancing*, transl. by R. Barton (London: Bull, 1830).

——, *An Elementary Treatise upon the Theory and Practice of the Art of Dancing* (Milan, 1820; re-ed. by Mary Stewart Evans, New York: Dover, 1968).

Börne, Ludwig, *Sämtliche Schriften*, ed. by Inge and Peter Rippmann, 5 vols (Düsseldorf: Melzer, 1964–1968).

Freud, Sigmund, *Standard Edition of the Complete Psychological Works of Sigmund Freud*, ed. by James Strachey in collaboration with Anna Freud, 24 vols (London: Hogarth Press, 1953–1974).

Gautier, Théophile, *Gautier on Dance*, ed. by Ivor Guest (London: Dance Books, 1986).

——, *L'Histoire dramatique en France depuis 25 ans*, I (Leipzig, 1858; repr. Geneva: Slatkine, 1968).

——, *Giselle ou les Wilis* (Paris: Librairie de l'Opéra, 1841).

Goethe, Johann Wolfgang, 'On the Laocoon Group', in Goethe, *Essays on Art and Literature*, ed. by John Gearey, transl. by Ellen von Nardroff and Ernest H. von Nardroff (New York: Suhrkamp, 1986), pp. 15–23.

Hegel, Georg Wilhelm Friedrich, *Aesthetics: Lectures on Fine Art*, transl. by T.M. Knox, 2 vols (Oxford: Clarendon, 1975).

Heine, Heinrich, *Selected Prose*, ed. and transl. by Ritchie Robertson (London: Penguin, 1993).

——, *Historisch-Kritische Gesamtausgabe der Werke*, ed. by Manfred Windfuhr et al., 16 vols (Hamburg: Hoffmann und Campe, 1973–97).

——, *The Sword and the Flame: Selections from Heinrich Heine's Prose*, ed. by Alfred Werner (New York: Thomas Yoseloff, 1960).

——, *Poetical Works*, transl. by Margaret Armour, 4 vols (London: Heinemann, 1917).

——, *The Works of Heinrich Heine*, transl. by Charles Godfrey Leland, Vol. 5 (London: Heinemann, 1892).

Hentschke, Theodor, *Allgemeine Tanzkunst* (Stralsund: Hausschildt, 1836; repr. Leipzig: Zentralantiquariat der DDR, 1986).

Herder, Johann Gottfried, *Sculpture: Some Observations on Shape and Form from Pygmaiion's Creative Dream*, ed. and transl. by Jason Gaiger (Chicago: University of Chicago Press, 2002).

Hoffmann, E.T.A., *The Life and Opinions of the Tomcat Murr*, transl. by Anthea Bell (London: Penguin, 1999).

——, *The Golden Pot and Other Tales*, transl. by Ritchie Robertson (Oxford: Oxford University Press, 1992).

——, *Musical Writings: Kreisleriana, the Poet and the Composer, Music Criticism*, ed. by David Charlton, transl. by Martyn Clarke (Cambridge: Cambridge University Press, 1989).

——, *Sämtliche Werke*, ed. by Wulf Segebrecht et al., 6 vols (Frankfurt am Main: Deutscher Klassiker Verlag, 1985–).

——, *Schriften zur Musik*, ed. by Friedrich Schnapp (Munich: Winkler, 1977).

——, *Selected Letters*, ed. and trans. by Johanna C. Sahlin (Chicago: University of Chicago Press, 1977).

——, *Tagebücher*, ed. by Friedrich Schnapp (Munich: Winkler, 1971).

——, *The Best Tales of Hoffmann*, ed. by E.F. Bleiler (New York: Dover, 1967).

——, *The Devil's Elixirs*, transl. by Ronald Taylor (London: John Calder, 1963).

Hogarth, William, *The Analysis of Beauty*, ed. by Ronald Paulson (New Haven: Yale University Press, 1997).

Kant, Immanuel, *Critique of Pure Reason*, ed. and transl. by Paul Guyer and Allen W. Wood (Cambridge: Cambridge University Press, 1998).

Kleist, Heinrich von, *Selected Writings*, ed. and transl. by David Constantine (London: Dent, 1997).

——, *On the Marionette Theatre,* trans. by Roman Paska, in *Fragments for a History of the Human Body Part I*, ed. by Michel Feher (New York: Zone, 1990), pp. 415–21.

——, *Sämtliche Werke und Briefe*, ed. by Ilse-Marie Barth et al., 4 vols (Frankfurt am Main: Deutscher Klassiker Verlag, 1987–97).

——, *Berliner Abendblätter* (Leipzig: 1925; repr. Stuttgart: Cotta, 1959).

Lauchery, Etienne, *Recueil des Ballets de Cassel par Mr. Lauchery*, 1768, held in the British Library, London.

Lessing, Gotthold Ephraim, *Laocoon: An Essay on the Limits of Painting and Poetry*, transl. by Edward Allen McCormick (Baltimore: Johns Hopkins University Press, 1984).

Mallarmé, Stéphane, 'Ballets', in *Igitur, Divagations, Un coup de dés* (Paris: Gallimard, 1976), pp. 191–7.

Mann, Thomas, *Tonio Kröger*, in *Death in Venice and Other Stories*, transl. by H.T. Lowe-Porter (London: Secker and Warburg, 1979), pp. 85–120.

Noverre, Jean-Georges, *Letters on Dancing and Ballets*, transl. by Cyril W. Beaumont (London: The author, 1930).

Schäffer, C., and C. Hartmann, *Die Königlichen Theater in Berlin: Statistischer Rückblick 1786–1885* (Berlin: 1886).

Schiller, Friedrich, *Gracefulness and Dignity*, transl. by Leon Richard Liebner (University Microfilms International, 1979).

Schlegel, August Wilhelm, *Vorlesungen über Ästhetik I*, ed. by Ernst Behler (Paderborn: Schöningh, 1989).

Schlegel, Friedrich, *Philosophical Fragments*, transl. by Peter Firchow (Minneapolis: University of Minnesota Press, 1991).

Schneider, Louis, *Geschichte der Oper und des Koeniglichen Opernhauses in Berlin* (Berlin: Duncker und Humblot, 1852).

Smith, Albert, *The Natural History of the Ballet Girl* (London: Dance Books, 1996).

Sulzer, Johann Georg, *Allgemeine Theorie der schönen Künste*, 5 vols (Leipzig: 1792–94; repr. Hildesheim: Olms, 1967–70).

Théleur, E.A., *Letters on Dancing Reducing this Elegant and Healthful Exercise to Easy Scientific Principles* (London: 1831).

Valéry, Paul, 'Philosophy of the Dance', in *The Collected Works of Paul Valéry*, ed. by Jackson Mathews, 15 vols (London: Routledge and Kegan Paul, 1958–75), XIII (1964), 197–211.

Wieland, Christoph Martin, *The History of Agathon*, transl. by John Richardson, 4 vols (London: Cadell, 1773).

Winckelmann, Johann Joachim, *Reflections on the Painting and Sculpture of the Greeks*, transl. by Henry Fusseli (Menston: Scolar Press, 1972).

Secondary Sources

Abra, Jock, 'The Dancer as Masochist', *Dance Research Journal*, 19/2 (1987/88), 33–9.

Allemann, Beda, 'Sinn und Unsinn von Kleists Gespräch *Über das Marionettentheater*', *Kleist-Jahrbuch* (1981/1982), 50–65.

Allroggen, Gerhard, *E.T.A. Hoffmanns Kompositionen* (Regensburg: Bosse, 1970).

Altenhofer, Norbert, 'Chiffre, Hieroglyphe, Palimpsest: Vorformen tiefenhermeneutischer und intertextueller Interpretation im Werk Heines', in Altenhofer, *Die verlorene Augensprache*, ed. by Volker Bohn (Frankfurt am Main: Insel, 1993), pp. 104–53.

——, 'Die exilierte Natur: Kulturtheoretische Reflexion im Werk Heines', in Altenhofer, *Die verlorene Augensprache*, ed. by Volker Bohn (Frankfurt am Main: Insel, 1993), pp. 174–206.

Anzieu, Didier, *The Skin Ego* (New Haven: Yale University Press, 1989).

Bakhtin, Mikhail, *Rabelais and His World* (Bloomington: Indiana University Press, 1984).

Bal, Mieke, 'Performance and Performativity', in *Travelling Concepts in the Humanities: A Rough Guide* (Toronto: University of Toronto Press, 2002), pp. 174–212.

Banes, Sally, *Dancing Women: Female Bodies on Stage* (London: Routledge, 1998).

Barthel, Wolfgang, ed., *Heinrich von Kleist und Achim von Arnim: Zwei Autographen aus dem Jahre 1810* (Frankfurt/Oder: Kleist Gedenk- und Forschungstätte Kleist-museum, 1995).

Barthes, Roland, 'Réquichot et son corps', in *Œuvres complètes*, ed. by Éric Marty, 3 vols (Paris: Seuil, 1993–95), II (1993), 1623–42.

Beaumont, Cyril W., *The Ballet Called Giselle* (London: the author, 1944).

Beaune, Jean-Claude, 'The Classical Age of Automata: An Impressionistic Survey from the Sixteenth to the Nineteenth Century', in *Fragments of a History of the Human Body*, Part I, ed. by Michel Feher (New York: Zone, 1990), pp. 431–80.

Benjamin, Walter, *The Origin of German Tragic Drama*, transl. by John Osborne (London: NLB, 1977).

Benthien, Claudia, 'Gesichtverlust und Gewaltsamkeit: Zur Psychodynamik von Scham und Schuld in Kleists *Familie Schroffenstein*', *Kleist-Jahrbuch* (1999), 128–43.

——, *Im Leibe wohnen: Literarische Imagologie und historische Anthropologie der Haut* (Berlin: Spitz, 1998).

Blamberger, Günter, 'Agonalität und Theatralität: Kleists Gedankenfigur des Duells im Kontext der europäischen Moralistik', *Kleist-Jahrbuch* (1999), 25–40

Böhme, Hartmut and Gernot Böhme, *Das Andere der Vernunft: Zur Entwicklung von Rationalitätsstrukturen am Beispiel Kants* (Frankfurt am Main: Suhrkamp, 1985).

Brandstetter, Gabriele, 'Choreography as a Cenotaph: The Memory of Movement', in *ReMembering the Body*, ed. by Gabriele Brandstetter and Hortensia Völckers (Ostfildern-Ruit: Cantz, 2000), pp. 102–35.

——, 'Transkription im Tanz: E.T.A. Hoffmanns Märchen *Nußknacker und Mausekönig* und Marius Petipas Ballett-Szenario', in *Jugend: Ein romantisches Konzept?*, ed. by Günter Oesterle (Würzburg: Königshausen und Neumann, 1997), pp. 161–73.

——, *Tanz-Lektüren: Körperbilder und Raumfiguren der Avantgarde* (Frankfurt am Main: Fischer, 1995).

——, 'Nachwort', in *Aufforderung zum Tanz: Geschichten und Gedichte*, ed. by Gabriele Brandstetter (Stuttgart: Reclam, 1992), pp. 401–24.

——, 'Psychologie des Ausdrucks und Ausdruckstanz: Aspekte der Wechselwirkung am Beispiel der Traumtänzerin Madeleine G.', in *Ausdruckstanz: Eine mitteleuropäische Bewegung der ersten Hälfte des 20. Jahrhunderts*, ed. by Gunhild Oberzaucher-Schüller (Wilhelmshaven: Noetzel, 1992), pp. 199–211.

——, '"Die Bilderschrift der Empfindungen": Jean-Georges Noverres *Lettres sur la Danse, et sur les Ballets* und Friedrich Schillers Abhandlung *Über Anmut und Würde'*, in *Schiller und die höfische Welt*, ed. by Achim Aurnhammer et al. (Tübingen: Niemeyer, 1990), pp. 77–93.

Bronfen, Elisabeth, *The Knotted Subject: Hysteria and its Discontents* (Princeton: Princeton University Press, 1998).

——, *Over Her Dead Body: Death, Femininity and the Aesthetic* (Manchester: Manchester University Press, 1992).

Bubner, Rüdiger, 'Philosophisches über Marionetten', *Kleist-Jahrbuch* (1980), 73–85.

Burt, Ramsay, *The Male Dancer: Bodies, Spectacle, Sexualities* (New York: Routledge, 1995).

Butler, Judith, *Bodies that Matter: On the Discursive Limits of 'Sex'* (London: Routledge, 1993).

——, *Gender Trouble: Feminism and the Subversion of Identity* (London: Routledge, 1990).

——, 'Performative Acts and Gender Constitution: An Essay in Phenomenology and Feminist Theory', in *Performing Feminisms: Feminist Critical Theory and Theatre*, ed. by Sue-Ellen Case (Baltimore: Johns Hopkins University Press, 1990), pp. 270–82.

Camus, Renée, 'Cancan: Blurring the Line Between Social Dance and Stage Performance', in *Proceedings of the Twenty-Fourth Annual Conference of the Society for Dance History Scholars* (Stoughton: The Printing House, 2001), pp. 6–10.

Carter, Françoise, 'Celestial Dance: A Search for Perfection', *Dance Research*, 5 (1987), 3–17.

Caruth, Cathy, *Unclaimed Experience: Trauma, Narrative, and History* (Baltimore: Johns Hopkins University Press, 1996).

——, ed., *Trauma: Explorations in Memory* (Baltimore: Johns Hopkins University Press, 1995).

Chambers, Ross, 'Two Theatrical Microcosms: *Die Prinzessin Brambilla* and *Mademoiselle de Maupin'*, *Comparative Literature*, 27 (1975), 34–46.

Chase, Cynthia, 'Models of Narrative: Mechanical Doll, Exploding Machine', *Oxford Literary Review*, 6/2 (1984), 57–69.

Cheauré, Elisabeth, *E.T.A. Hoffmann: Inszenierungen seiner Werke auf russischen Bühnen – Ein Beitrag zur Rezeptionsgeschichte* (Heidelberg: Winter, 1979).

Cixous, Hélène, 'Les marionettes: lecture de Kleist – le dernier chapitre de l'histoire du monde', in Cixous, *Prénoms de personne* (Paris: Seuil, 1974), pp. 127–52.

Clark, Maribeth, 'Bodies at the Opéra', in *Reading Critics Reading: Opera and Ballet Criticism in France from the Revolution to 1848*, ed. by Roger Parker and Mary Ann Smart (Oxford: Oxford University Press, 2001), 237–51.

Clark, T.J., *The Painter of Modern Life: Paris in Art of Manet and his Followers* (Princeton: Princeton University Press, 1984).

Clausen, Bettina, and Harro Segeberg, 'Technik und Naturbeherrschung im Konflikt: Zur Entzerrung einiger Bilder auch über Kleist und Goethe', in *Technik in der*

Literatur, ed. by Harro Segeberg (Frankfurt am Main: Suhrkamp, 1992), pp. 33–50.

Craig, Edward Gordon, 'The Actor and the Über-Marionette', in *Gordon Craig on Movement and Dance*, ed. by Arnold Rood (London: Dance Books, 1978), pp. 37–57.

Cunningham, Merce, 'Studio', <http://www.merce.org/studio.html> (accessed September 2004).

——, E.T.A. Hoffmanns Beethoven-Kritik und die Ästhetik des Erhabenen', *Archiv für Musikwissenschaft*, 38 (1981), 79–92.

Dahms, Sibylle, 'Étienne Lauchery, der Zeitgenosse Noverres', in *Mozart und Mannheim, Kongreßbericht Mannheim 1991*, ed. by Ludwig Finscher et al. (Berne: Peter Lang, 1994), pp. 145–55.

Davies-Cordova, Sarah, *Paris Dances: Textual Choreographies in the Nineteenth-Century French Novel* (San Francisco: International Scholars Publications, 1999).

Dempster, Elizabeth, 'Women Writing the Body: Let's Watch a Little How She Dances', in *Bodies of the Text: Dance as Theory, Literature as Dance*, ed. by Ellen W. Goellner and Jaqueline Shea Murphy (New Brunswick: Rutgers University Press, 1995), pp. 21–38.

Derrida, Jacques, 'Ellipsis', in *Writing and Difference* (London: Routledge, 1995), pp. 294–300.

——, 'Signature, Event, Context', in *Limited Inc.*, trans. Samuel Weber, (Evanston: Northwestern University Press, 1988), pp. 1–23.

Deufert, Kattrin, and Kerstin Evert, 'Der Torso im Tanz: Von der Destabilisierung des Körpers zur Autonomie der Körperteile', in *Körperteile: Eine kulturelle Anatomie*, ed. by Claudia Benthien and Christoph Wulf (Hamburg: Rowohlt, 2001), pp. 423–38.

Dotzler, Bernhard, 'Die Wiederkehr der Puppe: Szenenwechsel im Fin de Siècle', in *Puppen, Körper, Automaten: Phantasmen der Moderne*, ed. by Pia Müller-Tamm and Katharina Sykora (Cologne: Oktagon, 1999), pp. 234–47.

Douglas, Mary, *Purity and Danger: An Analysis of the Concepts of Pollution and Taboo* (London: Routledge, 1966).

Eilert, Heide, *Theater in der Erzählkunst: Eine Studie zum Werk E.T.A. Hoffmanns* (Tübingen: Niemeyer, 1977).

Engelstein, Stefani, 'Reproductive Machines in E.T.A. Hoffmann', in *Body Dialectics in the Age of Goethe*, ed. by Marianne Henn and Holger A. Pausch (Amsterdam: Rodopi, 2003), pp. 169–91.

Felman, Shoshana, and Dori Laub, *Testimony: Crises of Witnessing in Literature Psychoanalysis, and History* (London: Routledge, 1992).

Fischer-Lichte, Erika, 'Theatralität: Zur Frage nach Kleists Theaterkonzeption', *Kleist-Jahrbuch* (2001), 25–37.

Foster, Susan Leigh, 'Choreographies of Gender', *Signs: Journal of Women in Culture and Society*, 24 (1998), 1–33.

——, *Choreography and Narrative: Ballet's Staging of Story and Desire* (Bloomington: Indiana University Press, 1996).

——, 'Pygmalion's No-Body and the Body of Dance', in *Performance and Cultural Politics*, ed. by Elin Diamond (London: Routledge, 1996), pp. 131–54.

——, *Reading Dancing: Bodies and Subjects in Contemporary American Dance* (Berkeley: University of California Press, 1986).

Földény, László F., 'Die Inszenierung des Erotischen: Heinrich von Kleist, *Über das Marionettentheater*', *Kleist-Jahrbuch* (2001), 135–47.

Foucault, Michel, *Technologies of the Self: A Seminar with Michel Foucault*, ed. by Luther H. Martin et al. (London: Tavistock, 1988).

——, *Discipline and Punish: The Birth of the Prison* (London: Penguin, 1977).

——, 'Preface to Transgression', in *Language, Counter-Memory, Practice: Selected Essays by Michel Foucault*, ed. by Donald F. Bouchard (New York: Cornell University Press, 1977), pp. 29–52.

——, *L'ordre du discours* (Paris: Gallimard, 1971).

Frank, Manfred, *Einführung in die frühromantische Ästhetik: Vorlesungen* (Frankfurt am Main: Suhrkamp, 1989).

Gilbert, Sandra M., and Susan Gubar, *The Madwoman in the Attic: the Woman Writer and the Nineteenth-century Literary Imagination* (New Haven: Yale University Press, 1979).

Gilman, Sander L., *Creating Beauty to Cure the Soul: Race and Psychology in the Shaping of Aesthetic Surgery* (Durham: Duke University Press, 1998).

Greiner, Bernhard, *Eine Art Wahnsinn: Dichtung im Horizont Kants – Studien zu Goethe und Kleist* (Berlin: Schmidt, 1994).

——, '"Der Weg der Seele des Tänzers": Kleists Schrift *Über das Marionettentheater*', *Neue Rundschau*, 98/3 (1987), 112–32.

Grözinger, Elvira, 'Die doppelte Buchhaltung': Einige Bemerkungen zu Heines Verstellungsstrategie in den *Florentinischen Nächten*', *Heine-Jahrbuch*, 18 (1979), 65–83.

Guest, Ivor, *Two Coppélias: A Centenary Study* (London: The Friends of Covent Garden, 1970)

——, *The Ballet of the Second Empire 1847–1858* (London: Black, 1955).

Gumpert, Gregor, *Die Rede vom Tanz* (Munich: Fink, 1994).

Gustafson, Susan E., 'The Cadaverous Bodies of Vampiric Mothers and the Genealogy of Pathology in E.T.A. Hoffmann's Tales', *German Life and Letters*, 52/2 (1999), 238–54.

——, 'Beautiful Statues, Beautiful Men: The Abjection of Feminine Imagination in Lessing's Laokoon', *PMLA*, 108.5 (1993), 1 083–97.

Hart, Gail K., 'Anmut's Gender: The *Marionettentheater* and Kleist's Revision of *Anmut und Würde*', *Women in German Yearbook*, 10 (1994), 83–95.

Hellmann, Hanna, *Heinrich von Kleist: Darstellung des Problems* (Heidelberg: 1911).

Henn, Marianne, and Holger A. Pausch, 'Introduction: Genealogy and Construction of Body Identity in the Age of Goethe', in *Body Dialectics in the Age of Goethe*, ed. by Marianne Henn and Holger A. Pausch (Amsterdam: Rodopi, 2003), pp. 9–21.

Hertz, Neil, 'Freud and the Sandman', in Hertz, *The End of the Line: Essays on Psychoanalysis and the Sublime* (New York: Columbia University Press, 1985), pp. 97–121.

Heselhaus, Clemens, 'Das Kleistsche Paradox', in *Kleists Aufsatz über das Marionettentheater*, ed. by Helmut Sembdner (Berlin: Schmidt, 1967), pp. 112–31.

Hofmann, Michael, 'Veranschaulichung von Ambivalenz in Bildern des Tanzes: Dichotomien der Aufklärung und ihre poetische Bearbeitung bei Heine und Wieland', in *Aufklärung und Skepsis: Internationaler Heine-Kongreß 1997 zum 200. Geburtstag*, ed. by Joseph A. Kruse et al. (Stuttgart: Metzler, 1999), pp. 102–17.

Hopkins, Albert, *Magic: Stage Illusions and Scientific Diversions including Trick Photography* (New York: Arno, 1977).

International Encyclopedia of Dance, ed. by Selma Jeanne Cohen et al., 6 vols (Oxford: Oxford University Press, 1998).

Jowitt, Deborah, *Time and the Dancing Image* (Berkeley: University of California Press, 1988).

Junk, Viktor, *Grundlegung der Tanzwissenschaft* (Hildesheim: Olms, 1990).

Kant, Marion, 'Wo getanzt wird, da ist der Teufel', in *Giselle*, ed. by Staatsoper unter den Linden Berlin (Frankfurt am Main: Insel, 2001), pp. 36–75.

Kapp, Gabriele, *Des Gedankens Senkblei: Studien zur Sprachauffassung Heinrich von Kleists 1799–1806* (Stuttgart: Metzler, 2000).

Kindermann, Heinz, *Theatergeschichte Europas* (Salzburg: Müller, 1977).

Klein, Gabriele, and Christa Zipprich, 'Tanz Theorie Text: Zur Einführung', *Jahrbuch Tanzforschung*, 12 (2002), 1–14.

Knab, Janina, *Ästhetik der Anmut: Studien zur 'Schönheit der Bewegung' im 18. Jahrhundert* (Frankfurt am Main: Peter Lang, 1996).

Knauer, Bettina, 'Heinrich Heines *Florentinische Nächte*: Form und Funktion novellistischen Erzählens und esoterischer Allegorik', in *Aufklärung und Skepsis: Internationaler Heine-Kongreß 1997 zum 200. Geburtstag*, ed. by Joseph A. Kruse et al. (Stuttgart: Metzler, 1999), pp. 833–45.

Kolb, Jocelyne, 'Heine and Music: Let it Sound No More', *Heine-Jahrbuch*, 23 (1984), 90–113.

Košenina, Alexander, 'Will er "auf ein Theater warten, welches da kommen soll?" Kleists Ideen zur Schauspielkunst', *Kleist-Jahrbuch* (2001), 38–54.

——, *Anthropologie und Schauspielkunst: Studien zur 'eloquentia corporis' im 18. Jahrhundert* (Tübingen: Niemeyer, 1995).

Kracauer, Siegfried, *Jacques Offenbach und das Paris seiner Zeit* (Frankfurt am Main: Suhrkamp, 1976).

Krämer, Sybille, and Marco Stahlhut, 'Das "Performative" als Thema der Sprach- und Kulturphilosophie', *Paragrana*, 10/1 (2001), 35–64.

Kremer, Detlev, *E.T.A. Hoffmann: Erzählungen und Romane* (Berlin: Schmidt, 1999).

Kristeva, Julia, *Powers of Horror: An Essay on Abjection* (New York: Columbia University Press, 1982).

Kurz, Gerhard, '"Gott befohlen": Kleists Dialog *Über das Marionettentheater* und der Mythos vom Sündenfall des Bewußtseins', *Kleist-Jahrbuch* (1981/82), 264–77.

Lacan, Jacques, 'Le stade du miroir comme formateur de la function du Je', in *Écrits* (Paris: Seuil, 1966), pp. 93–100.

Leeker, Martina, 'Maschinen – Gnosis – Tanz', *Jahrbuch Tanzforschung*, 10 (2000), 33–66.

Levin, David Michael, 'Balanchine's Formalism', in *What is Dance? Readings in Theory and Criticism*, ed. by Roger Copeland and Marshall Cohen (New York: Oxford University Press, 1983), pp. 123–45.

Liebrand, Claudia, *Aporie des Kunstmythos: Die Texte E.T.A. Hoffmanns* (Freiburg: Rombach, 1996).

Lippe, Rudolf zur, *Naturbeherrschung am Menschen*, 2 vols (Frankfurt am Main: Suhrkamp, 1974).

Man, Paul de, 'Aesthetic Formalization: Kleist's *Über das Marionettentheater*', in de Man, *The Rhetoric of Romanticism* (New York: Columbia University Press, 1984), pp. 263–90.

Manning, Susan, 'The Female Dancer and the Male Gaze: Feminist Critiques of Early Modern Dance', in *Meaning in Motion*, ed. by Jane C. Desmond (Durham: Duke University Press, 1997), pp. 153–66.

Martin, Ralph, *Die Wiederkehr der Götter Griechenlands: Zur Entstehung des 'Hellenismus'-Gedankens bei Heinrich Heine* (Sigmaringen: Thorbecke, 1999)

Mauss, Marcel, 'Les techniques du corps', *Journal de Psychologie*, 3–4 (1935), pp. 271–93.

Mayer, Hans, 'Die Wirklichkeit E.T.A. Hoffmanns', in *Romantikforschung seit 1945*, ed. by Klaus Peter (Königstein: Hanstein, 1980), pp. 116–44.

McCarren, Felicia, *Dancing Machines: Choreographies of the Age of Mechanical Reproduction* (Stanford: Stanford University Press, 2003).

——, *Dance Pathologies: Performance, Poetics, Medicine* (Stanford: Stanford University Press, 1998).

McGeary, Thomas, 'Gendering Opera', *Journal of Musicological Research*, 14 (1994), 17–34.

Meyer-Sieckendiek, Burkhard, 'Scham und Grazie: Zur Paradoxie der "schönen Seele" im Achtzehnten Jahrhundert', <http://www.goethezeitportal.de/db/wiss/epoche/meyers_seele.pdf> (accessed August 2004).

Menninghaus, Winfried, *Ekel: Theorie und Geschichte einer starken Empfindung* (Frankfurt am Main: Suhrkamp, 2002).

——, 'Die frühromantische Theorie von Zeichen und Metapher', *The German Quarterly*, 62/1 (1989), 48–58.

Müller-Farguell, Roger, *Tanz Figuren: Zur metaphorischen Konstitution von Bewegung in Texten – Schiller, Kleist, Heine, Nietzsche* (Munich: Fink, 1995).

Neumann, Gerhard, 'E.T.A. Hoffmanns "Prinzessin Brambilla" als Entwurf einer Wissenspoetik: Wissenschaft – Theater – Literatur', in *Romantische Wissenspoetik*, ed. by Gabriele Brandstetter and Gerhard Neumann (Würzburg: Königshausen und Neumann, 2004), pp. 15–47.

——, 'Glissando und Defiguration: E.T.A. Hoffmanns Capriccio "Prinzessin Brambilla" als Wahrnehmungsexperiment', in *Manier – Manieren – Manierismen: Festschrift für Renate Lachmann*, ed. by Erika Greber and Bettine Menke (Tübingen: Narr, 2002), pp.63–94.

——, '*Der Sandmann*', in *Meisterwerke der Literatur von Homer bis Musil*, ed. by Reinhard Brandt (Leipzig: Reclam, 2001), pp. 185–226.

New Grove Dictionary of Music and Musicians, ed. by Stanley Sadie et al., 29 vols (London: Macmillan, 2001).

Niehaus, Max, *Himmel Hölle und Trikot: Heinrich Heine und das Ballett* (Munich: Nymphenburger, 1959).

Noll Hammond, Sandra, 'Searching for the Sylph: Documentation of Early Developments in *Pointe* Technique', *Dance Research Journal*, 19/2 (1987/1988), 27–31.

Nussbaum, Martha C., 'The Professor of Parody', *The New Republic*, 22 October 1999, <http://www.tnr.com/archive/0299/022299/nussbaum022299.html> (accessed December 2002).

Oreglia, Giacomo, *The Commedia dell'Arte* (London: Methuen, 1968).

Pfotenhauer, Helmut, 'Gemeißelte Sinnlichkeit: Herders Anthropologie des Plastischen und die Spannungen darin', in Pfotenhauer, Helmut, *Um 1800: Konfigurationen der Literatur, Kunstliteratur und Ästhetik* (Tübingen: Niemeyer, 1991), pp. 79–102.

Phelan, Peggy, *Mourning Sex: Performing Public Memories* (London: Routledge, 1997).

Poe, Edgar Allan, 'The Philosophy of Composition', in Poe, *Essays and Reviews* (New York: The Library of America, 1984), pp. 13–25.

Poesio, Giannandrea, 'Narrative Gesture & Speaking Music', *About the House*, 1/3 (2001), 40–3.

Preisendanz, Wolfgang, *Heinrich Heine* (Munich: Fink, 1983).

Price, David, *Cancan!* (New Jersey: Farleigh Dickenson University Press, 1998).

Purdy, Daniel, 'Sculptured Soldiers and the Beauty of Discipline: Herder, Foucault and Masculinity', in *Body Dialectics in the Age of Goethe*, ed. by Marianne Henn and Holger A. Pausch (Amsterdam: Rodopi, 2003), pp. 23–45.

Rabinbach, Anson, *The Human Motor: Energy, Fatigue, and the Origins of Modernity* (Berkeley: University of California Press, 1990).

Raraty, M., 'E.T.A. Hoffmann and his Theatre', *Hermathena* (1964), 53–67.

Rauze, Elias de, '*Coppélia*' *Revue et gazette musicale de Paris*, 28 May 1870, p. 170.

Richter, Simon, *Laocoon's Body and the Aesthetics of Pain: Winckelmann, Herder, Lessing, Moritz, Goethe* (Detroit: Wayne State University Press, 1992).

Ringler, Susan J., 'Heine's *Florentinische Nächte*: The Autograph Manuscript', *Heine-Jahrbuch*, 25 (1986), 42–60.

Ruprecht, Lucia, 'Dance Goes Public: The Romantic Ballet and its Critics', in *The Cambridge Companion to Ballet*, ed. by Marion Kant (Cambridge: Cambridge University Press, 2006).

——, 'Heinrich Heine's *Florentinische Nächte*: A Tale of Transgression', in *Field Studies: German Language, Media and Culture (CUTG Proceedings 5)*, ed. by Holger Briehl and Carol Fehringer (Oxford: Peter Lang, 2005), pp. 139–56.

Rushing, James A., 'The Limitations of the Fencing Bear: Kleist's *Über das Marionettentheater* as Ironic Fiction', *The German Quarterly*, 61/4 (1988), 528–39.

Sarasin, Philipp, *Reizbare Maschinen: Eine Geschichte des Körpers 1765–1914* (Frankfurt am Main: Suhrkamp, 2001).

Saße, Günter, 'Die Karnevalisierung der Welt: Vom "chronischen Dualismus" zur "Duplizität des irdischen Seins" in Hoffmanns *Prinzessin Brambilla*', *E.T.A. Hoffmann Jahrbuch*, 9 (2001), 55–69.

Saul, Nicholas, 'Body, Language, and Body Language: Thresholds in Heinrich von Kleist' in *Schwellen: Germanistische Erkundungen einer Metapher* (Würzburg: Königshausen & Neumann, 1999), pp. 316–32.

——, 'From "Ideendichtung" to the *Commercium Mentis et Corporis*: The Body in German Literature around 1800', *German Life and Letters*, 52/2 (1999), 116–22.

Schlesier, Renate, *Mythos und Weiblichkeit bei Sigmund Freud: Zum Problem von Entmythologisierung und Remythologisierung in der psychoanalytischen Theorie* (Frankfurt am Main: Europäische Verlagsanstalt, 1981).

Schmidt, Ricarda, 'Klassische, romantische und postmoderne musikästhetische Paradigmen in E.T.A. Hoffmanns *Ritter Gluck*', in *'Seelenaccente' – 'Ohrenphysiognomik': Zur Musikanschauung E.T.A. Hoffmanns, Heinses und Wackenroders*, ed. by Werner Keil and Charis Goer (Hildesheim: Olms, 2000), pp. 12–61.

Schmitz-Emans, Monika, 'Eine schöne Kunstfigur? Androiden, Puppen und Maschinen als Allegorien des literarischen Werkes', *arcadia*, 30 (1995), 1–30

Schneider, Helmut J., 'Standing and Falling in Heinrich von Kleist', *MLN*, 115 (2000), 502–18.

——, 'Deconstruction of the Hermeneutical Body: Kleist and the Discourse of Classical Aesthetics', in *Body & Text in the Eighteenth Century*, ed. by Veronica Kelly and Dorothea von Mücke (Stanford: Stanford University Press, 1994), pp. 209–26.

Schulz, Walter, *Metaphysik des Schwebens: Untersuchungen zur Geschichte der Ästhetik* (Pfullingen: Neske, 1985).

Sembdner, Helmut, ed., *Heinrich von Kleists Nachruhm: Eine Wirkungsgeschichte in Dokumenten* (Bremen: Schünemann, 1967).

Sibony, Daniel, *Le corps et sa danse* (Paris: Seuil, 1995).

Siegmund, Gerald, 'Gedächtnisraum: Die Ballette William Forsythes', *Jahrbuch Tanzforschung,* 12 (2002), 397–411.

Simonis, Thomas, 'Zwischen(Ohn)macht und Begehren: Männlichkeitsinszenierungen im populären Tanzfilm, *Jahrbuch Tanzforschung,* 12 (2002), pp. 273–87.

Smith, Brittain, 'Pas de Deux: Doing the Dialogic Dance in Kleist's Fictitious Conversation About the Puppet Theater', in *Compendious Conversations: The Method of Dialogue in the Early Enlightenment,* ed. by Kevin L. Cope (Frankfurt am Main: Peter Lang, 1992), pp. 368–81.

Smith, Marian, 'What killed Giselle?', *Dance Chronicle: Studies in Dance and the Related Arts,* 13/1 (1990), 68–81.

Sparshott, Francis, *Off the Ground: First Steps to a Philosophical Consideration of the Dance* (Princeton: Princeton University Press, 1988).

Starobinski, Jean, 'Ironie et Melancholie (II): la *Princesse Brambilla* de E.T.A. Hoffmann', *Critique,* 22 (1966), 438–57.

Steig, Reinhold, *Heinrich von Kleist's Berliner Kämpfe* (Berlin: Spemann, 1901).

Sternberger, Dolf, *Heinrich Heine und die Abschaffung der Sünde* (Hamburg: Claassen, 1972).

Stokes, Adrian, 'Tonight the Ballet', in *What is Dance? Readings in Theory and Criticism,* ed. by Roger Copeland and Marshall Cohen (New York: Oxford University Press, 1983), pp. 244–54.

Sträßner, Matthias, *Tanzmeister und Dichter: Literaturgeschichte(n) im Umkreis von Jean-Georges Noverre, Lessing, Wieland, Goethe, Schiller* (Berlin: Henschel, 1994).

Swift, Mary Grace, *A Loftier Flight: The Life and Accomplishments of Charles-Louis Didelot, Balletmaster* (Connecticut: Wesleyan University Press, 1974).

Webber, Andrew, 'Mann's Man's World: Gender and Sexuality', in *The Cambridge Companion to Thomas Mann,* ed. by Ritchie Robertson (Cambridge: Cambridge University Press, 2002), pp. 64–83.

——, *The 'Doppelgänger': Double Visions in German Literature* (Oxford: Clarendon Press, 1996).

Weder, Christine, 'Ein medizinisch-literarisches Symptom: Zum Schwindel bei E.T.A. Hoffmann und im Kontext des medizinischen Diskurses der Zeit', *E.T.A. Hoffmann Jahrbuch,* 10 (2002), 76–95.

Weickmann, Dorion, *Der dressierte Leib: Kulturgeschichte des Balletts 1580–1870* (Frankfurt: Campus, 2002).

Weigel, Alexander, 'Das imaginäre Theater Heinrich von Kleists: Spiegelungen des zeitgenössischen Theaters im erzählten Dialog *Ueber das Marionettentheater*', *Beiträge zur Kleist-Forschung,* 14 (2000), 21–114.

——, 'Der Schauspieler als Maschinist: Heinrich von Kleist *Über das Marionettentheater* und das 'Königliche Nationaltheater'', in *Heinrich von Kleist: Studien zu Werk und Wirkung,* ed. by Dirk Grathoff (Opladen: Westdeutscher Verlag, 1988), pp. 263–80.

——, 'König, Polizist, Kasperle... und Kleist: Auch ein Kapitel deutscher Theatergeschichte, nach bisher unbekannten Akten', in *Impulse: Aufsätze,*

Quellen, Berichte zur deutschen Klassik und Romantik, Vol. 4, ed. by Walther Dietze and Peter Goldammer (Berlin: Aufbau, 1982), pp. 253–77.

Weigel, Sigrid, 'Zum Phantasma der Lesbarkeit: Heines *Florentinische Nächte* als literarische Urszene eines kulturwissenschaftlichen Theorems', in *Lesbarkeit der Kultur: Literaturwissenschaften zwischen Kulturtechnik und Ethnographie*, ed. by Gerhard Neumann and Sigrid Weigel (Munich: Fink, 2000), pp. 245–57.

White, Hayden, 'Bodies and Their Plots', in *Choreographing History*, ed. by Susan Leigh Foster (Bloomington: Indiana University Press, 1995), pp. 229–34.

Wiese, Benno von, *Signaturen: Zu Heinrich Heine und seinem Werk* (Berlin: Schmidt, 1976).

Winkler, Markus, *Mythisches Denken zwischen Romantik und Realismus: Zur Erfahrung kultureller Fremdheit im Werk Heinrich Heines* (Tübingen: Niemeyer, 1995).

Wittkowski, Wolfgang, 'E.T.A. Hoffmanns musikalische Musikdichtungen *Ritter Gluck, Don Juan, Rat Krespel*', *Aurora*, 38 (1978), 54–74.

Wittmann, Gabriele, 'Dancing is not Writing: Ein poetisches Projekt über die Schnittstelle von Sprache und Tanz', *Jahrbuch Tanzforschung*, 12 (2002), 585–96.

Woitas, Monika, 'Anmut im Rhythmus und Dichtung als Spiel: E.T.A. Hoffmann und das Ballett', in *Jacques Offenbachs 'Hoffmanns Erzählungen': Konzeption – Rezeption – Dokumentation*, ed. by Gabriele Brandstetter (Laaber: Laaber, 1988), pp. 389–420.

Wolff, Janet, 'Dance Criticism: Feminism, Theory and Choreography', in *Resident Alien: Feminist Cultural Criticism*, ed. by Janet Wolff (Cambridge: Polity Press, 1995), pp. 68–87.

Wright, Elizabeth, *Psychoanalytic Criticism: A Reappraisal*, 2nd edn (Cambridge: Polity Press, 1998).

Wyss, Beat, *Trauer der Vollendung: Zur Geburt der Kulturkritik* (Cologne: Dumont, 1997).

Zelle, Carsten, 'Maschinen-Metaphern in der Ästhetik des 18. Jahrhunderts (Lessing, Lenz, Schiller)', *Zeitschrift für Germanistik*, 3 (1997), 510–20.

——, *Die doppelte Ästhetik der Moderne: Revisionen des Schönen von Boileau bis Nietzsche* (Stuttgart: Metzler, 1995).

Zima, Peter V., 'Friedrich Schlegels Romantik: Eine Dekonstruktion avant la lettre?', in Zima, *Die Dekonstruktion* (Tübingen: Francke, 1994), pp. 10–15.

Index